# The Political Psychology
# of Appeasement

# The Political Psychology of Appeasement

## Finlandization and Other Unpopular Essays

Walter Laqueur

Transaction Books
New Brunswick (U.S.A.) and London (U.K.)

Copyright © 1980 by Transaction, Inc.
New Brunswick, New Jersey 08903

All rights reserved under International and Pan-American Copyright Conventions.
No part of this book may be reproduced or transmitted in any form or by any
means, electronic or mechanical, including photocopy, recording, or any information storage and retrieval system, without prior permission in writing from the
publisher. All inquiries should be addressed to Transaction Books, Rutgers—The
State University, New Brunswick, New Jersey 08903.

Library of Congress Catalog Number: 79-64854
ISBN: 0-87855-336-3 (cloth)
Printed in the United States of America

**Library of Congress Cataloging in Publication Data**

Laqueur, Walter Ze'ev, 1921–
    The political psychology of appeasement.

    1.    World politics—1945-     —Collected works.
I. Title.
D.843.L284        327'.09'045        79-64854
ISBN 0–87855–336–3

# Contents

9-25-80

# Acknowledgments

The author gratefully acknowledges the following publishers for granting permission to reprint copyrighted material:

"Europe: The Specter of Finlandization," *Commentary,* December 1977.
"Finlandization: A Reply," *Commentary,* May and October 1978.
"The Fall of Europe?," *Commentary,* January 1972.
"'Eurocommunism' and Its Friends," *Commentary,* August 1976.
"Russia — Beyond Brezhnev," *Commentary,* August 1977.
"Six Scenarios for 1980," *The New York Times Magazine,* December 19, 1971.
"The Next Ten Years," *Harper's Magazine,* December 1974.
"Karl Heinzen and the Origins of Modern Terrorism," *Encounter,* August 1977.
"The Futility of Terrorism," *Harper's Magazine,* March 1976.
"The Continuing Failure of Terrorism," *Harper's Magazine,* November 1976.
"Second Thoughts on Terrorism," *Washington Quarterly,* Autumn, 1978.
"The Psychology of Appeasement," *Commentary,* October 1978.
"The World and President Carter," *Commentary,* February 1978.
"America and the World: The Next Four Years," *Commentary,* March 1977.
"The Issue of Human Rights," *Commentary,* May 1977.
"Third World Fantasies," *Commentary,* February 1977.
"Fascism — The Second Coming, *Commentary,* February 1976.
"Peace With Egypt?," *Commentary,* March 1974.
"Is Peace Possible in the Middle East?," *Commentary,* March 1976.
"Is Peace Still Possible in the Middle East? The View from Tel Aviv," *Commentary,* July 1978.
"Israel's True Believer (The World of Mr. Begin)," *Times Literary Supplement,* July 1978.
"Hannah Arendt in Jerusalem — The Controversy Revisited," *Encounter,* November 1978.

# Preface

The essays included in this volume were written over a number of years and reflect the preoccupations and interests of the author during this period. They are comments on current affairs, even if, in some instances, this has led me into reflections about past events and in others toward speculation on the future. The essays are published here without change; I would not have done so had I not felt that I have been more often right than wrong. I am glad in retrospect that in the "Scenarios for 1980" and in "Looking Backwards," written in the early 1970s, I spotted the appointments to high office of Messrs. Szeczinski and Harmke, but also predicted the exile to Urumtchi of Mao's widow — not yet a widow at the time. On a more serious level, I pointed to the limits of detente when this was not fashionable. I noted that SALT, whatever its other merits, would not make the world a much safer place; that nine years later the Europeans would still be discussing the question of a common currency; that by 1980 the Chinese danger would loom larger than ever in Soviet eyes; that Aden had become a base for Russians operating from the Horn of Africa; and that the ambition of the Shah to bring prosperity and stability to his people had not succeeded. H.G. Wells and other futurists have done better, but then they were not preoccupied with politics.

Have I been, on the whole, too pessimistic? Is it not true that, Murphy's law notwithstanding, not everything that may go wrong does actually go wrong? I have never accepted fashionable theories of doom. The writing and the publication of books and articles would be a senseless endeavor in any case if the future was foreordained. My concern was with the dangers ahead, and that these dangers existed, and continue to exist, is no longer seriously disputed. Thus, on rereading these essays I find little that I would put differently even now. Among experts on terrorism these writings have been blamed, on the contrary, for an optimism considered almost reckless, for they stress the limited effect of terrorist activities at the present time. Many experts in this field took in the past a far more somber view.

If, on occasion, judgment in these essays has been unduly harsh, this reflects a feeling of frustration when facing, quite often, an obstinate resistance to accept unpleasant realities in world affairs. Such resistance has not much lessened over the years nor has the feeling of frustration. Secondly, there is always the danger to overrate the speed with which events happen on the international scene. In the real world, in contrast to the realm of abstract reasoning, there are always retarding factors: events sometimes unfold more or less as one thought they would, but quite often only months or even years later. Or, to put it in the shortest possible way — in foreign politics, for better or worse, everything takes longer.

I find it surprising, in retrospect, that with the exception of the essay on Finlandization, and the articles on peace in the Middle East, these articles have not been seriously challenged. But this is not to say they were universally welcomed; on the contrary, they were not too popular and I suspect that re-publication will not gain many new friends to the author. No one likes to be reminded that he has been wrong, even though such reminders actually cause little harm. I find it difficult to think of reputations that have been tarnished among either actors or pundits in the field of foreign affairs as the result of having been mistaken. Anyone but the absolute beginner in this field knows that the decisive test is not to be right, but to be right at the right time. Careers have been spoiled because those concerned were prematurely right. Having been wrong in good company has never prevented anyone's rise to high office or the acquisition of a brilliant reputation. This is a fascinating phenomenon which deserves further study, but the general lesson seems obvious: in foreign policy, success involves sticking fairly closely to the *Zeitgeist*, the general mood of the period. If one does, the rewards are obvious, but woe to those either naive or obstinate enough to ignore it. But the *Zeitgeist* is not shaped by a dispassionate analysis of foreign political trends, it is strongly influenced by domestic concerns, by passing intellectual fashions, by various fears and hopes.

It is one of the paradoxes of our time that with all the technological advances in the means of communications, the quality of information and comment has deteriorated. This is one of the reasons why debate in foreign policy has become more difficult. Government is quite properly criticized for its intelligence failures, but it can hardly be denied that foreign policy coverage in the American media is by and large worse than in other democratic societies; it is worse even in comparison with the state of affairs in this country twenty or forty years ago: important developments abroad are sometimes reported with delay or are altogether ignored, editorials and columns sometimes voice statesmanlike platitudes and at other times extreme opinions. How often do they contribute to the enlightenment of the public? The lack of discrimination is sometimes frightening. Arrant nonsense on foreign affairs is published and broadcast side by side with sound and well informed comment and treated with equal respect. In domestic affairs ridicule sometimes still kills, but this seems to no longer apply to foreign affairs. These are not trivial weaknesses for they have greatly contributed to the prevailing confusion.

It is perfectly true that democratic societies have an inbuilt inclination toward both somnambulism and inertia; sometimes they are saved by the presence of a major danger, at others a good fairy seems to protect them. But does this suffice as an explanation for intellectual confusion? It could be argued that logical thought and conceptual clarity have not necessarily been the norm in history, but it is also true that if students of science had behaved with similar recklessness and lack of discrimination in their intellectual pursuits, mankind would still live in caves. A typical example, one unfortunately out of many, is the use of terms such as "left" and "right", "progressive", "liberal" and "conservative" in the foreign political debate. In these discussions appeasement of aggression has become an attribute of progressive political thought; a poor Lebanese Christian mountain villager is "right wing", Colonel Khadafi and his theological friends in Iran are at least "objectively" men of the left, or "liberals", so of course are the Russians and Fidel Castro. Since criticism of Soviet policy is thought to be always "conservative" and "hawkish" in inspiration, the Chinese are transformed into men of the right and Mr. George Kennan becomes a representative of the left. There seems to be no limit to this kind of lunacy. Spinoza once noted that many errors mainly consist in the application of the wrong names to things, but Spinoza unfortunately was quite wrong. There are many kinds of mistakes and ignorance and those attempting to infuse some clarity in the foreign political debate face an uphill struggle which in some respects resembles that facing the psychoanalyst. Sometimes, admittedly, there is room for legitimate dispute and there are basic differences of outlook. But far more often the realities are only all too obvious, only there is great psychological resistance against accepting them. To wear down such resistance is neither a popular nor an easy task and if one succeeds, this has usually less to do with the strength or the persuasiveness of arguments but a shock of sorts, against which the victim had been warned, but which, he confidently felt, would never happen . . . .

A famous ancient historian opened his great work with the statement that the study of history is the training *par excellence* for political life; he could, in fact, envisage no other. Few will accept now a prescription of this kind about the interaction between the study of history and the conduct of politics. Much of history now written trains neither for politics nor indeed anything else. Some historians, under various fashionable guises, have turned to antiquarianism, collecting and analyzing irrelevant facts; others have rewritten history according to their political prejudices without any pangs of conscience. There are, of course, no ready-made answers to contemporary problems in the past; to transfer more or less mechanically past situations to the present day makes for both bad history and bad politics. Not only political scientists have warned against the dead hand of the past, as it is so easy to invoke false "historical lessons." But in present day America a surfeit of history is certainly not the foremost danger. On the contrary, the neglect and the ignorance of history has gone much too far and as a result many contemporary political scientists have removed themselves effectively from participation in the debate on real issues of present day concern. History, it is true, always acts as an antidote to sanguine optimism and to exaggerated hope, and it is perhaps for this reason that some have suggested to abolish this, essentially reactionary, discipline. But there is more to history than the follies and the crimes and the despair of mankind; it is equally the record of achievements and hope, and thus in the end one always returns to history as the fullest reflection of the human spirit and the human condition.

*Washington, June 1979*

# Europe

# Finlandization

## My Finnish Adventures: An Introduction

Habent sua fata libelli—the reprint of a chapter from a book of mine on the subject of Finlandization became the focus of a heated controversy inside Finland in 1978 and of polemics which still continue. The drawbacks of polemics are well known. There is always the tendency to magnify the bones of contention, to score debating points, and above all, perhaps be side-tracked: polemics frequently create more heat than light. But they also have their advantages, for they tend to bring out some of the issues that have been swept under the carpet. It can hardly be denied that whatever their other merits, some of the world's greatest under-the-carpet-sweepers reside at present in Helsinki.

My essay discussed with some sympathy the difficult dilemma facing contemporary Finland—to combine neutrality with a special relationship vis-à-vis the Soviet Union and the price that has to be paid for the preservation of freedom inside Finland. Among the questions asked in this article were whether collaboration with the Soviet Union had gone beyond the inexorable necessities of Finland's geographical location, a small country bordering on a superpower, whether Finnish neutrality was moral and ideological as well as political, and whether the special relationship was likely to become a general pattern in Europe as indeed it has been frequently suggested by Soviet leaders. The term "Finlandization" has been offensive to most Finns and it is difficult not to sympathize with them. There is always an element of distortion when a geographical term is used to describe a political phenomenon and a good case can perhaps be made to eliminate it from our vocabulary. But a change in our dictionary will hardly affect the realities of world power. There will still be the desire on the part of weaker nations to accommodate their powerful neighbors, sometimes far beyond objective needs. Sometimes such accomodation will also involve domestic "adjustment," such as the need to behave "responsibly" (i.e., with self censorship) and the election to high office only of candidates that are trusted by the powerful neighbors.

Such practices have, of course, been known since time immemorial. What is new is the smoke screen of political make believe, the pretense of equality between states. When the Romans established their client states they did not bother about appearances, whereas in modern international relations a spade has always to be called an agricultural implement. Those who do not observe this elementary rule are violating basic standards of politeness like the child in Andersen's story about the Emperor's new clothes. Hence the anger expressed by Mr. Kekkonen, the Finnish president, and his political friends on yet another essay about Finlandization, a subject they believed to be safely buried—or at least swept under the carpet. Thus the search began for its author: was he influential or just a light-weight maverick? Why should a foreigner reveal such an unhealthy interest in Finnish affairs? Perhaps he did not exist at all, perhaps he was a second "Komissarov"? (A few years earlier a book had been published in the Soviet Union which greatly displeased most Finns because it argued that the Soviet Union had the right to interfere in Finnish affairs to a much larger extent than they always argued. Upon closer investigation it appeared that Comerade Komissarov did not exist, but was the pen name of one, or more, Soviet officials.)

Once it had been established that Mr. Laqueur did exist, and that it was not a pseudonym for either Mr. Brzezinski or Mr. Kissinger, the line taken by one part of the Finnish press was that while the author of the notorious article had shown less than complete familiarity as far as the intricacies of Finnish domestic affairs were concerned, he still had touched upon some very real and painful problems, and that little was to be gained by claiming that these problems did not exist. For there has been of late, for the first time in many years, outspoken concern from almost all the parts of the political spectre inside Finland about the slow, almost imperceptible but still very real retreat from independence—not just in foreign affairs but also on the domestic front. To provide but a few examples: Kyosti Skyttä, who bitterly attacked my Finlandization article, had himself previously compared contemporary Finland ("Kekkolandia") with Wilhelmian Germany; Professor Ilkka Heiskanen defined Finland as "autocratic"; Professor Veli Menkoski wrote about Finland as a "non democracy"; Professor Osmo Jussila said that Finland is on its way to a "kind of monarchy"; Sakari Talvitie wrote in "Kanava" that "not only politicians but newspapermen too" try to "hear even the faintest whisper from inside the Soviet embassy"; and Tor Högnäs, a Swede and one of the very few foreign correspondents permanently stationed in Helsinki, noted that "A strange fear is spreading . . . anxiety and prostration towards the Soviets are very much in evidence."

The picture that emerged was not compatible with the official version and it may have been also for this reason that the Finlandization article became the focus of so much attention. The counterattack, in many dozens of articles, claimed firstly that any attempt to invoke the spectre of Finlandization could only be based on the political doctrine of the extreme right. The logic is curious, for if criticism of the Soviet Union (or its absence) is made the yardstick, the Chinese suddenly move to the extreme right whereas Mr. G. Kennan becomes the spokesman of the far left. But there are, or course, mitigating circumstances; the asinine concept that a critical attitude towards the Soviet Union has to be equated with a right wing philosophy can be found equally often in the writings of American columnists and editorialists. For this reason, if for no other, one should not be too hard about some of the Finns. Next, the task became more delicate: It was claimed at one and the same time that the foreign author was totally ignorant—and that he knew suspiciously much about Finland. His ignorance was attested by an obliging American professor who had published a book on recent Finnish history. The syndrome is well known among area specialists, though in the past it has been associated mostly with Third World countries. The expert has been to Ruritania and he wants again to go there in future, nor does he want to find any doors closed to him. The least he can do is to extend a little help to the people whose hospitality he has enjoyed only yesterday — *sapienti sat*.

The obverse argument is more interesting, but also more disquieting. For if the critic of Finlandization is so well informed and if he derives his information not from official American sources, surely he must have some people inside Finland aiding and abetting his evil designs, people befouling their own nest, besmirching the good name of Finland (one recalls having heard this tune before!) by supplying him with translations from the Finnish press. Who are these men (or women)? A search is started, the guessing game spills over into the columns of the Finnish press, names are bandied about, pictures are published, rumors appear, ridiculous and quite untrue. But what if they were true? Is it implied that the translation of articles from newspapers not easily obtainable abroad is a crime against the state or, at the very least, unpatriotic behavior? And so the search for motives continues. The author is interviewed by leading Finnish newspapers and each time his "Jewish connections" are more or less subtly mentioned and not just once, in case that some of the inattentive readers may have missed the point. Perhaps this is just a case of Israeli retaliation for some Finnish votes in the U.N. Poor author, it will never be believed in Turku and Tampere that he has not the faintest idea how the Finns voted in the United Nations or whether they voted at all. One writer dismissed the tiresome search for motives: probably the author of the notorious article just wanted to earn a few dollars . . . At last an expert who really knows the United States, who remembers how eagerly American editors look forward to publishing articles about Finland, and what huge sums they will shower on those willing to write on this subject, and how the reading public in America waits with bated breath for every new comment on a speech by Virolainen, and Björklund and all the others . . .

The debate on Finlandization triggered off by my article is probably drawing to its close. At a safe distance it has been the source of some amusement, but for those more exposed to the icy winds it has been, and will be, no laughing matter. As an editor of the *London Times* recently (November 3) noted following a visit to Helsinki: "President Kekkonen has created a situation where the Russian question unnecessarily dominates Finnish politics. The president is said to regard support for this Russian policy as a permanent litmus test of peoples political reliability in every other sphere." And, this, the writer concludes, is what Finlandization is all about. President Kekkonen is now eighty and may soon retire. With all his insistence on the special relationship with the Soviet Union, with all the concessions, necessary and unnecessary, made in foreign politics and on the domestic scene, it is also true that he has been a very stubborn man. But a certain pattern has been established under his rule, and the system will be tested under his successor; it can only be hoped that one's worst fears will not come true.

The real significance is, of course, in Finland's role as a model. We may want to banish "Finlandization" from our vocabulary but this does not change the fact that the Russians have behaved during the last year almost with contempt vis-à-vis the Europeans. Norwegian rights in the North Sea have been disregarded, Germany has been admonished on a variety of subjects, Britain has been warned of the horrible consequences of the sale of some Harrier aircraft to China. (Before that the new British ambassador was kept waiting for seven months until Mr. Gromyko could spare half an hour for meeting him for the first time.) British newspapers have complained that the Soviet leaders would not have behaved in such a peremptory way to the last of their satellites. But why blame the Soviet leaders? There must have been, after all, some reason that led them to believe that Western Europe would on its free will accept the kind of relationship which exists between Finland and the Soviet Union. The Finns, unlike the Europeans, have been acting from a position of weakness; their only fault is to have contributed to the general obfuscation about the real state of affairs, belittling the extent of Soviet indirect intervention. This from the Finnish point of view is psychologically only too understandable, but the consequences as can now be seen, have been unfortunate. And the "friends of Finland" who, acting no doubt from the best motives, wish to perpetuate this obfuscation have a great deal to answer for.[1]

## II

### The Specter of Finlandization

The term "Finlandization"—meaning that process or state of affairs in which, under the cloak of maintaining friendly relations with the Soviet Union, the sovereignty of a country becomes reduced—has entered the political dictionary despite the protests of Helsinki, Helsinki's Western well-wishers, the Russians, and some American neo-isolationists. There is an element of injustice whenever geographical terms acquire a political meaning—not everything in Byzantium was Byzantine, not everything in the Levant was Levantine, not everyone in Shanghai is shanghaied, and if the Balkans were balkanized, it was largely the fault of outside powers. "Finlandization," in any case, is here to stay: it has become the subject of articles, books, and even doctoral dissertations.

Though the term is of recent date, its origins are by no means certain. The phenomenon was allegedly first described in 1953 by the Austrian Foreign Minister Karl Gruber, warning his government not to follow the Finnish example. He did not, however, actually coin the term. Professor Richard Lowenthal said in a 1974 interview with *Time* magazine that he may have been the first to use the term sometime in 1966, when the Warsaw Pact countries, at their meeting in Bucharest, suggested the dissolution of all military blocs. Subsequently, the term was used by Pierre Hassner, myself, and many other writers.

To speak of Finlandization is, of course, considered highly offensive and detrimental to national prestige in Finland itself. But outside observers too have warned against the use of the term. Some have argued that it conveys a false picture of Finland's real situation. Others have maintained that Finland is a unique case, and to apply the term to other countries is misleading. Still others have claimed that the process of Finlandization is not something to be decried but is rather a positive phenomenon, worthy of emulation. And lastly, a few optimists have expressed the belief that Western Europe, at all events, so far has little to fear from Finlandization, certainly less than do Russia's East European satellites.

Coming to grips with the phenomenon of Finlandization is made all the more difficult by the circumstance that so little is known in the West about Finland itself, and hence about exactly what sort of example it offers to other nations. There is no systematic press coverage from Helsinki and the existing scholarly literature in languages other than Finnish is not extensive; it is also not altogether reliable, because the self-censorship practiced inside Finland has infected Western publications on that country.[2]

Finland, which gained independence in 1917, was attacked by the Soviet Union in 1939 and defeated after stubborn resistance. It had to cede part of its territory. To regain what it had lost, Finland joined Germany in the attack on Russia in June 1941; in 1944 it made a separate peace with the Soviet Union and turned against the German army.

Stalin could have annexed Finland in 1944-45, but he preferred not to do so. There were several possible reasons for this magnanimity. The war, after all, had not yet ended, and the annexation of Finland at this date would have precipitated a conflict with the West. Strategically, moreover, Finland was less important than other territories annexed by the Russians. Then, too, the Russians had a healthy respect for the Finns, who had stubbornly fought for their freedom for a long time and who would have been more difficult to digest than, for instance, the Latvians and the Estonians. Nor is it unthinkable that Stalin wanted to keep Finland as a showcase for Russia's benevolent intentions toward the rest of the world.

Whatever the reason, Finland did not become a Soviet republic. But a price had to be paid, and continues to be paid to this very day.

What is that price? Finland, first of all, is a neutral country, but not vis-à-vis the Soviet Union, toward which it has special obligations. It must not oppose any major Soviet foreign-policy initiative or enter into any commitments without Soviet approval, and it is expected to give active support to some aspects of Soviet foreign policy.

Secondly, Finland is permitted to have an army, but only within the limits set by the Soviet Union.

Thirdly, only those political parties approved by the Soviet Union can participate in the government, and the same applies *a fortiori* to the president and prime minister. There is no censorship by the Soviets, but the Finns are supposed to exert self-censorship. Communist participation in the government is not absolutely required, but Finnish statesmen are informally required to make frequent declarations stressing their friendly and mutually beneficial relations with the Soviet Union.

Fourthly, Finland is expected to have close commercial relations with the Communist bloc, but in this respect there are no hard and fast rules, and pressure has been more sporadic than in other fields—perhaps in view of Finland's limited importance as a trading partner and COMECON's limited capacity for supplying consumer goods.

Lastly, it is part of the whole process to deny its very existence. Only ignorant or malicious foreign observers, the Finns are expected to say, would find anything ominous or even out of the ordinary in Finland's relations with the Soviet Union.

   To begin with the issue of neutrality, this is perhaps the least important aspect of the Finnish predicament (although it has been discussed endlessly). According to the Soviet-Finnish Treaty of 1948 and subsequent agreements, Finland has certain definitive commitments to the Soviet Union. It is true that Finnish spokesmen, such as Max Jakobson, have argued that the treaty does not bind Finland to anything beyond the defense of its own territory. Unfortunately, this interpretation has not been accepted by the Russians—Mr. Jakobson's book on the subject was bitterly attacked in the Soviet press—and given the facts of political and military power, it is the Soviet interpretation that counts. (When Mr. Jakobson was a candidate for the post of Secretary General of the UN some years ago, the Soviet Union vetoed his appointment; that he is of Jewish origin probably did not help, but the decisive consideration was no doubt that he was not thought to be politically "safe." That is, he was suspected of taking neutrality seriously.) The frequent claims of Finland's President Kekkonen that "all great powers have explicitly recognized Finnish neutrality" are a statement of intent, not of fact.

   What is more significant than neutrality is the issue of freedom, which is of immediate practical relevance to the political, social, and cultural life of the Finnish people. Compared with Russia's East European satellites, Finland is both independent and free. It has many political parties (ten), and many (too many) elections. Its institutions are democratic, its constitution is scrupulously observed. There are no arbitrary arrests; in fact, no one ever has been sent to prison for political reasons. Finns can freely travel abroad. The larger part of the Finnish economy is not nationalized. There is a vigorous cultural life, and Soviet influence on it is certainly not overwhelming. Foreign books and newspapers are widely available. Finland, in short, enjoys the same freedoms as the Western nations.

   But there is another side to the picture, less visible but always present, which is a consequence of the Kekkonen "line" that Finland's survival can be assured only by maintaining Soviet trust. To provide but a few examples: when the United Nations voted for the withdrawal of Soviet troops from Hungary after the Soviet invasion in 1956, the Finnish government did not join the majority but insisted that it was up to the governments of the Soviet Union and Hungary to reach an agreement. When Kekkonen visited Prague one year after the Soviet invasion of 1968, he admonished his hosts to behave in such a way as not to give rise to conflicts. Foreign Minister Leskinen, speaking in 1971, said that the handling of the Czechoslovak crisis by the Warsaw Pact and by NATO was a "triumph of European understanding." And so forth.

   If Soviet confidence could be retained at the price of foreign political concessions alone, the cost for Finland might be bearable; it would be understandable, in any case, in view of Finland's geographical position. But according to the Kekkonen line, it is also imperative that Finnish political leaders, parties, the media, and individual citizens all behave "responsibly"; otherwise they will endanger the very survival of the country. To act "responsibly" means to refrain from doing *anything* the Russians may not like, and this involves not only self-censorship but also the need to anticipate Soviet wishes, and even a willingness to accept a Soviet veto if self-censorship breaks down.[3]

The existence of a Soviet veto is denied quite brazenly in the face of the truth by proponents of the Kekkonen line. But there have, in fact, been quite a number of Soviet vetoes during the last two decades; if they have become fewer in recent years, it is precisely because of the Finnish government's willingness to refrain from actions that might provoke one. The most blatant cases of Soviet intervention occurred in 1958, when the Soviet Union demanded the resignation of the Social Democratic Fagerholm government, and in 1961, when it threatened to invoke the 1948 treaty unless Kekkonen were reelected president. Seen in retrospect, Finnish compliance with Soviet wishes in 1958 was quite unnecessary, but it legitimized Soviet interference in Finnish domestic affairs (as distinct from foreign and defense policy) and made it that much harder to resist further such pressures in the future.

Other Soviet interventions have been less dramatic than these, principally because these had served to establish the rules of the game. Thus, although a Finnish president or prime minister or member of the cabinet is democratically elected, he also has to be "approved" by the Soviet embassy in Helsinki or the appropriate institution in Moscow. Parties and personalities who have not been approved may be represented in parliament, but they must not be in a position of influence or decision-making. After the 1958 crisis, the Finnish Social Democrats—the biggest party in the country—became eligible to serve in the government only after their old leadership had resigned and the younger leaders had wholeheartedly embraced the Kekkonen line.

Despite the self-censorship exerted by Finnish political leaders and the media, however, Soviet complaints about Finnish transgressions continue almost without interruption. These complaints are reinforced by warnings on the part of Kekkonen and his supporters, such as Kalevi Sorsa, the leader of the Social Democratic party. But Soviet blame has also been mixed with praise—for example, for those Finnish leaders who have supported Soviet foreign-policy initiatives like the appeal for the neutralization of Norway, which, if successful, would clearly be against Finland's best interests.

Typical of the official policy of "confidence-building" are Kekkonen's frequent speeches and statements, published in Russian and English every few years, whose tenor is that Soviet-Finnish relations are excellent and are getting better all the time. Upon receipt of the Lenin prize, Kekkonen—who is not a Marxist or even a man of the Left—praised Lenin for his great role in granting Finland independence. At the time of the Communist youth festival in Helsinki, he expressed admiration for the enthusiasm with which the Finnish national anthem was sung. On another occasion, he claimed that the anxiety of the Russians in the face of the West was real "because I have read in the history of Russia that she has been attacked fourteen times in the last 150 years and that Minsk, the capital of White Russia, has been in enemy hands 101 times" (this is sheer fantasy).

It has been argued by Kekkonen's supporters that such abject statements should not be taken too seriously. If certain declarations, made to preserve Finland's freedom, happen to be untrue they have after all worked. Who would have benefited if, as the result of acting according to their conscience, the Finns had lost their freedom? Having convinced the Russians that the present Finnish leadership can be trusted, Finland has received special dispensation to be an associate member of the European Free Trade Association (EFTA) and to sign an agreement with the EEC. Even Kekkonen's policy of bringing Communists into the government, his supporters maintain, has not had fatal consequences; on the contrary, the Communist party split, and the more liberal wing denounced the Soviet invasion of Czechoslovakia in no uncertain terms—very much in contrast to the Finnish government itself. And when a Soviet ambassador too blatantly supported the Stalinist fraction of the Communist party, he was withdrawn following Finnish representations to Moscow.

One could cite other instances showing that the Finns have been adept in handling the Russians. But with all its apparent achievements, the Kekkonen line has undermined the Finns' willingness to resist Soviet encroachments on their sovereignty. For even if only half of the wonderful things said about the Soviet political and social system in Kekkonen's speeches were true, it would be difficult to explain to a younger generation of Finns why they should still try to keep their distance and not become part of the Soviet Union, that "great federation of free people," as their Karelian brothers have already done. Finnish *sisu* (roughly translated as guts) has been frequently praised by outside observers, but the constant repetition of a basically fraudulent official ideology is bound to have its effect. As Carl-Gustaf Lilius has written: "In the prevailing atmosphere it becomes easy for hypocrisy and apathy to spread, with the pretense that everything is as it should be. And a mentality of this kind entails a measure of corruption, detrimental to the spirit of national self-assertion."

Throughout history, small countries have had to accommodate their policies to the wishes, interests, and whims of their more powerful neighbors. The attitude of small nations has traditionally ranged from refraining from provoking the great power nearby to paying tribute and actively appeasing it in every possible way. As for the great powers, they have routinely interfered in the domestic affairs of their weaker neighbors, picked their own candidates for leaders, and ostracized those whom they did not trust. As Edward N. Luttwak has recently shown in *The Grand Strategy of the Roman Empire,* the rulers of eastern client states did not actually have to *see* Roman legions marching toward their cities in order to respond to Rome's commands, for they could imagine what the consequences of disobedience would be. Nor is self-censorship an unprecedented phenomenon. It had to be practiced, for instance, in the countries defeated by Napoleon, and in Switzerland and Sweden after the outbreak of World War II, when newspapers were called upon by the authorities to behave "responsibly" in writing about Nazi Germany in terms virtually identical to those used in recent years by President Kekkonen in relation to the Soviet Union.

Given Finland's geographical location and its small size (it has fewer than five million inhabitants), it is obvious that to survive as an independent nation, it has to take Soviet foreign-policy interests into account and has to act with great circumspection: "So far from NATO, so near the Soviet Union," to alter a famous saying of a Mexican president. Finland has had to be silent when other, more distant nations have been able to speak up without fear. But when all these circumstances have been taken into account, it is still true that it was a fatal mistake to legitimize Soviet interference in Finnish domestic affairs. While it is admirable that so much freedom has been preserved, Finland is not independent in any accepted sense of the term. It is, as Soviet leaders have themselves long contended, a country in a category apart, neither satellite nor neutral, a country whose "adaptation" to the dictates and wishes of the Soviet Union has become part of the national fabric.

Which brings us back to the debate over Finlandization. George F. Kennan, in his latest book, *The Cloud of Danger,* praises the Finns for what he sees as their composure and firmness in dealing with the Soviet Union, and objects to the common usage of the term "Finlandization" as signifying something humiliating and spineless. Along somewhat similar lines, President Kekkonen, in two different speeches a few years ago, conceded that there was indeed such a thing as Finlandization, but went on to say that it should be seen as a positive phenomenon. The same position has been taken by others: far from being an object of pity, Finland, they contend, has benefited from its "adaptation" by getting the best of both worlds. It has excellent relations, including economic ties, with both West and East; its security is guaranteed as a result of the defense pact with the Soviet Union; and it has done more than its share of working for détente and closer cooperation between the power blocs. Thus Finlandization is not something to be deplored but actually offers a model for other countries that must live with the Soviet Union.

A Washington *Post* columnist, writing in 1972, maintained that Finland was "where most of Europe wanted to be," a country not relying on the presence of foreign troops and having both security and more real freedom than some of the countries now in fear of being Finlandized. On the scholarly level, Professor David Vital, in *The Survival of Small States,* called Finland a paradigm for the future—a solution to the problem facing an isolated minor state pitted against a great military power. Mr. Vital, in contrast to the Washington *Post* columnist, did not have Europe in mind but especially the Middle East, which he saw falling "slowly under the preponderance of a single power—in this case the Soviet Union." In the circumstances, the continued survival of a minor (Middle Eastern) state would depend first and foremost on its ability to maintain "a balance of restraint and pressure between it and the preponderant power in whose sphere of interest it falls, as does Finland." While Mr. Vital did not specify what minor state he had in mind, it is unlikely that he meant Libya.

A diametrically opposite view to these has been taken by John P. Vloyantes, an American political scientist and author of a book on Soviet-Finnish relations, *Silk Glove Hegemony* (1975). According to him, it is nonsense to talk about Finlandization, because Finland's situation is unique. Mr. Vloyantes writes that is "fantastic" to assume that Russian influence could possibly replace American influence in Europe, and he cites as corroboration a "European revival," as well as growing French, Italian, and British political and economic power.

That a strong Europe need not fear Finlandization goes without saying, but how strong is Europe? Time has not dealt kindly with Mr. Vloyantes's evidence of growing European power. It may well be that the Soviet Union would not make specific demands on Western Europe under the threat of force. But there were no Soviet threats of force in 1958 either, when the Finns caved in despite their vaunted fearlessness and strong nerves—which, to put it cautiously, are not found in equal measure in other European countries.

The case of Finland *is* in some respects unique. The country was defeated in World War II; at the end of the war it was clearly within the Soviet sphere of influence; and the West never indicated that it would be able or willing to extend support to Finland in the case of conflict with its eastern neighbor. The other European countries by contrast, either belonged to NATO or had no common border with the Soviet Union. (Austria was an exception, but it was in a more fortunate position inasmuch as the Soviet Union was not the only occupying power—there was also a Western presence.) All this only means, however, that the Finnish analogy, like any analogy, has its limits. But it is certainly not a "myth," as some have claimed.

For when all allowances for the uniqueness of the Finnish case have been made, it is still true that Finland is something of a model and that the Soviet leaders regard it as such. If Poland or Hungary constitute one example of a close relationship between the Soviet Union and its smaller neighbors, Finland provides another. Under certain conditions, this kind of relationship might spread to other parts of the globe.

Those "certain conditions" are to some extent already visible in Europe. In its present state Europe is weak and disunited, and there are legitimate doubts with regard to its political resolve. Much damage has been done by the centrifugal pressures, the narrow nationalist interests, which have made closer integration impossible, and the domestic difficulties now facing Italy and France may have repercussions affecting the rest of Europe. But above all, there is that mixture of lethargy and hypochondria which has bedeviled the continent for a number of years.

There is nothing inevitable or irreversible about the decline of Europe, but at the present time one still searches in vain for a turning of the tide. On the other hand, one does *not* have to look hard for signs of accommodation, of a lack of courage whenever some challenge or threat from the outside has to be faced. The incidents themselves may appear trivial —a Soviet attempt to change the program of the Venice film festival; Soviet expressions of displeasure over the size of the French defense effort; Soviet pressure on Spain not to join NATO; Soviet advice to the Austrians not to modernize their army, and to the Turks not to be so fussy about violations of their air space; Soviet pressure on all European countries not to provide facilities to Radio Free Europe and Radio Liberty; Soviet efforts to erode the status of West Berlin. But if there is nothing startling or new about these and other Soviet initiatives, what is new is the subtle change in attitude toward them on the part of influential circles in Western Europe, the increased endeavor not to give offense to the Russians.

European reaction to President Carter's early initiative for human rights is an example; while this policy was (and is) quite popular among Europeans in general, some leading newspapers have reacted with extreme concern or anger. President Giscard d'Estaing was the only one to express his disapproval publicly, but other heads of government privately said more or less the same thing. It was not that they opposed human rights, but they feared that their domestic problems might be aggravated as a result of annoying the Russians; more important yet, they seem to have been frightened by the idea of moving off the defensive in the ideological struggle. In these circles it has come to be regarded as legitimate for the Soviet Union to receive foreign Communist leaders and to cooperate with foreign Communist parties, but it is considered bad taste if a Western statesman sees leading Soviet dissidents or expresses support for their activities. By the same token, Soviet broadcasts in Western languages are considered legitimate, but extreme prudence is called for with regard to Western broadcasts in the languages spoken by the peoples of the Soviet Union.

It may be said that while such behavior is not very courageous, it only reflects Europe's diminished place in today's world, and the fact that the policy of accommodation, of adopting a low profile, is applied not just toward the Soviet Union but toward everybody, East and West, North and South. When issues of principle are discussed, the argument always recurs that Britain (or France) is a country whose economic survival depends on foreign trade, and that good customers must be kept happy. Nations that depend on the good will of others have to adjust their policies accordingly.

Such adjustments are undertaken by individuals as well as by whole societies whenever there is a radical change in the balance of power, or when such a change is anticipated. Students of Nazi Germany are familiar with the famous *Gleichschaltung* bandwagon of 1933, when millions of Germans suddenly joined Hitler's party; they were not faced with an ultimatum, nor had they necessarily to fear for their jobs and positions. They simply did it as an act of insurance, just as some Italian newspapers and intellectuals have for the last few years prepared themselves for the "historic compromise" either by joining the Italian Communist party or at least by refraining from criticizing it. They have not even had to be advised, as Finnish journalists were by their president, to behave "responsibly"; they have felt the need to do so in their bones.

It is true that at the present time, *direct* foreign interference in the domestic affairs of any European country would not be tolerated. European political parties and their leaders do not need the stamp of Soviet approval; in this sense Europe has not yet been Finlandized, or even (with the possible exception of Italy) self-Finlandized. Should the present situation become permanent, perhaps some new term will have to be found to define Europe's status in the world—something less than Finlandization, but also something less than the independence it has enjoyed until now. But time does not stand still. If the economic crisis deepens, if nationalism and Communism continue to prevent closer European cooperation, if NATO, shrunk or weakened, no longer offers effective protection, and if the paralysis of political will is not overcome, accommodation seems bound to turn into appeasement, and appeasement to lead to a diminution of sovereignty for which the term "Finlandization" continues, all things considered to seem appropriate.

*December 1977*

## III

## Finlandization: A Reply

*One:*

Readers might be interested to learn of the widespread comment which my article, "The Specter of Finlandization" [December 1977], attracted in Finland itself. A long excerpt was published in *Helsingin Sanomat,* Finland's leading newspaper, and this was followed by an editorial in the same newspaper, critical of the article but moderate in tone. Subsequently, editorials and columns, some of them increasingly agitated and strident, appeared in many newspapers and periodicals. The sheer volume of the reaction made it clear that my article had touched on an issue that, notwithstanding declarations from official Finnish circles, continues to trouble a great many people in Finland. It was, of course, impossible for me to reply to every critical remark, but I did attempt a general response. Here are two excerpts, the first from my letter to the editors of *Hufvudstadsbladet* and *Suomen Kuvalehti* and the second from my letter to the editor of *Helsingin Sanomat:*

> A recent article of mine on Finlandization has been widely commented upon in many Finnish newspapers and periodicals, and though this did not come as a total surprise, the implications of such a reaction are a little disturbing. I can think of several explanations for the outcry. If a foreigner has grossly slandered a country, it is, of course, the duty of every patriot to demonstrate his loyalty by denouncing him. But I do not think that my article falls into this category—not being involved in Finnish domestic affairs, I wrote about the subject with some detachment; my wish was not to attack, but to understand and to analyze. It is perfectly true that I was interested not only in Finland's internal but also in its external affairs; in this, however, I was following the advice frequently given by Finland's powerful neighbor, that the relationship between Finland and itself is worth studying as a model which other countries would do well to follow. Surely I cannot be blamed for accepting the advice of Messrs. Brezhnev, Kosygin, and Suslov.
>
> A second possible explanation for the publicity given to my article surely does not apply in this case. In an authoritarian political system the media are orchestrated; instructions are given to deal, in a hostile or friendly spirit, with certain subjects. But since there is freedom of the press in Finland, such an interpretation is unwarranted.

Lastly, there is the possibility, indeed the likelihood, that however inoffensive in approach, my article touched a nerve; those who now take such pains to refute me (and my name, after all, is not a household word in Finland) must feel in their hearts that beyond all the official rationalizations there is a genuine question: in what direction has Finnish democracy been moving? The violent reaction to my article in some quarters shows a certain unease over this question.

It would be unprofitable to cover the same ground again, but permit me to make some general observations. While foreigners have no right to interfere in Finnish policy, or in that of any other country, they certainly have the right to observe and to comment; only dictatorships expect that such comment will always be laudatory. I was concerned with the internal "adjustments" in Finnish politics, and since it is my view that these have gone well beyond the limits imposed by Finland's geopolitical position, my remarks were hardly acceptable to those who favor such "adjustments" and even want to improve upon them. But as good democrats, they might show a little tolerance for views which differ from their own.

I have been criticized for having adduced only one slender volume in defense of my arguments. But the essay published in *Commentary* was an abridged version of a chapter in a book; it is not customary in an essay to cite all one's references. Although I have not read everything, many books and articles pertaining to the subject were translated for me. Incidentally, when I started out, my own views on Finlandization were not unlike those of George F. Kennan, until I began to study the texts of the major speeches of Finland's political figures, freely available in English and Russian translation. It was only then, when I compared the "official ideology" with the reality, that the discrepancies between theory and practice became obvious to me. In short, my doubts arose as a result of reading the official documents rather than as a result of the strictures of critics of Finlandization.

You refer to the remarks of George F. Kennan on Finland in his recent book, *The Cloud of Danger*. Mr. Kennan, like Voltaire's Pangloss, seems to believe that everything is for the best so far as democracy in Finland is concerned. I think it a mistake to attribute too much weight to Mr. Kennan's views; he would be the first to admit that he is not really familiar with the Finnish domestic situation. I still admire some of his works, but just as I cannot share his defense of official South African policy (and, until recently, Rhodesian policy), I cannot accept what he says on Finlandization, though in fairness to him it should be noted that his references to Finland consist of three or four sentences in a book of two hundred pages. The reviewer in the London *Times* called *The Cloud of Danger* a flawed, superficial collection, filled with defeatist generalizations. This is a harsh judgment, for a book covering the whole world cannot possibly deal in depth with every subject. But it is true that the book does exhibit a defeatist undertone.

This brings me to my last point. One of your writers published a most revealing article, "Sven Tuuva's Time Is Over." Sven Tuuva, if I remember correctly, is the legendary hero in Runeberg's *Ensign Steel's Tales* who fell in the war against the Russians in 1808-9, fighting alone on a bridge against a whole platoon of Cossacks. I could not agree more that in our nuclear age the time for such heroics is clearly over. But we should perhaps spare an occasional thought for those poor, misguided heroes of a bygone age who were willing to give their lives for their country. Without them, Finland (and quite a number of other countries) would probably not enjoy independence today. The real point is that, between the Joan of Arcs on the one hand and the Pétains and Lavals on the other—between the extremes of foolhardy and suicidal defiance of a stronger power and obsequious collaboration—there is still some middle ground. It is my impression, however, that Finland at present is not faced with the danger of too great a pendulum swing in the direction of the Sven Tuuvas of this world.

*   *   *

The editorial in *Helsingin Sanomat* says that at times an outsider (meaning myself) may see a truth "which we do not lightly admit to ourselves." But the editorial also says that my article shows how difficult it is for a stranger to give an unbiased account of Finland. Not reading Finnish, I depend on friends who translate for my benefit articles from the Finnish press and speeches by politicians, and admit that I am frequently mystified. I understand the words but the meaning is not always clear. But I suspect that I would still be puzzled even if I were able to read the original text. It is my impression that Finnish political language has become Aesopian, full of hints and allusions, devoid of open, let alone blunt, speaking; this does make it difficult for strangers to understand Finnish realities.

But is not the language part of the political reality, does it not reflect it? Are the reasons for the ambiguities and the lack of precision and openness mainly linguistic? I fear this is not the case, and this leads me to my next point. You seem to believe that only a conservative of the extreme Right would express concern over Finlandization, or even use the term. Nothing could be further from the truth. May I assure you that events in Finland are followed with increasing interest by men and women representing every part of the political spectrum in many countries, who are motivated not by hostility but a feeling of sympathy and genuine concern?

A few illustration should suffice. I have no reason to doubt that President Kekkonen is the greatest living Finnish statesman and also a most fervent patriot. But I am not aware of any other country in which one man has been elected President for twenty-four years in a row. As a historian and student of politics, I know, of course, of countries in which leaders are elected by a majority of 90 per cent, but these are usually not democratic societies. You will argue that Finland is a special case. Perhaps so, but the Finnish case seems to become more and more special every day, and this is bound to cause increasing bewilderment among foreigners.

Or let us take the "changes" undergone by the Finnish Social Democrats during the last ten or fifteen years. (I could think of a much more fitting term, but how easy it is to slide into Aesopian language.) Perhaps the Social Democrats have good reason to admire Communism as it is practiced in the Soviet Union; it is clearly not for an outsider to criticize them. But what puzzles the outsider is the fact that despite their rapprochement with the Communist party of the Soviet Union, despite the fact that they are now less independent and less critical of it than the Italian or French (let alone the Spanish) Communists, they continue to stress their attachment to the ideals and values of social democracy, they are still members of the Socialist International, and they try, admittedly without much success, to convert other social-democratic parties to their policy. One might wish for some clarification of the apparent contradictions here.

To choose another example at random, take the case of the so-called "Black Dozen." This groups of moderate politicans has been harshly attacked and denounced as "unacceptable" to the Soviet Union, despite the fact that they have not deviated from the Paasikivi-Kekkonen line where Finnish foreign policy is concerned, but have simply followed a somewhat independent line in domestic politics. But—what is even more significant—no Finnish newspaper, to the best of my knowledge, has published their statements in full. How often, in recent Finnish history, has it been insinuated that someone or other is "unacceptable"? Under the circumstances, you will have to excuse the perplexity of foreign observers: on the one hand, we are assured that Finlandization is a figment of our imagination; on the other hand, there are many facts which cannot be explained away.

No one in his right mind would blame Finland because its relationship with the Soviet Union, for obvious reasons, is of a special character. The real issue is the "adjustments" that have taken place in Finnish domestic politics as a result of this relationship. Permit me to end this letter in a manner befitting an outside observer, with a question rather than an assertion: can it really be maintained that there has been no erosion of political freedom in Finland?

*Two:*

My article, "The Specter of Finlandization," has continued to create agitation in Scandinavia and I am grateful to Anja Hansen for the opportunity to add a postscript. She will forgive me if I dwell only briefly on her observations, which range from the correct (but irrelevant) to the ludicrous (her description of the 1958 crisis). Mrs. Hansen is quite right—the Social Democrats were not the strongest party in Finland for a while in 1958, and had indeed split a few months earlier. But what possible bearing does this have on my argument? Mrs. Hansen appears to be more pro-Kekkonen than some of the Finns. (In this connection, an article in the May issue of the Finnish periodical *Kanava,* for example, noted certain imprecisions in my article but went on to add: "In fact, however,

Laqueur has met in advance most of the counterarguments brought up by the Finnish critics.'')

Mrs. Hansen is wrong in saying that according to my evidence President Kekkonen could be characterized as a Communist fellow-traveler, or that Sovietization is a more apt term for what I was talking about than Finlandization. It is not a question of Sovietization, and President Kekkonen is not a Communist fellow-traveler. He is a Finnish patriot who believed, up till Stalingrad, that a pro-German orientation was the only possibility for his country and then changed his line in 1943. For no obvious reason Mrs. Hansen quotes a speech made by Kekkonen in Stockholm in late 1943, a speech which was reprinted in Helsinki in 1955 and happens to be readily available. Not wishing to cause any further embarrassment, I shall refrain from quoting what Kekkonen said in this speech about the Russian intention of destroying Finland's independence, about the war of 1941 being only a continuation of the Russian attack of November 1939, and so forth. All that matters in the present context is that Kekkonen in the Stockholm speech sensibly advocated a return to the neutrality policy of 1939. He did not advocate Finnish neutrality 1978-style. Since Mrs. Hansen quotes from old speeches and articles, why not go even further back and quote from articles written by Kekkonen (under the pen name Pekka Peitsi) for the Swedish and Finnish press before the tide turned in World War II? The result could be both illuminating and entertaining.

But the case of President Kekkonen, however interesting, is not really the central issue—after all, he may be replaced by someone more obsequious. Far more important is the general question of appeasement. Now it is true that a policy of appeasement may be perfectly legitimate for a small country facing a powerful neighbor. But appeasement is (a) frequently carried far beyond what is necessary, and (b) is often advocated not as an unfortunate necessity, but as a panacea for the resolution of political conflict, and a policy of wisdom, maturity, and responsibility.

What is troubling about Mrs. Hansen's letter is that it is so obviously a case of rationalizing weakness, so typical of a certain strand of political thought in Scandinavia. With all their shortcomings, the Scandinavian societies are among the most civilized the world has known. The absence of fanaticism and brutality are striking, the standards of democratic behavior, of social justice, of honesty and decency, of lack of corruption in public life are unparalleled. And yet these same admirable people who have shown such maturity in arranging their domestic affairs have for generations been the world's most wishful thinkers in foreign affairs. Examples abound: their belief in the League of Nations in the 1920s, their trust in Germany's peaceful intentions in the 1930s, their doctrine of bridge-building between West and East in the 1940s, their faith in the

United Nations in the 1950s and 1960s, and their belief in the Helsinki "Final Act" in the 1970s. Could it be perhaps that the very qualities which have made for Scandinavian maturity at home in some way hamper understanding of the world outside? I do not know. But I do know the consequences of this wishful thinking, for the history of Scandinavian appeasement does not begin in the late 1950s. Since Mrs. Hansen writes from Denmark, she might have found some excellent illustrations in recent Danish history, such as the case of the Social Democrats and the Radicals in the 1930s, who were staunch opponents of Hitler but even stauncher opponents of defending themselves against Hitler. There was Peter Munch, for instance, the leader of the Danish Radicals and Danish Foreign Minister, who loathed the Nazis and everything they stood for. But this did not prevent him from casting his vote against the League of Nations' condemnation of Hitler's rearmament (ineffectual as it was) in 1935, or from voting against sanctions against Nazi Germany in 1936, or from signing a nonaggression pact with Hitler in 1939. There was also Thorwald Stauning, the grand old man of Danish socialism, who was for many years Prime Minister, and a man of great dignity as well as a staunch anti-fascist. But this did not prevent him from succumbing to a Vichy mentality after the Nazi invasion, or from believing that Germany would be Europe's leading power after the war. In the meantime he cooperated with the Germans to make Denmark a model protectorate. These men, and many others like them, were good patriots who sincerely believed there was no other way for their country, and this led them to Finlandization *avant la lettre*.

History has judged them, but memories are short. So we now hear in Mrs. Hansen's letter echoes from the past expressing concern about "Soviet sensitivity to any increase of NATO activity in Scandinavia," as though we had not been over this ground once before. Views like these are quite prevalent in Scandinavia today. Fortunately, they are not the only views.

Finally, there is one statement in Mrs. Hansen's letter which really cannot be allowed to pass. Mrs. Hansen could have argued that some form of self-censorship in Finland is inevitable, that the whole issue is extremely sensitive and complicated, or even that the American press would not be worse for a little censorship. But to say that the Finnish press is free and does not practice self-censorship is simply an untruth. She must know this. Why then does she say it?

*October 1978*

## NOTES

1. The most recent contribution on the subject has been made by Vice President Mondale who commented on the occasion of a visit to Helsinki (April 1979) not only on the beauty of the Finnish landscape but also on Finlandization: "The use of the term interferes with accurate communication because it is charged with emotions." If this was meant to say that the term is disliked inside Finland, Mondale was, of course, right. But according to this logic most of our political vocabulary would have to be abolished for it is also charged with emotions. The Vice President did not suggest a more neutral, less offensive term.
2. Studies on Finlandization include Nils Orvik's book, *Sicherheit auf Finnisch* (Security, Finnish-style), and George Maude's recent *The Finnish Dilemma,* London 1976.
3. See Carl-Gustaf Lilius, "Self-Censorship in Finland," *Index on Censorship,* Spring 1975.

# The Fall of Europe?

Never in its history has Europe suffered from so large and perceptible a discrepancy between economic strength on the one hand, and political and military impotence on the other. It is true that economic predictions for 1972 are not too sanguine and that Britain for instance is still in the throes of a severe economic crisis, but the foreign visitor would be hard put to discover signs of it in the streets of London or elsewhere. Italy's economy has taken a downward turn, but a traveler crossing from Italy into Switzerland, or the other way around, would not observe a great difference in prices or in the standard of living on the two sides of the line. A heated debate recently held on French television between a leading Gaullist and the new Secretary General of the French Communist party focused on the issue of whether the average French income has trebled (as the Gaullist claimed) or only doubled (according to the Communist thesis) in the last two decades.

On paper, the new Europe is a major world power: with a total population of 250 million, a combined GNP of some $640 billion (about two-thirds of the American GNP and considerably larger than that of the Communist bloc), it accounts for some 40 per cent of world trade. But there is something profoundly askew about this continent which for the past twenty-five years has lived on borrowed time, incapable of mustering sufficient strength to overcome national particularism and establish some form of political unity. Europe now finds itself in a perilous political and military situation. It is usually said that 1973 will be the European year of decision, when the general elections that are scheduled to be held in France, West Germany, and Italy will produce new governments, armed with a mandate to engage in more decisive and far-reaching policies. Yet even if all should go well from this point of view in 1973, Europe will still find itself only at the start of a long-drawn-out march toward political unity, and if that march is not undertaken, it is doubtful whether even the Common Market will manage to survive.

In recent days there has been a great deal of movement in European politics. Only a few months ago the entire Continent was agitated over the issue of Britain's entry into the European Economic Community, but by early October the debate had fizzled out even in Britain itself, where the issue had been regarded as the gravest the nation had to decide upon in this century. When, on October 28, the House of Commons finally voted to join the Common Market, the rest of Europe hardly noticed, so many more important problems having intervened and taken precedence: Brandt's *Ostpolitik,* the impact of America's new economic policies, the Soviet drive for a European Security Conference. Still, had the vote on October 28 gone *against* joining the Market, it would have meant not just the further decline of Britain but very probably the beginning of the end for Europe as a whole.

The debate over Britain's entry into the EEC is closely connected with the other problems facing Europe. West Germany's growing independence, both in economic matters and in areas of foreign policy, contributed decisively to Pompidou's decision to make British entry possible. To put it in somewhat oversimplified terms, whereas in the 1950s and 1960s the French needed West Germany as a counterweight to British influence, in the 1970s Britain herself has become for France the counterweight to West Germany. Moreover, the French, notwithstanding official declarations, now share British skepticism with regard to Soviet intentions in Europe. In view of the near certainty of American troop reductions in the years ahead, it has become clear to the French government that only a common defense policy can prevent what is now commonly referred to as the Finlandization of Europe. In this respect, as in others, the pendulum has swung far since the era of Charles de Gaulle.

Though Parliament voted in favor of entry, the majority of Englishmen were against joining Europe. In this sense the decision was undemocratic, but before drawing alarming conclusions from this fact one should bear in mind that, according to recent polls, seventy-seven percent of the British electorate would also vote in favor of restoring capital punishment, and in addition would no doubt have stopped non-white immigration into Britain long ago. The opposition to joining the EEC consisted of a strange assortment of extreme right-wing Tories and extreme left-wing Labourites, both of which groups exploited all the free-floating conservatism, fear, distrust, envy, and xenophobia abroad in British society. For once Bernadette Devlin and Ian Paisley were on the same side of the barricade.

One of the basic arguments employed by left-wing critics was that British social services would suffer as a result of entry into the EEC. The Welfare State and the National Health Service have been the pride of Britain for several decades. What is less well known is that all the European

Community countries have overtaken Britain and now spend a higher proportion of their GNP on social welfare. In absolute terms the discrepancy is even more striking: Britain spends $285 per person per annum, West Germany $507; a British worker gets between sixteen and twenty paid holidays a year, an Italian worker between twenty-nine and forty-seven. No European government spends less on housing than Britain does, and France spends almost three times more. Family allowances on the Continent are more than double Britain's.

But, opponents argued, the Common Market was inward-looking, parochial, oblivious of its duty to the countries of the "Third World." Here too a closer look reveals that every European country contributes at least as much as Britain to the Third World, and many contribute more. The Common Market, these critics went on, is right-wing, reactionary, dominated by the super-cartels. This argument may have had some force five years ago, but West Germany, the most powerful European country, today has—what Britain does not—a socialist-dominated government; Social Democrats are also represented in the Italian government, as well as in Benelux. But, still another group of critics said, Britain is likely to lose the Commonwealth, or the special relationship with the United States, or above all its sovereignty, the time-honored traditions that have always set England apart from Europe. The truth is, however, that the Commonwealth has for a long time been a fiction, the special relationship with America was lost years ago, and the idea of British "apartness" did not even come into being until the nineteenth century.

The economic argument (non-Communist variety) against entry can be summarized under two headings: (a) the scheme would not work; and (b) the price of Britain's entry was too high. It would not work because British industry, being outdated, poorly managed, and strike-ridden, cannot compete any longer with the rest of the world. For this reason Britain would not be in a position to exploit the economic advantages of the Common Market (the availability of a wider market, lower tariffs against industrial goods, etc.). There is no denying that this is a real consideration. But even assuming, on the basis of the defeatist argument, that Britain is destined to become Europe's depressed area, a second Ulster, the country would still probably be better off inside the European community than out in the cold. For, once inside, it can count on the help of the other members. The real nub of the matter is the price of Britain's entry, estimated by the government at $250 million in 1973 and rising to twice that sum in 1977. Will not this outlay devastate the country's recently-restored balance-of-payments position and thus inhibit economic growth? Why should Britain support the Common Market agricultural policy which, whatever its original intentions, has done nothing but subsidize inefficient farming at a ruinously high cost? Will not the British housewife end up paying the price of British entry into the Market?

There does seem to be general agreement that food prices in Britain are bound to rise substantially once entry into the Common Market is effected, though why this should be so is not altogether clear. During a recent visit to the Continent I found that, butter aside, food prices in France, Switzerland, and Italy are more or less the same as in Britain: fruit and vegetables are a bit cheaper, meat is a little more expensive but of better quality. It is taken for granted that whereas the benefits of having joined will not be felt for a long time, the toll, in the form of higher food prices, will make itself felt almost immediately. Maybe so, but on the other hand an increase of even a half of one percent in Britain's growth rate would more than cover the membership fee. And since exports will unquestionably increase as a result of the merger, the inordinate amount of time being wasted in the debate over the future price of butter already seems a little ridiculous.

The Tory campaign in favor of joining was helped along by the fact that the Labour party had only two years earlier favored British entry into the EEC on conditions that were certainly no better than those finally obtained by Prime Minister Heath. If anything, the Conservatives were hampered by a lack of enthusiasm in their own ranks; their new Europeanism, however loudly proclaimed, is limited in scope and not altogether convincing. Certainly the propaganda put out by the Conservative Central Office in defense of joining Europe would be disquieting to anyone who regards Europe as something other than a free trade zone, an economic convenience. One pamphlet, in trying to allay public fears of a "faceless bureaucracy" and a reduction in the prerogatives of Parliament and the Queen, noted comfortingly that there "has been no progress yet toward closer political unity," and that there was little likelihood of any pooling of sovereignty in the foreseeable future.

This argument is self-defeating because the case for Britain's entry rests in the last resort precisely on political, not economic, premises. The real issue is not the price of butter and sugar, not even the rate of growth, but the simple viability of the various countries of Western Europe. Taken one by one these countries do not count for anything politically, they are defenseless militarily, and they are economically highly vulnerable. European unity is the only way to overcome these weaknesses and to prevent the suicidal infighting which has so far in this century caused two world wars. In a recent article, Andrew Shonfield rightly complained about the apparent lack of concern with international relations manifest in the British debate over the Common Market. For if a slowdown should occur in the growth of international trade in the years to come, would there not be an overwhelming temptation for individual

European nations to seize short-term advantages at the expense of other nations, unless a firmly established framework existed to contain and regulate economic tensions? The same goes, *a fortiori,* for the recrudescence of violent nationalism in any European country. Seen in this light, the trouble with the Common Market is not that it has moved too far and too fast toward supranationality, but that, on the contrary, movement in that direction has been agonizingly slow.

It is of course quite possible that political and military cooperation in Western Europe wil proceed independently of economic development. In a press conference in early 1971, President Pompidou ridiculed the idea of Europe as a third force in world politics. But the fact of American disengagement from Europe, combined with traditional distrust of Soviet intentions and the fear of a deal between the two superpowers at Europe's expense, may well cause a quickening in the pace of cooperation outside the economic field. The political argument for British entry seems so overwhelming on the face of it that future generations will no doubt be puzzled that it took so long to accept the obvious and that England had to be pulled into Europe kicking and screaming. The cost of joining may be high, but the cost of not joining would in the long run be insupportable.

## II

The course of Soviet-German talks in recent months highlights the dilemmas involved in the current phase of European politics. For more than two decades Germany was the main battlefield of East-West confrontation in Europe. It is clear in retrospect that the official German attitude was too rigid; Bonn should have accepted long ago, unilaterally if necessary, such consequences of World War II as the Oder-Neisse line, and it should have renounced the Munich agreement of 1938. Instead of insisting on the Hallstein Doctrine (threatening to break with all countries recognizing East Germany) it should have put up with the fact that an East German state had come into being and would not disappear in the foreseeable future. It was argued for too long that for domestic reasons—the opposition mounted by refugee organizations—any accommodation with the East would have suicidal consequences for the party in power.

But if it was not really necessary to wait until the great coalition came into being in late 1966 for an initiative in German *Ostpolitik,* it is also true that up until that time the Soviet Union continued to threaten West Germany with military intervention (on the basis of paragraphs 53 and 107 of the UN charter) and had launched a massive propaganda attack (with accusations of "neo-Nazism," revanchism, etc.) against Bonn. Not until the spring of 1969, when the Soviet diplomatic offensive aimed at the establishment of a European Security Conference was stepped up, did hints emerge that the Russians were willing to engage in serious negotiations. This coincided with the advent to power in Bonn of a new government; when Willy Brandt became chancellor in September 1969 he devoted much of his energy to the discussions which led to the Soviet-German treaty of August 1970. This treaty, very broadly speaking, envisaged closer relations between the two countries on the basis of the recognition of the status quo in Europe. But it was to come into force, as the Germans insisted with full NATO support, only after a satisfactory solution had been found for the thorny Berlin issue; and this finally occurred in August 1971.

There is some promise in the new German *Ostpolitik,* and there are many dangers. Brandt can rightly claim that he did only what was in the long run inevitable, and what his predecessors, lacking courage and foresight, had failed to do—that is, to recognize, *de jure,* that Germany had lost the war. He can claim furthermore to have defused a potentially dangerous situation. West Germany is no longer the main villain of Soviet foreign policy; on the contrary, Brandt was praised in almost extravagant terms by Brezhnev in the latter's recent talks with Tito. This is a far cry from the past situation and it is only human for the architects of the *Ostpolitik* to believe that—far from having given anything away—they have restored to their country ("an economic giant but a political dwarf") much greater freedom of maneuver than anybody would have dreamed of even a year ago. Once the outcast, the pariah of European politics, Germany has again become a respected member of the family of nations in East and West alike.

Yet West Germany may one day have to pay a heavy price for these achievements. However often Brandt and Scheel may profess their loyalty to their Western allies, there is a great deal of free-floating distrust in Europe of Germany's reemergence as a leading power. Some of this apprehensiveness is exaggerated if not downright hysterical; Brandt and his colleagues are good Europeans and they have had too many dealings with the Communists in their own lifetime to join a Popular Front on the interstate level, as a few commentators have implied they might. But the distrust persists; the recent French-British rapprochement was caused at least partly, as noted above, by French fears of Germany's growing role in Europe.

Potentially more dangerous than these relatively harmless rivalries, however, is the general climate of make-believe concerning Soviet intentions to which Brandt and his colleagues have succumbed and also contributed. The German Social Democrats may in fact have taken their stand on a slippery slope. For if Brandt and his government fail to live up to Soviet expectations in the political and economic fields, the Soviets will not hesitate to bring strong pressure to bear. Brandt realizes that but for a militarily credible American presence in Europe his deal with the Russians is bound to turn sour; his government has been among those protesting most loudly against any American troop reductions. But at the same time the *Ostpolitik* has given invaluable ammunition to American Senators and Congressmen who favor troop withdrawal below the point of credibility. After all, U.S. troops were kept in Europe mainly to defend Germany against Soviet encroachments; if Germany has reached an agreement with Russia which supposedly guarantees its security, what further need can there be for an American presence? According to a public opinion poll taken a few days after Brandt received the Nobel Peace Prize, fifty percent of the German people now favor neutrality and only thirty-eight percent support the Western alliance; why should they be prevented from having it their own way? Brandt knows of course that neutrality is just not practical so far as Germany is concerned, and that, the balance of power in Europe being what it is, the only alternatives are either close collaboration with the West or gradual absorption into the Soviet sphere of influence. But he has already to some degree fallen captive to the illusions nursed by too much loose talk concerning Soviet-German rapprochement.[1]

### III

The signing of the agreement on Berlin has been seen by some as an official acknowledgment, so to speak, that the post-war era is over. But periodization is an enterprise of dubious value in the best of times, and these are not the best of times. When, for example, did the previous postwar era end? The question is of course unanswerable. In one sense it ended in 1923, in another it lasted until the outbreak of World War II. With equal justice, it can be claimed that the second postwar period ended in 1948-9, when the European economy had once again attained its pre-war levels and the location of the Iron Curtain was fixed. Yet most of the problems created by the war remained unsolved. As a consequence of World War II the balance of power in Europe underwent a radical shift; the resulting situation has continued in force despite years of East-West dialogue, diplomatic activity, security conferences, unilateral and multilateral talks, and no end of new schemes, ideas, and approaches. In other words, to a very real extent the postwar era is *not* over: Europe remains divided, the Soviet Union is the dominant military power, and but for the military alliance between Western Europe and the United States it would be the dominant political power as well. Such are the harsh facts, and no new formulas, however ingenious, no theoretical legerdemain, can make them disappear.

The age of dialogue, we are told, has replaced the age of confrontation. This is only partly true. Western Europe no longer fears a Soviet invasion, but on the other hand neither the fundamental assumptions nor the political aspirations of the Soviet Union have changed. It is the age of détente—not, unfortunately, a détente that signals real peace and security, but a détente in the more narrow meaning of a "period that succeeds a period of crisis in the Cold War."[2] For European security since the end of the war has rested not on dialogues and mutual understanding but on the existence of a certain balance of military power, and this balance, never complete or perfect, has in recent years been radically upset.

The facts are not in dispute: the Soviet Union and its allies now have three times as many tanks in Europe as does NATO, and 3,500 more tactical aircraft. From 1962 to 1968 American forces in Europe were reduced from 462,000 to 300,000, whereas the number of Soviet divisions has grown during the last four years from 26 to 31. The number of American ICBM's has remained static since 1967 at 1,054, while during the same period the number of Soviet missiles has almost doubled, and now stands at 1,500.[3] The build-up of the Soviet fleet is well publicized and need not be described in detail. In sum, between 1967 and 1970 the military expenditures of NATO decreased by ten billion dollars, those of the Warsaw Pact countries rose by five billion. The Soviet Union now spends two to three times more per capita than NATO on military affairs.

These facts, to repeat, are not in dispute. What is at issue is their significance. Thus, for example, it has been said that they are of no great political consequence: the Soviet Union is too engrossed with its allies and with domestic problems to desire any further expansion. All the Russians need in Europe—at any rate so long as the conflict with China continues—is security and recognition of the status quo. Having acquired the necessary strategic parity with the United States, the Soviet Union is unlikely to engage in a ruinous arms race in order to gain a superiority which, in the age of modern nuclear warfare, might well prove specious. On the contrary, proponents of this line of reasoning find much evidence that the Soviet Union wishes to expand trade relations with the West, and they suggest that the West make the most of the situation and work for a *modus vivendi* in Europe that will help establish a climate of mutual trust and security.

The argument is alluring but many of the premises on which it is based are debatable, and some are manifestly wrong. First, the Soviet military build-up is by now well in excess of what can be reasonably considered essential for Soviet security in Europe. Second, and more important, the argument rests on the assumption that the Soviet Union (like the United

States) is now a status quo power. This is simply not the case, and those who think it is are merely succumbing to the escapism which these days pervades political thinking in the United States and Western Europe alike.

True, Chinese pressure may induce the Kremlin to make certain concessions—on SALT, for instance—and as a short-term goal the Russians do also wish closer economic ties with Europe. But beyond this, the Soviet Union has more ambitious plans of which it has never made a secret. As the greatest European power it aspires to political, economic, and military hegemony, and it hopes to achieve this goal by inducing Western Europe to relax its political cohesiveness and military vigilance, by encouraging an accelerated program of American disengagement, and by preventing all moves toward closer political and military cooperation or integration among European countries.[4]

The main instrument of Soviet foreign policy in Europe in recent years has been the demand for the establishment of a European Security Conference.[5] The basic concept dates back a long time, having made its first appearance in 1954-5 as part of the Soviet plan to prevent the consolidation of NATO in Europe. When this failed, various schemes for disengagement were introduced (such as the Rapacki plan), all of which were widely discussed but in the end discarded by the West because they were thought to contain no elements which would have contributed to real security in Europe. The Soviet aim all along was to dissolve both NATO and the Warsaw Pact and to create something like a European co-prosperity sphere. But the scheme was too crude, the lack of symmetry all too apparent: the Communist countries of Eastern Europe were tied together by bilateral defense agreements which would have remained in force, whereas Western Europe had no such arrangement. Furthermore, if hostilities broke out, American forces would have had to cross the Atlantic, while Soviet divisions merely would have had to move two hundred miles eastward.

Gradually the scheme became more sophisticated: in July 1966 the Warsaw Pact leaders issued a declaration on peace and security in Europe which included some concrete proposals. But the Soviet invasion of Czechoslovakia two years later put an end, temporarily at least, to negotiations. It was only October 1969 that talks began in earnest on an agenda proposed by the Soviets "to insure European security, to renounce the use or threat of force in mutual relations, to expand commercial, economic, scientific-technical, and cultural relations for the purpose of developing political cooperation among European states."

By this time the project had begun to make a more solid and thoughtful impression. Skeptics still argued that, given the character of the

Soviet regime, vague talk about the renunciation of the use or threat of force lacked credibility. Moreover, since both the Soviet Union and the West European countries were already signatories to a declaration to the same effect—the United Nations Charter—what was to be gained by affirming these principles yet another time? As for expanding trade relations, the Soviet Union's interest in this matter was never in doubt; the Russians badly needed (and need) Western computers and other modern equipment. Cultural relations, the free flow of people and ideas across international borders, posed a more problematical issue, raising, in the Soviets' view, the possibility of ideological infection, of "peaceful invasion." Brezhnev and other Soviet leaders have stressed time and time again (most recently at the 24th Party Congress) that there can be no coexistence in the ideological sphere. This raised the old problem which has bedeviled East-West relations for so long: if Soviet doctrine does not in the long run envisage coexistence with political systems differing from its own, how can anyone be expected to take seriously the constant Soviet invocation of an era of "mutual trust and security"?

Despite all these reservations and other, procedural, misgivings, NATO at its meetings in Reykjavik, Lisbon, and Rome (May 1970) decided to take up the Soviet suggestions and explore them further. The NATO Council made its participation conditional on the further improvement of the situation in Central Europe. Such improvement appeared to be rapidly forthcoming: with the Soviet-German treaty, the Berlin agreement, the prospects for further advance in the SALT talks, and Soviet hints concerning discussions on Mutual and Balanced Force Reductions (MBFR), it was decided last October to delegate Mario Brosio, the outgoing NATO Secretary, to explore Soviet intentions in Moscow.

The West has been strongly urged to participate in the European Security Conference, not only by the Soviets but by East European leaders as well. The interest of some of the latter is obvious: while the Soviets negotiate, any military initiative against Rumania and Yugoslavia, for example, would be self-defeating. Since the talks would last a long time, perhaps several years, Rumania and Yugoslavia would gain, at the very least, a breathing space. Other East European leaders, notably in Poland and Hungary, think that they, too, would gain more freedom as a result of ESC, but the position of these particular states would more likely worsen; for the Soviet Union, fearing that its allies might go too far toward rapprochement with the West, would be inclined to tighten rather than loosen its hold over them.

Another group of lobbyists for the ESC is made up of politicians from neutral countries. Some of these sincerely desire to act as mediators and bridge-builders; with others ulterior motives may be at work. Not much need be said about Finland in this context; in view of its relationship with Russia it cannot very well refrain from supporting its powerful neighbor. Swedish foreign policy has pursued a middle line between West and East which, if not morally reprehensible (as the late John Foster Dulles claimed), does not reflect either superior moral courage or wisdom: but for the existence of a balance of power in Europe, Sweden could not afford to be neutral. There is a tendency in Sweden to forget its unfortunate record of dealings with Nazi Germany between 1938 and 1944; there may or may not be lessons to be drawn from that record for the present time, but it might be hoped that study of the period would nevertheless serve to curb the Swedish habit of moralizing about situations involving the security of others.

The British and French attitude has been one of "polite reserve," in the words of one observer, though not necessarily for the same reason. The French prefer bilateral talks to mass circuses; de Gaulle certainly would not have approved of a scheme as lacking in substance as this one. In most British eyes, American disengagement from Europe seems likely to produce in the long run a situation more dangerous to peace than the present state of affairs. In Italy, Norway, and Denmark, on the other hand, the idea of ESC has found a considerably more friendly reception. The Italian government, in its insistence on responding to the Soviet initiative, has taken account of the fact that one-third of Italy's electorate votes regularly for parties which oppose NATO and which, in contrast to the situation in France, constitute a very real political factor. These parties are eager to find compromise formulas in their opening to the Left—and it is far easier to find them in matters of foreign policy than in matters of domestic policy. "Neutralism" is an important factor in Norway and Denmark as well; recent elections in both countries saw an increase of support for anti-NATO parties. While these two governments in general exhibit an awareness of just to whom it is they owe their independence, public opinion is not so clear on this point. Soviet intimidation too has had a certain effect here; Russia has tried hard, and not entirely unsuccessfully, to demonstrate that it is the strongest military power in the area and that American help cannot be relied upon.

The advocates of ESC in Western Europe maintain that dialogue with the East, even if limited at first to areas like oceanography and the environment, will gradually gather momentum and lead to an improvement in the general political climate. Some of the main obstacles toward such dialogue were removed by Willy Brandt's *Ostpolitik*. Brezhnev's announced approval last summer of the NATO proposals for balanced troop reductions seemed yet another step in the right direction. It is, however, by no means certain that the Soviet leadership has accepted the Western demand that troop reductions be asymmetrical (because the conventional forces of Western Europe are so much weaker than those of the East). Even so, the signals from Moscow encouraged President Nixon and other Western leaders to probe Soviet intentions further.

Nevertheless, it is not altogether certain that a conference is what the Russians really want. It is obviously in their interest to prolong the present "talks about talks" for as long as possible; a conference that is bound to reveal disagreement on the one issue that really matters, namely who is going to dominate Europe, would constitute an anti-climax after the present upsurge of expectations.

It can be argued that the pessimism expressed here is unwarranted. To be sure, the resolutions of the last Soviet Party congress mention the "consolidation and *extension* of the Soviet ['socialist'] order"—but why take at face value the ritual invocations of a basically conservative leadership that has no use for revolutionary fervor and no expansionist aims? The answer is that a regime need not be revolutionary in character to aim at expansion, provided the temptation is strong enough and the risks involved not too high. It may well be that Soviet leaders are willing to make certain concessions in order to achieve their principal aim in Europe—the removal of American forces. They do not, for instance, insist any longer on the exclusion of the United States from the proposed conference. Similarly, as the threat from China increases—more Soviet divisions are now stationed on the Chinese border than in Eastern Europe—it is not unthinkable that the Soviet Union may evince a willingness to engage in more meaningful talks with the West. And it is also not impossible that if this state of affairs were to last long enough, the Soviet Union would give up its more ambitious aims in Europe altogether.

But this optimistic outlook presupposes one of two conditions, neither of which unfortunately exists at present: the continuation of a strong American presence in Europe, or alternatively, the existence of a strong Western European defense community. So far as the first is concerned, domestic pressures in the U.S. for disengagement from Europe are no secret to the Soviets; and as for the second, nobody in Western Europe seems ready to shoulder the cost in money and manpower necessary to bring West European conventional forces up to a level roughly equal to that of the Warsaw Pact forces.

It would take a Soviet invasion of Rumania or Yugoslavia, or Soviet participation in a Middle Eastern war, to galvanize West European public opinion on this point. This the Russians of course know, and they will no doubt refrain in the near future from actions which may cause disquiet in the West. In the meantime, while the Russians greet unilateral American troop reductions and cuts in American defense spending with polite and reassuring professions of good will and peaceful intentions, we may be sure that they are not about to make any far-reaching concessions of their own.

In the face of all this, the only alternative would seem to be appeasement or, in more refined language "accommodation." Whatever the term used, the likely result will be the gradual growth of Soviet power in Europe. At present, there are not many outright advocates of Soviet hegemony in Europe, even among the Communist parties. But if the American retreat continues and if Western Europe proves incapable of strengthening its own defenses fairly rapidly, the argument will increasingly be heard that accommodation with the Russians, being inevitable, should be sought sooner rather than later.

What would Soviet hegemony mean in practical terms? Certainly not the physical occupation of Western Europe. Europe would be expected, however, to help with the economic development of the Eastern bloc. The Soviet Union would not necessarily insist on the inclusion of Communists in every European government, but (as in Finland) it would surely demand that untrustworthy political leaders or parties be excluded from positions of power and influence, and it would expect a ban on any criticism of Soviet policies. To a limited extent it is possible to discern something of this pattern already emerging. Soviet leaders have declared unequivocally that they would take it as a threat to peace if the German *Bundestag* should fail to ratify the Soviet-German treaty. Broadcasting stations critical of Soviet policy have been called a danger to European security and Soviet demands have been issued for their removal from the air; needless to say, no such restrictions have been suggested with regard to Soviet broadcasts. Similarly, the Soviet Union regards interference with the activities of its intelligence agents in Western Europe as a hostile act; protests are brushed aside or dismissed as cold-war propaganda or even a threat to peace. (After the recent expulsion of some ninety Soviet agents from London, it was sadly observed in Bonn and Paris that such drastic action would now be almost unthinkable in any other European capital.)

There is still a chance that out of the present confusion a new European defense community will emerge, based on Anglo-French nuclear cooperation and the combined conventional forces of ten European countries. Attempts to establish a European defense force date back to the early 1950s; they were voted down by the French National Assembly while Pierre Mendès-France was Prime Minister and they failed to kindle much enthusiasm in any of the other countries in question. For twenty years Europe lay under the American nuclear guarantee, and by a stroke of unique good fortune resulting from the Soviet conflict with China, the Continent has now received a second respite. No one knows how long this breathing space will last, or indeed whether it can be successfully exploited. Pooling their resources, the West European countries could muster a sum total of $23 billion by way of a military budget (as against the $63 billion spend by the Warsaw Pact), and a force of about two million men and 300 combat vessels. Still, if one takes into account the Soviet Union's commitments in other parts of the world the overall picture is not as hopeless as it appears at first sight.

But would a European defense community be of any consequence without an independent nuclear deterrent? The immensely complex issue of Anglo-French nuclear cooperation has recently been analyzed in some detail by Ian Smart.[6] Britain has had much longer experience than France with nuclear weapons, whereas the French have made more progress in producing their own missiles. The French tactical nuclear artillery (Pluton) will be deployed in Germany later this year. The main obstacle is not, as is frequently thought, an economic one; Britain has spend less than 0.2 percent of its GNP on strategic weapons, France about 0.6 percent. France's progress has been hampered in recent years above all by certain technical difficulties which will, no doubt, be overcome in due course. But there are immense political problems. Should Germany and other European countries participate in this program? Leaders of the German CDU have in the past welcomed the concept of a British-French pool as an important step toward an all-European deterrent. But it is doubtful whether the present German government would risk incurring Soviet displeasure and thus the achievements, real and imaginary, of the *Ostpolitik* by making a financial contribution. Moreover, how credible would an Anglo-French deterrent be? In Smart's view, the only threat such a deterrent could pose would be the threat of retaliation either for a Warsaw Pact military action which could be held to endanger vital British or French interests, or for a strategic nuclear attack by the Soviet Union. "The former threat is one which entails suicide, the latter a blow from the grave." Nevertheless, a European capacity to retaliate, however small, would not be lightly dismissed by the Warsaw Pact countries.

Considerations of this nature will, of course, appear outdated and irrelevant (if not altogether heinous) to those who have decided to their satisfaction that the cold war has ended at long last and a new era of peace and cooperation is automatic and inevitable. But there is still a distinct danger that by unilateral concessions and disarmament those who strive for peace will undermine the very basis on which the prospects for peace and security in Europe rest—namely the ability of Europe to defend itself. A European Defense Organization could play a decisive role in bringing about a real détente. If, on the other hand, the Europeans put their trust in high-sounding but basically meaningless dialogues and security conferences, while at the same time failing to take adequate measures to insure their own defense, the outcome, short of a miracle, will be only too predictable.

*January 1972*

## NOTES

1. To provide but one example, Brandt's Foreign Minister declared in an interview in late November that "structural changes inside the Soviet Union in recent years" could provide a good basis for a further reduction of tension. Even Communists outside the Soviet Union have been hard put to discover the presence of any such "structural changes."
2. Philip Windsor, *Germany and the Management of Détente,* London, 1971.
3. The impact of nuclear parity has been discussed in considerable detail in Walter Slocombe's recent study, *The Political Implications of Strategic Parity,* London, 1971.
4. Michael Palmer, *The Prospects for a European Security Conference,* London, 1971, p. 18.
5. Several recent studies analyze Soviet policy on this matter in detail: Karl Birnbaum, *Peace in Europe,* London, 1970; "Europe and America in the 1970s," *Adelphi Papers 70/71,* London, 1971; Hans Peter Schwarz, ed., *Europäische Sicherheits Konferenz,* Opladen, 1970; Thomas W. Wolfe, *Soviet Power and Europe,* Baltimore, 1970.
6. "Future Conditional: The Prospect for Anglo-French Nuclear Cooperation," *Adelphi Paper 78,* London, 1971.

# "Eurocommunism" and Its Friends

The problem of cooperation between democratic and Communist parties is not new. Originally, in the 1920s, it was a major doctrinal issue for the Communists, but lately it has ceased bothering them and has now mainly become a problem for their prospective democratic partners. Sir Harold Wilson—until recently Prime Minister of the British Labour government, and a man who has never been accused of being either an alarmist or a cold warrior—warned not long ago against collaboration between democratic socialists and Communists, which he said was bound to endanger democracy, and not only in the country in which the alliance is consummated. In the United States, by contrast, many voices have been advocating an accommodation with West European Communism, or "Eurocommunism," as it is coming to be called. Some have argued that Italian Communism in particular is essentially moderate and reformist and will become even more so, provided of course that an intransigent American foreign policy does not reject the outstretched hand and thus strengthen the influence of the pro-Soviet elements in the PCI. Others, such as George Ball, have maintained that the rise to power of Italian Communism is inevitable, and that if Washington only plays its cards right, the United States may actually benefit if and when a new situation is created in Rome.

These American advocates of an accommodation with the PCI are not generally known for their attachment to the values of democratic socialism—a fact which has sorely tried the patience of some Italians. One prominent Italian jounalist was tempted, he said, to remind American readers that the rise of fascism under Benito Mussolini was also welcomed at the beginning by a large number of Americans, including intellectuals and journalists.[1] This in turn provoked a pained outcry: to draw even an implicit analogy of this kind was scandalous. Obviously no one wants to be compared with the early defenders of Fascism. But is the analogy really so self-evidently wrong, or does it perhaps help to throw a bit of light on present-day attitudes to the emergence of a new, strange, and in some ways attractive political movement which has the one drawback of being non-democratic in character?

In this connection it is essential to recall that Fascism in 1922, and for quite a few years thereafter, did not yet have the purely negative connotations it later acquired and still has now. The old system, as the London *Times* wrote on October 31, 1922 (the day Mussolini was made Prime Minister), had been "very corrupt," and the New York *Times* commented on the very next day that the new rulers were after all of a "relatively harmless type." Winston Churchill was more positive. "If I had been an Italian," Churchill told a group of Fascists, "I would have been wholeheartedly with you from the beginning." He had been charmed, he said, by Signor Mussolini's gentle and simple bearing and by his calm and detached demeanor—clearly Mussolini was a man who thought of nothing but the lasting good of the Italian people. Other observers saw Fascism as a genuine movement of national regeneration, an attempt to restore order and cohesion to a country torn by bitter internal strife. Mussolini was making the trains run on time, suppressing the Mafia, and cleaning up the cities (as Lord Howard, a visiting Englishman wrote: "Under Fascism Italians no longer spit in public").

Sympathy for Fascist Italy was by no means limited in the early days to the right and to big business. Not a few well-wishers could be found among the liberals and on the Left. George Bernard Shaw was a fervent supporter for many years. H. G. Wells said that there was something in Fascism "of a more enduring type than most of the other supersessions of parliamentary methods"—it insisted on discipline and service. The editor of the *Observer,* leader of liberal opinion in Britain, wrote that Mussolini was a "volcano of a man." And in a little book on *The Historic Causes of the Present State of Affairs in Italy* (Oxford, 1923), G. M. Trevelyan, the author of a monumental biography of Garibaldi, declared:

> Let us not be impatient with Italy if she is for a moment swerving from the path of liberty in the course of a very earnest attempt to set her house in order and to cope with the evils which the friends of liberty have allowed to grow up. Signor Mussolini is a great man and according to his lights a very sincere patriot. Let our prayer for him be not that he victoriously destroy free institutions in Italy, but that he may be remembered as a man who gave his country order and discipline when she most needed them, and so enabled those free institutions to be restored in an era happier than that in which it is our present destiny to live.

Reaction in America too was frequently enthusiastic. Lincoln Steffens was an admirer of Mussolini. Charles Beard thought Mussolini was a populist and that he represented "destiny riding without any saddle and bridle across the historical peninsula." Horace Kallen counseled understanding in the *New Republic,* which, in an editorial, admonished its readers that harsh judgments of the present regime in Italy would be a great mistake. The view that Fascist Italy was an interesting social experiment was shared by Stark Young, Herbert Croly, and other Progressives of the day, and Jo Davidson produced an impressive bust of Mussolini. And when Smedley Butler, a U.S. army general, made a speech critical of Fascist Italy, he was court-martialed and bitterly attacked by both the New York *Times* and *Time* magazine.[2]

All this makes embarrassing reading today, but it is also true that one can think of a great many mitigating circumstances. The former government *had* been corrupt, and Fascism indeed restored order; the well-wishers simply failed to realize that while corruption was bad, it was not the only evil threatening Italy, and perhaps not even the worst. Fascism was not a "bad good thing," as H.G. Wells wrote in 1933; it was a bad thing *tout court*. But again, measured against the abominations of Fascism elsewhere, Italian Fascism was a mild form of dictatorship—"Fascism with a human face," as one might say. Not many political opponents were killed. Cultural censorship was relatively relaxed and the great majority of Italian intellectuals, including many who after 1943 became fervent anti-Fascists, at first collaborated with the regime. Those who predicted early on that Fascism would inescapably lead to war were proved right, but only because Fascist regimes emerged elsewhere in Europe as well. Had this not been the case, it is doubtful whether the Duce would have dared to invade Ethiopia, and of course there would have been no World War II. Perhaps the regime would have mellowed in time, perhaps it would have developed after several decades into a freer society. But the Fascist wave did spread and we have to face the fatal consequences to this day.

The political landscape has changed since 1922, but the inclination toward wishful thinking remains. There still is the same tendency among outside observers to give non-democratic parties the benefit of all possible doubts. After the last Congress of the French Communist party, for example, the Washington *Post* said that the new slogans "sound positively Jeffersonian." And the paper added: "It is poor taste to jeer at other people's sudden conversion." This, of course, is very true indeed, but whether the same rule applies to the first exhibition of a "new look" at a fashion show is less certain. It is more important to consider whether and to what extent the new democratic professions of some of the West European Communist parties can be taken at face value, and, above all, to ponder the likely course of action of these parties once they become part of a government coalition.

That there are ideological differences between the European Communists and the Russians is by now well known. The Russians regard the dictatorship of the proletariat as the "supreme form of democracy," while the Italians and the French, much to the chagrin of Moscow, have dropped the concept. The Russians stress proletarian internationalism—meaning obedience to Moscow—whereas the French at their recent party Congress proclaimed *socialisme aux couleurs de la France,* the Italians propagate "critical solidarity," and the Spanish have declared that the old-style internationalism is dead altogether and that they alone will be responsible for the "Spanish march to socialism." The final document issued at the conference of European Communist leaders in June made no mention of proletarian internationalism. According to Santiago Carillo, the head of the Spanish Communist party, given Europe's different (meaning more democratic) historical tradition, socialism in Western Europe is bound to differ from socialism in the USSR; this, he said, "is not a question of tactics and propaganda."

The economic and social programs of the Western Communist parties are anything but revolutionary. The Italians do not insist on immediate large-scale nationalization, which is perhaps not very surprising when one considers that about half of Italy's major industries now belong to the state anyway. The program of the French Socialists is in some respects more radical than that of the French Communists, and the same goes for the Spanish Socialists. Above all, Western Communists have strongly emphasized their devotion to democratic values: according to French Communist leader Georges Marchais, there can be no democracy and no liberty without political pluralism or without freedom of speech.

So far as foreign affairs are concerned, the Italian and Spanish Communists do not oppose the Common Market, and they have even modified their attitude toward NATO. Only a few years ago they took the position that NATO had to be fought so as to liberate Europe from U.S. hegemony. More recently they have stated that the dissolution of power blocs can only come about through détente, and meanwhile there should be no reversal of alliances. To quote Carillo again: "One day the Americans will leave Spain, but this should be envisaged only when the Russians withdraw from Czechoslovakia."

All these developments are very interesting. They would be even more reassuring if they were not repeat performances. The French Communists were very discreet about the dictatorship of the proletariat when they entered the Popular Front in the 1930s, and again in 1945. At that time their leader, Maurice Thorez, gave an interview to the London *Times* in which he announced that France would not follow the Russian road to socialism, but that of the French people, "rich in glorious tradition," would find its own way. The glorious tradition did not prevent the French party from reembracing Stalinism soon after.

There is no denying that the West European Communist parties have learned from past mistakes and that they have become more modern and more pragmatic in their approach. But they have not become more democratic, and it is difficult to imagine that parties which are still strictly authoritarian in their own internal structure could become guardians of liberty in the sphere of national politics. When Carillo was asked recently what in view of the doctrinal changes were the remaining differences between the Communists and the social democrats, he answered quite truthfully that in the final analysis his party was Leninist. This, of course, is the crux of the matter. There is so far no known case of a Leninist party becoming democratic in its own operations. "Democratic centralism"—that is, the suppression of all dissent—remains the guiding principle of all Communist parties, including the Italian party under Enrico Berlinguer and the French party under Marchais.

Nor is the meaning of some of the doctrinal innovations at all clear. The Russians, to do them justice, have never insisted that other Communist parties should "slavishly imitate" the Russian pattern. They have always conceded, at least in theory, that there are "national peculiarities" which should be taken into account. But they have even more forcefully stressed that all Communist parties are obliged to learn from the Soviet experience gained in the progress toward socialism. The question whether the "national peculiarities" or the "Soviet lessons" are more important has been left open.

Having dropped the concept of the dictatorship of the proletariat, the French have replaced it with a new notion—that of the "hegemony of the working class"—and it may take a great deal of semantic effort to sort out the distinctions. The Italians have vowed their attachment to pluralism; what they mean by this may perhaps be inferred from the praise Gian Carlo Pajetta, one of their more enlightened leaders, has accorded the multi-party systems of East Germany and Poland. (Only specialists will recall that in these countries, as in Czechoslovakia and Hungary, there exist to this day three or four "non-Communist" parties; their political influence is, roughly speaking, comparable to that of the Foreign Ministry of the White Russian Soviet Republic.) And even Santiago Carillo has declared that while his party should remain in the *Junta Democratica,* everyone will go his own way once the immediate objectives are reached, and that the friends of today will be the enemies of tomorrow. The Italian Communists have expressed warm support for European cooperation, very much in contrast to the French who only last month bitterly attacked the Polish Prime Minister for having praised the European Economic Community. But even the Italians have said that they would like to transform the "small" into a "big" Europe, taking a neutral position between East and West.

Given these and many other ambiguities, the question invariably arises whether the significance of recent ideological changes has not been overrated by Western observers, forever in search of the proverbial silver lining. It is impossible to give a clear answer, partly because Communist explanations have been contradictory, partly because conditions vary from country to country. The French party is the most orthodox and its foreign policy is still, by and large, dictated by Moscow, except on rare occasions when it is angered by what it considers excessive Soviet professions of friendship toward the French government. The Italians are more independent; they find little to admire in the Soviet system and comments made in private by some of their leaders have been very outspoken indeed. The Spanish are even more extreme in this respect; Carillo once said that if Russia were to attack Spain as it invaded Czechoslovakia, he would not hesitate for a moment to give the order to resist.

As for Italy, it is perfectly true that the PCI no more wants Soviet bases on Italian soil than a repetition of the recent earthquake, and there would be no dancing in the streets of Rome and Milan if Moscow regained a foothold in Yugoslavia and Albania. But when Berlinguer talks about the "iron link" uniting the Communist party of Italy with the Soviet Union, and when he proclaims that those who expect a "break between us and the Soviet Union will forever be disappointed," he is merely expressing the exigencies of his own political situation. Internally, the legitimacy of the Communist party, despite all its reservations, still rests on the Soviet connection; a break would split the party, partly because the rank and file is more fundamentalist in its political convictions that the leadership. This explains the apparent paradox that the erstwhile "right-wing" critics of the Soviet Union such as Amendola and Pajetta are now much more restrained in their approach as compared with Ingrao, the head of the left-wing faction, who is more outspoken about the senior partner in the Communist camp.

The relation of forces in France is, of course, altogether different. There is on the one hand the prospect of an electoral victory with the Socialists in 1978 on the basis of the *program commun*. But the French Communists are now the junior partner in the alliance; unlike the Italians they have been unable to break out of the working-class ghetto. Their share of the electorate has gone down from twenty-eight percent in 1946 to twenty percent or perhaps even less, whereas the Socialist party has made an astonishing recovery in recent years. But the Socialists have far less cohesion and discipline than the Communists, the attachment of their radical wing (CERES) to parliamentary democracy is not above suspicion, and there is always the chance of a split, with a minority of Socialists joining forces with the Communists. Jean-François Revel, author of *La Tentation Totalitaire,* recently wrote that the Socialists under Mitterrand have gained arithmetically, but ideologically it is the Socialists who have been Stalinized. This may be too harsh, and in any case whereas the non-Communist structures in Italy are in a state of decomposition, in France the democratic tradition is considerably stronger and not limited to political parties. Nor has the French Communist leadership shown a political acumen equal to that of their Italian comrades.

Predictions concerning the fortunes of Spanish Communism are most difficult of all because everything now depends on the outcome of the struggle for power in that country, a struggle reflected in but not likely to be resolved by the recent appointment of a new Prime Minister. The moderation shown by the Spanish Communist leadership has been noted, but as in Italy the moderates are challenged by more radical elements among the rank and file, particularly in Catalonia and the Basque region. Spanish politics has witnessed in recent months both growing polarization between right-wing and leftist forces and also an almost incredible fragmentation of parties, groups, and *groupuscules.* The popular basis of Spanish Communism is as yet relatively narrow, but the Communists dominate the trade unions and they have made considerable inroads among the intellectuals (and the media).

Advice has freely been offered as to how the United States should deal with the new offensive of West European Communism. Some of it is based on predictions that need hardly be taken very seriously—for instance, the idea that the advance of the Western Communists is bound to strengthen the liberal trend in world Communism and inside the Soviet Union itself. It is just possible (but quite unlikely) that the deviations of Western Communism could have a certain impact on some East European countries, and that as a result the Soviet leaders would again be preoccupied with restoring order in their own back yard. But far from encouraging a liberalization within the Soviet sphere, such a development would lead to a tightening up. As to whether it would limit Soviet forward operations in other parts of the globe, that is another question.

Zbigniew Brzezinski, in an interview with the Italian weekly *L'Espresso,* has said that a new American government will interpret the changes that have taken place in Europe in recent years as positive signs and not as symptoms of decadence and crisis. Zygmunt Nagorski, Jr. of the Council on Foreign Relations, writing in the New York *Times,* has claimed that new Europe is emerging and that America is failing to adjust itself. Europe's democratic institutions, he says, "require new concepts and new flexibility. They also need to be overhauled in view of the rising demands of highly developed, highly structured, highly stratified societies. . . . The new power levers are about to move that country [Italy] either away from us or closer to the Atlantic Alliance. . . . It is time to look toward the new European political and social requirements leading toward a different world."

It is not at all clear what positive changes Mr. Brzezinski has in mind, nor what Mr. Nagorski's "European political and social requirements" are, let alone what highly structured and highly stratified societies have to do with the present problems; the Delphic Oracle was a paragon of precision and clarity in comparison with pronouncements of this kind. But they are wrong in any case. The American proclivity to generalize about Europe as if it were, like the United States, one country, one nation, one society, always leads to confusion. The problems facing Spain have nothing in common with those confronting Scandinavia. If the trend in Italy has been to the Left, in Britain, West Germany, and Sweden it is at present to the Right, or perhaps more correctly, to the center. It is regrettable, no doubt, that generalizations about Europe are invariably wrong; this is, in fact, part of the European problem. But it is quite meaningless to call for an American adjustment to the "new European political and social requirements," when the various parts of Europe are moving in different directions.

The same lack of specificity applies to the complaint that America has not shown sufficient sympathy for the forces of democratic socialism in Europe. Broadly speaking this is not true, except perhaps for the fact that Margaret Thatcher was invited to the White House and Mitterrand was not. But on the other hand, U.S. relations with the social democrats in Bonn and London have always been closer than with right-of-center governments in Paris. The problem facing the United States in Europe is not in any case to refrain from showing favoritism in the confrontation between the Left and the Right; it is the non-democratic character of the Communist parties and their Russian connection.

More specifically, it has been claimed that American intransigence toward the Italian Communists is bound to drive them back into Moscow's arms. This may or may not be true: all that can be said is that past experience, paradoxically, seems to point the other way. American attitudes toward Communist China in the 1950s were excessively hostile, but this did not prevent the Sino-Soviet split. Up to 1948 Yugoslavia was considered the most contrary Soviet satellite (with the possible exception of Albania) by the Western powers, yet the Yugoslav and Albanian leaders quarreled with the Kremlin anyway. Conversely, American sympathy for Castro in his early days did not prevent Cuba from embracing the Soviet Union.

Another claim is that the hard line taken by the United States on Italian Communism will offend and alienate sectors of Italian public opinion which have traditionally been pro-American. Such warnings, however, have more often emanated from New York and Washington than from Rome and Milan. Close observers of the Italian domestic scene like Enzo Bettiza, editor of *Il Giornale Nuovo,* have declared that, on the contrary,

Italians have been convinced by American newspapers such as the Washington *Post* and the New York *Times* "that public opinion in the U.S. about the credibility of the Italian Communist party has fundamentally changed." And when someone like George Ball tells the Italians, as he did in an interview with the weekly *Il Mondo,* "We cannot change a process that is now irreversible," it is easy to imagine the effect at a time when the demand for postdated Communist-party membership cards has been on the increase anyway. Who wants to resist an inevitable and irresistible historical process?

It has been said, quite rightly, that Italy is first and foremost a European problem and that it would be far easier to solve it if Europe were united. But Europe is not united and one cannot reasonably expect a decisive initiative from these quarters. On the contrary, Chancellor Schmidt's critical comments on the Italian situation have caused a mini-crisis. The Italian Christian Democrats have resented the aspersions cast on them, and it is of course true that the German Chancellor should have castigated above all the Italian Socialists, for it is their inability to provide a viable alternative to Christian Democratic rule which is at the bottom of the present situation.

The issue most frequently discussed is the future of Italy in NATO—and the future of NATO in general. It has been said that Iceland remained in NATO even under a Communist coalition, and that there is no reason why Italy should not also remain so long as Communists are not in key positions that have a bearing on national security. But Italy is not Iceland, and in the modern world there are few ministerial offices that do not have a bearing of one kind or another on national security.

The future of NATO depends on how its functions are interpreted, whether one regards it as a club or a trading company with limited liability—in which case there are indeed no insurmountable difficulties ahead. But if it is considered, as in the past, a defensive alliance based on the assumption that an attack against one is an attack against all, and if it is recalled that Italy, *inter alia,* is a member of the Nuclear Planning Group, the complications immediately become apparent. It can be taken for granted that even under a coalition including the Communists, Italy would still be interested in remaining under the NATO umbrella; if something untoward should happen to Yugoslavia, this desire might become even stronger. But what active part would Italy play in the alliance, and to what extent would its representatives be trusted by the other members of NATO?

Italy, moreover, happens to be located on the critical southern flank of NATO. An Italian government with Communist participation might well (as it has been argued) pursue Italian interests more forcefully, but this is about the last thing that is needed at a time when there is little, if any, momentum left in the movement toward European political cooperation. The Communists would at best perpetuate this stagnation; more likely, they would undermine the fragile balance of power which at present constitutes the sole guarantee of Europe's relative immunity from Soviet pressure.

Some commentators have argued all along that NATO may no longer be needed since détente is so deeply rooted, since military power does not really count in the modern world, and since the Soviet Union is so preoccupied with its East European allies. Those who maintained only a short while ago that the danger of Finlandization in Europe was a figment of the imagination now claim that Finland, everything considered, is not doing so badly after all. Others, less remote from the realities of the European scene, have been proposing the establishment of an inner and outer circle in NATO with, say, Western Germany and Britain as the core, and other countries more loosely associated. But aside from the technical difficulties involved in such a transformation, it would certainly weaken the alliance, and it would also again increase the pressure in the U.S. for withdrawl of American troops from Europe. For even if a new West European Communist power center should emerge as a counterweight against Soviet pressure—a most unlikely proposition in the foreseeable future—it would not be easy to persuade the citizens of Iowa or Colorado that one kind of Communist bloc should be defended against another.

Lastly there is the argument that Italy is different, that Americans are too crude and ignorant to understand the intricacies of Italian politics, that they are unaccustomed to coalition governments and therefore fail to see the difference between a *Putsch* and the sharing of power. Once the Italian Communists enter the government, it is said, they too will be sucked into the quagmire of Italian intrigues like so many well-meaning politicians before them. We are advised, in short, to rely not so much on the moderation and liberal character of Italian Communism as on the changes that will set in once the party is no longer in opposition but part of the "system." Given the facts of Italian life—the civilized level of political intercourse on the one hand, and the corrosive impact of intrigues and corruption (in the widest sense) on the other—such a possibility can by no means be ruled out. But the chances of a development on similar lines in France or Spain, or indeed in any other European country, are minimal.

Meanwhile, the prospects are that Italy will stagger on from crisis to crisis. The Communists have improved their position but the dramatic breakthrough has not occurred. The Christian Democrats are still the strongest party; public order is still breaking down; the country is still saddled with an inflated and inefficient government apparatus, enormously increased labor costs, a capitalist class which regards tax evasion as a national sport, and a big nationalized sector in the economy which is so wasteful that even the Communists want partly to dismantle it. The Communists may not be too unhappy that they have not yet been called to share full responsibility for this sorry state of affairs; they did not want elections in 1976 in the first place and they know that, in any case, the country cannot be run without some tacit understanding between them and the Christian Democrats. Thus they will have some real power without too much responsibility for the results. And of course well-meaning Western observers will, as the Socialist Saragat (a former President of the Republic) puts it, continue to regard Italian Communism as a quaint and not too dangerous piece of Mediterranean folklore, or—in the words of Claire Sterling—a unique party which, unlike all other political parties, really means everything it says and which promises a most exciting social and political experiment.

The question remains to be asked whether it is too late even now for the emergence of a democratic alternative to the Communists and the Christian Democrats. Certainly recent Italian experience has not been encouraging, and the usual intrigues of professional politicians apart, this has been to a significant extent the fault of the intellectuals and, in particular, the media. After 1945, with the memory of their deplorable record under Fascism still fresh, there was a great deal of breast-beating among the intellectuals and of solemn promises to serve the ideals of political freedom with loyalty and fervor. Yet barely three decades later, when a Communist victory seemed virtually assured, a strange silence descended over the Italian scene, and in many circles there was an almost indecent haste not to be overtaken by the wave of the future. Some of these bearers of the conscience of the nation may have been afraid of losing their jobs, others were perhaps responding to social pressures, fearful of no longer being considered *uomini di cultura* (to quote Renzo de Felice, the leading historian of Fascism). But whatever the motives may have been, the old conformism reappeared with a vengeance. Indeed, some foreign observers even reached the conclusion that the *Gleichschaltung,* something akin to self-Finlandization, had already taken place, and that it was a foretaste of how much political and cultural freedom would ultimately survive under a government with Communist participation.

*August 1976*

## NOTES

1. Marino de Medici, in an exchange with Peter Lange, *Foreign Policy,* Spring, 1976.

2. The examples given above are mainly drawn from R. Bosworth, "The British Press, the Conservatives, and Mussolini: 1920-1934," *Journal of Contemporary History,* 2, 1970, and from John P. Diggins, *Mussolini and Fascism,* Princeton, 1972. Similar examples from Germany, France, and other parts of the world could easily be listed.

# Russia Beyond Brezhnev

Almost every new Russian ruler for the last two centuries has been hailed as a liberator upon acceding to power, and in almost every case initial euphoria has given way to disappointment, and worse. When Nicholas I died in 1855, even the harshest critics of the Russian system (the exiled Alexander Herzen among them) welcomed his successor, Alexander II, in glowing terms, especially after a few reforms were announced. Within six or seven months their enthusiasm had waned: "We confess our mistake. . . . This is the same regime, sweetened by molasses."

The pattern repeated itself when Stalin came to power in the late 1920s. Some Western observers hailed the event as a long-awaited return to normalcy after the excesses of Lenin and Trotsky. This, for instance, was how Sir Bernard Pares, an Englishman and one of the most distinguished early Sovietologists, saw it, not only at the time but even fifteen years later when Russia under Stalin appeared to him "as a nearer approach to true democracy than the liberal movement before the revolution." And when Stalin died in 1953, needless to say, expectations of a bright new future were even higher.

In many ways, the optimism that accompanied Stalin's death was justified. There was every reason to assume that his successors would follow a policy more rational, less arbitrarily cruel and oppressive, than that of the murderous "father of peoples," who had clearly become mentally unbalanced during the last years of his life. One of the most optimistic voices at the time was that of the late Isaac Deutscher, who wrote that the coming epoch might bring with it a "breathtaking reversal of the process by which the Soviet democrary of the early years of the revolution had been transformed into autocracy." Deutscher thought that the economic needs of the country made the progress toward liberalization more or less inevitable; economic change would result in political change. "The nation has outgrown authoritarian tutelage," Deutscher wrote, and a return to socialist democracy was just around the corner: "For decades freedom was banned from Russia, because it was, or was supposed to be, the enemy of socialism. . . . But freedom may once again become the ally and friend of socialism; and then the forty years of wandering in the desert may be over for the Russian revolution.''

It was a heartwarming vision, but, alas, it was not to be. Yet the question of where and why Deutscher went wrong is still (or again) of considerable interest. Was it his Marxist faith that led him astray? For he was of course naive, to put it no more strongly, to assume, in the light of the Fascist and Stalinist experience, that industrialization and modernization were bound to lead to greater political freedom. Yet Deutscher's Marxist faith had a curious admixture of subjectivism and voluntarism. In any other country Deutscher would have discovered historical laws and necessities and class interests; in Russia, he could see only regrettable aberrations, individual mistakes, accidents of history which could be easily rectified. Historical materialism, in short, did not apply to the Soviet Union, a country about which Deutscher, in common with many others to this day, felt free to write like an old-fashioned Hegelian idealist.

Now that yet another change in leadership is taking place in the Soviet Union, new commentators in the tradition of Sir Bernard Pares and Isaac Deutscher have appeared. One of them is Jerry F. Hough, who teaches political science at Duke University. In a recent article on the Soviet succession (Washington *Post*, April 17, 1977), he presents arguments reminiscent of his illustrious predecessors.

Not that Professor Hough thinks everything is rosy in the Soviet Union, but by and large it has become in his opinion a more liberal and democratic society. A real diffusion of power has taken place, he writes, with more and more people participating in decision-making—as shown by the fact that over 50 percent of the college-educated males between the ages of thirty and sixty are members of the Communist party. The position of the poor and of the dissidents has also, he tells us, steadily improved since 1964. As for the future, there is a strong natural tendency toward a ''more relaxed type of authoritarianism,'' such as is practiced in Poland. From this it follows, in Professor Hough's view, that America should support those who work inside the regime for a ''Polish'' solution, and should not support the dissidents, who are dangerous people because they call for strict observance of the Soviet constitution—a constitution which ''is not to be taken seriously''—and because they stand for ''revolutionary change.'' (On another occasion, at a conference in Washington, Professor Hough went so far as to compare the Soviet dissidents to Jerry Rubin and Abbie Hoffman who, he said, once spread comparable exaggerations abroad about repressive conditions in America.) He recommends that the Carter administration soft-pedal the human-rights aspects of the Helsinki accords, reassure Soviet leaders

—who suffer from a "deep sense of military inferiority"—with mutual gestures of arms restraint, and scale down or perhaps discontinue the activities of Radio Free Europe and Radio Liberty.

Soviet leaders would no doubt be amused by this effort to ascribe to them a deep feeling of military inferiority, which must be so deep as to be hidden from themselves as well as from the rest of the world, especially that part of it which has lately been feeling the effects of this "inferiority." Equally amusing is the idea that membership in the Communist party is somehow bound up with the Soviet decision-making process (it is simply a prerequisite for getting and keeping positions of any importance in most fields of human endeavor in the Soviet Union). Poland, moreover, is the worst possible example Professor Hough could have chosen for his thesis: "authoritarianism" there may be relatively weak, but it is not at all relaxed. The Polish regime has managed to alienate the workers, the Church, the peasants, and the intelligentsia; having no political base, it is kept in power simply by the fear of open Soviet intervention. Then there is a statement like the following: "We have been too quick to assume that the increase in military spending [in the Soviet Union] denotes a leadership plan to achieve military superiority, and we have failed to consider that it may be part of the evidence that the leadership has relatively few conscious policy intentions and is primarily mediating among specialized elites." As the Duke of Wellington said: if you can believe this, you can believe anything.

This curious mixture of naive misreading of domestic trends in the Soviet Union and open cynicism (the Soviet constitution "is not to be taken seriously") is difficult to explain. Mitigating circumstances can be found in the case of Pares, for the Soviet system had been in existence for only a short time when he wrote about it, and even perhaps in the case of Deutscher. When it comes to Professor Hough, one is bound to agree with his own statement (although he does not appear to mean to apply it to himself) that "our misunderstanding of the Soviet regime is now probably greater than at any time since World War II."[1]

It is instructive to compare Professor Hough's euphoria with the far more somber analysis presented by leading European Communists. Thus, Santiago Carrillo, head of the Spanish Communist party, writes in a book published earlier this year that the Stalinist political system of the Soviet Union has not been transformed, has not been democratized, and even remains coercive in its relations with other Communist states, as was brutally demonstrated by the military occupation of Czechoslovakia (*Eurocomunismo y Estado,* Barcelona, 1977).

Misconceptions and wishful thinking aside, it is of course undeniable that real changes have taken place in the Soviet Union since Stalin's days.

Neither the Khrushchev cult nor, subsequently, the Brezhnev cult has been remotely comparable to the adulation of Josef Stalin. There have been no bloody purges for many years; the few courageous dissenters have been harassed, arrested, and imprisoned, but apparently not one of them has been shot. Power is no longer wielded by one man: the Soviet Union is ruled today by the twenty members and alternate members of the Politburo, the eleven secretaries of the Central Committee (six of whom also belong to the Politburo), and the 426 members and alternate members of the Central Committee. (The Central Committee is convened but rarely, if only because its members are dispersed all over the Soviet Union.) Within the Politburo there is an inner group made up of the four senior members, all of them over seventy years old: Brezhnev, Suslov, Kirilenko, and Kosygin (there were five prior to Podgorny's ouster last May). There has been on the whole a great deal of continuity since the Khrushchev era; only five Politburo members have lost their positions for political reasons in over a decade.[2]

Below the supreme leadership are the district and regional party secretaries and the central and local party and state apparatuses—altogether a bureaucracy consisting of some three million persons. But to this day all orders emanate from the center: if Khrushchev made a modest effort to decentralize and to give greater autonomy to local representatives of the party, the process has been reversed. In this respect as in others, de-Stalinization ended with Khrushchev, and Deutscher's vision of freedom of speech, even within the party, is still a chimera.

The party secretaries rule a population which is largely apolitical. The observation, made by foreign visitors to Czarist Russia, that the Russian government always treated the people as minors, not fully competent to look after their own affairs, is as true now as it was at the turn of the century. Appeals for mass participation, to be sure, are issued almost without interruption, but these are always combined with calls for iron discipline and the need to strengthen the state and the party. Mass participation there is—in order to demonstrate conformity. A few observers of the Soviet scene have drawn encouragement from the fact that some local issues—such as the number of hospital beds to be provided, or of kindergartens—are decided locally, and sometimes are even accompanied by discussion; the supreme leadership cannot any longer impose totally arbitrary or unrealistic schemes on the population. This, however, was also true in the past. Even Stalin was not all-powerful; the shortcomings of human nature (and sometimes simply of nature), place a limit on the ultimate effectiveness of decrees issued from the center. There has always been *some* debate in the Soviet Union, on questions ranging from abortion to linguisitics; it is on issues of political significance that there has never been any debate at all, as is illustrated by the present "discussion" of the new Soviet constitution.

A great many things have changed since Stalin's day, then, but the monopoly of political power, the character of the institutions, the instruments of propaganda and control have been streamlined, but they have not been liberalized, and they are not likely to be in the foreseeable future. The idea that modernization would bring about a diffusion of power, that in an increasingly complex society, experts (the "intelligentsia") would play an ever more important political role, has so far been disproved by events.

But is it not possible that pressure from below will eventually result in far-reaching changes in the Soviet system? Some who argue that it will mainly have in mind the unsatisfactory economic situation and the aspiration of the national minorities. As to the economy, Soviet performance, measured by official promises, has certainly been less than brilliant. According to the party program of 1961, per-capita production in the Soviet Union was supposed to overtake the United States by 1970, but in 1977 the per-capita GNP is still (not quite) on the level of Greece and Spain. There has been, and will continue to be, a relative decline in the production of consumer goods. Furthermore, the Soviet economy faces considerable difficulties in its endeavor to increase productivity and capital formation.

The Soviet economy has, it is true, been less violently shaken by cyclical ups and downs than the economies of non-Communist nations. There is no unemployment (except the hidden one, which is not extensive), and the mineral wealth of the country will make it far less vulnerable to crises in the years to come than most other industrialized countries.[3] On the other hand, it will have to extend considerable help to its less fortunate allies and satellites.

In short, the Soviet regime provides its citizens with a living standard which is still low by comparison with the West, even though it offers more security. The real problem facing the Soviet leadership in this respect is not an acute crisis but the fact that human beings are notoriously ungrateful, that unfulfilled promises give additional impetus to rising expectations, that even the most accomplished propaganda cannot make up for shorter working hours, more ample living conditions, or a greater supply of consumer goods. Popular dissatisfaction may well bring about economic reforms at a future date, reforms that were vaguely discussed in the late 1950s and early 1960s but then shelved. It is not at all clear, however, that economic reform need or would affect the monopoly of political power.

The problem of the nationalities, with their manifold claims and aspirations, is on the other hand in many ways more threatening to that monopoly. According to the last Soviet census, Russians constituted 53.4 percent of the population of the USSR. Since there is reason to believe that this figure is slightly exaggerated, and since the rate of population growth is considerably higher among the Turkish peoples of the Soviet Union than among the Slavs (the former having increased by fifty percent since 1960, the latter by only about fifteen percent), it is no longer certain whether the Russians actually constitute a majority. This would be of little interest if it were true, as is officially maintained, that the peoples of the Soviet Union coexist and collaborate with each other in a spirit of friendship and solidarity unprecedented in the history of mankind, thus creating a new and higher type of national community. But in fact there are many indications that ethnic tensions persist in the Soviet Union and have been reinforced by the global trend toward nationalism.

Soviet nationalities policy under Stalin was one of undisguised, forced, often brutal Russification; this was modified after his death, but since the early 1960s warnings have been voiced against bourgeois nationalism among the non-Russian peoples (even though it is not easy to understand how such nationalism could possibly exist among peoples who have no bourgeoisie now, and for the most part had none in the past). In some Russian circles, on the other hand, there has been within the last decade something akin to a cult of the Russian past—the village tradition, Russian folk customs and art, and so forth. Even if mainly cultural in character and strictly unofficial in inspiration, this trend too points to a revival of nationalism, at the very least on the emotional level.

The main problem is not the resistance of the non-Russian peoples to a cultural program that aims to force them to accept the Russian language and all that goes with it; the gradual emergence of Russian as a *lingua franca* is a natural process. Nor is it correct to say that the non-Russian peoples have been culturally neglected; higher education has in fact spread more quickly among them than in the Russian republic. But as experience in Ireland and in other parts of the globe has shown, linguistic assimilation by no means makes for political solidarity; on the contrary, the emergence of highly educated local cadres creates new tensions—in the Soviet case reinforcing the pressure for the de-Russification of the local party and state apparatus. Russia, in any event, was never really a melting pot, and the political limits of cultural assimilation are now clearly discernible.

Soviet nationalities problems have on the whole been handled with considerable expediency. While there seems to be an awareness of the potentially explosive character of these issues, they are hardly ever discussed in public. What is true with regard to Soviet Jews and Germans applies by and large to the Soviet nationalities policy in general: the number of exit visas has been increased, but at the same time the militants have been arrested. The purges of leading cadres have been more frequent and more thoroughgoing in the non-Russian republics than in Moscow, but by way of compensation there has been a deliberate effort to co-opt more non-Russians into the Politburo (including the secretaries general of Kazakhstan, Azerbaijan, Uzbekstan, a Balt, and, of course, some leaders of Ukrainian origin). Russian leaders no doubt harbor few illusions of a truly integrated Soviet nation in the near future. Present policy is to defuse the inevitable conflicts by establishing close collaboration with the leadership of the non-Russian nationalities, in order to create an identity of material interests and to make them feel that they have no future except inside the wider framework of the Soviet Union. Given the circumstances, it is a realistic policy, but there is no guarantee it will succeed.

While the Russian republic has grown richer over the last two decades, most of the non-Russian peoples (except the Balts), being less in- dustrialized, have grown relatively poorer. Non-Russian leaders are treated in Moscow with respect, but it is also true that none of them plays a role in the party leadership even remotely comparable to that once played by a Stalin, a Beria, or even a Mikoyan; the same seems to be true with regard to the supreme army command and the state security organs. Nor is it certain to what extent the collaborating elites in the national republics can be politically relied upon in Moscow; their own ambitions apart, they have to represent, at least to some degree, the claims of their fellow nationals, so as not to lose their credibility at home. This is not at all easy to accomplish, for at a time when even the smallest national groups in Asia and Africa have attained independence, with seats in the United Nations and diplomatic recognition, Uzbeks and Georgians, Azerbaijans and Kazakhs want at the very least to be masters in their own house. The Soviet Union is the last surviving multinational empire, and hence potentially quite vulnerable. Whatever concessions will have to be made could produce a momentum of far greater political significance than economic reforms. Hence the enormous sensitivity shown by Soviet leaders to separatist propaganda from outside.

None of this is meant to imply that the days of the Soviet domestic em- pire are numbered; empires disintegrate only when their rulers lose self- confidence and nerve, and there are no signs that this is happening in the Kremlin. Nor is there a united front of non-Russians, as there was, at least for a little while, in 1917. On the contrary, the claims of some of the non-Russian groups collide with the interests of others, and this opens a great many possibilities for a policy of divide-and-conquer, as was prac- ticed by the Czarist regime. Still, it is fairly safe to predict that as centrifugal trends increase the new Soviet leadership will have to devote far more attention than in the past to nationalities policy.

By comparison, the challenge represented by the intelligentsia is almost insignificant. Once upon a time the Russian intelligentsia was a revolutionary force, but the qualities that made it so—loyalty to great ideas, a willingness to fight and to sacrifice—were confined to a small number of people. It is true that the intelligentsia turned decisively against the Czarist government toward the end of the century. By the same token, there are very few members of the intelligentsia today who are not critical of at least some aspects of the regime. But this kind of opposition, consisting of critical mumblings and anti-establishment jokes, is easy enough and occasional promises will keep the intelligentsia in line.

Indeed, aside from some individuals of exceptional courage, the record of the Soviet intelligentsia as a class has not been much better than that of intellectuals under other dictatorships. Some Soviet intellectuals have joined the ruling group and become *nachalniki,* bosses of one sort or another; others, not the best or the brightest, have offered fulsome praise to the historical mission of the party and its giant achievements. The great majority, while paying lip-service to official slogans, have tried not to get involved in politics. Talented young people of integrity are not encouraged to choose a political career. Among the younger members of the intelligentsia, official ideology is treated with skepticism, even open cynicism. But skeptics and cynics, lacking firm beliefs and values, will not, as a rule, choose the path of open defiance, with all the dangers involved. Rather than risk their careers, they will opt for the "private sphere" and invest their energies in their respective professional fields. They may be better informed about politics than the average Western intellectual, but they will essentially be passive onlookers. This general passivity of the intelligentsia is felt in the cultural sphere perhaps most acutely; even the late 1950s were an artistically exciting period in comparison with the 1970s.

Twenty years ago it was widely believed among Soviet experts in the West that the Soviet Union could not possibly stand still: it would either be transformed or it would degenerate. Yet there was a third possibility, as the years since have shown. Economic development has been coupled with political, social, and cultural stagnation at home, and a cautiously activist policy abroad. This combination could endure for a very long time.

What will the future leadership of the Soviet Union look like? In the near future, after Brezhnev goes, it seems likely that there will be a reshuffle among members of the old guard. But any such arrangement would be provisional; effective power sooner or later will pass into the hands of the younger members of the Politburo and the Secretariat. The transition may be smooth, for Brezhnev has placed his protégés in strategically important positions in the party and state apparatus, but it is equally possible that a struggle for power will break out, as happened after Stalin's death. The Central Committee may try to reassert its authority, as it did on at least two occasions in the past (in 1957 and in 1964), by deposing some of the present leaders and promoting new ones. But it is also not certain that any of this really matters; it would be of importance only if the struggle for power resulted in a one-man dictatorship, something that seems unlikely except perhaps in a national or international emergency. The trauma of the Stalinist era (and to a far lesser extent of Khrushchev's rule) has taught the upper bureaucratic crust the obvious lesson that its tenure, indeed its physical survival, cannot be assured under conditions of totally arbitrary rule; hence the necessity for a balance of power in the top leadership.

The generation that will succeed Brezhnev, Suslov, and Kosygin knows little about the outside world. This is not to say that the new leaders will be "Russia firsters." The fact that the Soviet Union is a superpower has a logic of its own, and Soviet leaders are drawn into foreign affairs as irresistibly as are American Presidents. In this respect there is bound to be continuity with the immediate past, since the new leaders will certainly want to strengthen the Soviet military potential and make the most of Western weaknesses without causing a breakdown in détente. They may in fact be more dynamic in the pursuit, partly because younger people are usually more enterprising than their elders, but also because, in contrast to their predecessors, they have yet to prove themselves. In addition, the fact that Soviet domestic problems are so difficult to deal with, not to say intractable, may in itself contribute to a strong emphasis being placed on foreign policy, a field where striking successes may appear more likely. This is a well-known historical syndrome, and one not limited to Communist regimes.

Thus, the new leaders are unlikely to give up on the traditional ideological ambitions of the Soviet regime. The notion, in any case, that any Soviet leaders—whether those currently in place or those who will succeed them—no longer wish to see Communists coming to power in certain other countries because this is bound to cause tension and conflict within the communist world, is based on a profound misunderstanding of Soviet psychology and policy. The Soviet Union is, after all, still the leader of the Communist camp; if it were not to press for the victory of Communism on a global scale, it would lose all credibility.

Nor, finally, are the Soviet leaders of the next generation likely to cut back on their military forces. The Soviet Union is a superpower, but not by virtue of its economic performance or the irresistible attraction of its official ideology. It has achieved the status of a superpower through its military strength. No Soviet leader is unaware of this fact, or can afford to disregard it. And the maintenance of a large military establishment carries with it the additional advantage of justifying economic short-comings and political dictatorship—all said to be necessary to protect the achievements of "socialism" from powerful enemies even at a time of détente.

Political and social systems can remain stagnant for amazingly long periods of time. I have stressed some of the destabilizing factors threatening the Soviet political regime, but there are others pointing in the opposite direction. Thus the growing complexity (and vulnerability) of human societies reinforces in the long term toward strict controls, toward the concentration of power in a few hands, and toward political domination by a relatively small elite. If there is discontent in the Soviet Union there is also a substantial part of the population, counting perhaps in the millions, which has a vested interest in the regime and which will oppose any change out of the fear that change will adversely affect its own status and privileges. This refers not only to those in the key posi-tions of party and state, the economy, the army, and the security organs, but also to the lesser secretaries, officers, instructors, and bureaucrats, in whose hands lie the tools of coercion and propaganda. Although, histori-cally speaking, dictators and ruling groups do sometimes lose their hold, such a prospect is not overly likely in a regime in which the dictatorship has been deeply institutionalized, and which can rejuvenate itself biologically if not ideologically.

The truth is that the Soviet regime is without precedent, not because the revolution from above accomplished its aims but because for the first time in history the political results of revolution have been successfully "frozen." True, there are enormous differences between the situation now and in 1950, and between 1950 and 1925. There have been periods of senseless slaughter, and others in which a bare minimum of violence was used. But the decisive lesson is that all these changes have taken place within clearly defined parameters, all scheduled to keep the regime in power, if possible with little coercion, if necessary by brutal means.[4]

Of course, all things, and all political and social regimes, are subject to change, and the Soviet Union is no exception. But if one day there is to be a movement toward freedom in that country, it will be triggered by forces and will take place in circumstances that cannot be foreseen today. As far as the Soviet Union is concerned, freedom is still the enemy of socialism and socialism is still thought to be possible without democratic institutions. The wandering still continues in a desert which has officially been declared an oasis.

*August 1977*

## NOTES

1. An equally strange theory of Soviet liberalization has recently been propounded by Victor Zorza, quoting Alexander Yanov, a Soviet emigré writer. According to Zorza, Yanov warns that a breakdown in détente would lead to the replacement of the present, "centrist" leadership by a Communist-nationalist regime which would follow an isolationist policy "and could evolve into a Russian Nazi system." The only way the "centrist" leadership can overcome the threat from the "little Stalins" is by allying itself with the managerial technocracy, or new class, which itself is attempting to secure its position by limiting the absolute power of the top Kremlin rulers. The West should therefore help the new class to "assert and extend its own authority in the interest of producing a stable regime able and willing to cooperate in a new international system." Détente, in other words, is needed to prevent the "danger" of Soviet isolationism. If the logic of this argument seems a little doubtful, the historical parallel to Nazism borders on the incredible—although the thought of isolationism as a pronounced feature of Nazism is certainly a novel one.

2. Brezhnev's recent elevation to the Presidency does not mean the restoration of one-man rule but, on the contrary, the opening of a new, more acute phase in the struggle for succession.

3. A comparison of the Soviet growth rate with that of the other six leading industrial nations shows that in 1971 the Soviet Union ranged third (after Japan and France); in 1972 it was seventh and last; in 1973 and 1974 it was second; in 1975 it led the field—but this was a year of general crisis. In 1976 and 1977 Soviet rates of growth have been (or promise to be) about average in comparison with other industrialized nations.

4. It is this element of stability which no doubt helps to account for the curious fact that in the West favorable comments on the Soviet Union are likely to come today more often from conservative circles than from the Left. The writings of George Kennan are an example; more recently, Enoch Powell, the eloquent spokesman of the extreme Right in Britain, has published an almost glowing account of his recent trip to the Soviet Union (London *Times,* June 21, 1977). Mr. Powell notes with approval that "here is a state at once intensely conservative and intensely nationalist," and he observes with equal approval that "it is self-evident to the Russians that the citizen belongs not merely to the state but to a specific part of the state, and has no right to leave his home or his country at will." It is quite obvious what there is in Soviet society to attract these conservatives—stable order and discipline imposed by a strong authority.

# Essays in Futurism

# Six Scenarios for 1980

When you have eliminated the impossible, Sherlock Holmes told his friend Watson, whatever remains, however improbable, must be the truth. But the master sleuth was commenting on the past; as far as the future is concerned there is more than the truth. Or as Prof. Karl Popper put it in the third of his statements on Indeterminism: We cannot predict the future course of human history. But even though we cannot predict we can guess and anticipate, bearing in mind, of course, that there is always more than one possibility. Individuals may refrain from thinking about the future, but a state, a society cannot. And every form of planning ahead is, of course, based on certain assumptions; even the philosopher who has proved that prediction is a priori impossible will retire from his chair only on the assumption that he will receive a pension. There are, in other words, degrees of probability.

The number of political alternatives in the next decade seems unlimited. And as every futurologist knows from bitter experience, one little error, one miscalculation, one unexpected event is sufficient to undermine a whole tower of predictions, however ingeniously constructed and seemingly foolproof. But if, following Sherlock Holmes's advice, we eliminate the impossible—say, the emergence of Sierra Leone or Outer Mongolia as a superpower by 1980—the number of possibilities that remain is limited, give or take an admittedly endless number of minor variations.

In what follows six such scenarios are developed; a good case could be made for extending that number, but I doubt whether it could be substantially reduced. Nuclear war between the superpowers has been disregarded not because it is impossible but because speculation beyond that point is not attractive. The consequences of an American-Soviet alliance directed against China are likewise not discussed. Such a course of action would not make sense from the American point of view for the simple reason that China is likely to remain the lesser danger for a long time to come.

### 1980: Scenario I, Or, New Faces but More of the Same

The United States, the Soviet Union and China are still the only global powers that count, and each is trying to prevent the other two from ganging up against itself. The Soviet Union has surpassed the United States by a wide margin in all modern weapons systems. In his speech on Nov. 6, 1979, Marshall Razruzhnikov, the Soviet chief of staff, referred with biting irony to the "daydreams" of American generals unwilling to recognize the crushing Soviet military superiority. (He compared them with the cat who thought it was a lion in Krylov's famous fable.) At the end of his speech the marshall stated that the Soviet Union was always willing to enter meaningful talks on arms reduction, and as a token of goodwill he suggested the immediate removal by each side of 1,000 I.C.B.M.'s (of which the U.S.S.R. had by that time 5,000, the U.S. 1,100).

However, among the political leaders in Moscow counsels are divided on such topics as what constitutes "acceptable damage," "assured destruction," "counterforce capability." Some argue that it is virtually certain that the Soviet Union has acquired a first-strike capability. Others maintain that "virtually" is not good enough, that there is no certainty that the Soviet Union will ever gain a certain, foolproof first-strike capability. But in view of the enormous superiority in conventional weapons and the greater mobility of Soviet forces, the further construction of I.C.B.M.'s can now be discontinued and the money saved invested in industry. (The Soviet G.N.P. in 1979 was still only 60 percent of the American.)

The SALT talks had ended in partial success in the mid-seventies with an agreement to stop the production and deployment of certain costly "excess weapons." However, much to the disappointment of some observers in the West, it now appears that, apart from this welcome money-saving operation, SALT has not made the world a safer place.

The European Security Conference is now in its seventh year, having become a permanent institution. The first three years were devoted to debates on such issues as who should be represented, where the meetings should be held, the language to be used, and, above all, the conference agenda. Subsequently there had been three years of discussion on air pollution, oceanography and trade relations.

The Common Market continues to exist but has not made progress beyond the establishment of a free trade zone; the question of a common currency and taxation system is still under discussion. The Werner report was succeeded by the Dumoulin report in 1974; when no agreement was reached on this basis, Professor Mueller was asked to prepare yet another working paper in 1977. Work on this paper is still in progress.

There has been no progress toward closer European unity. The West Germans were willing in principle to take an active part, but once it came to practical details they shied away because it might have endangered the achievements of the *Ostpolitik.* The British were lukewarm; even the Europeans in London regarded it mainly as an economic convenience. Relations between Britain and France are closer now than ever before; the Queen has not failed to attend a single horseshow in Paris since 1973, and with the opening of the Dover-Calais tunnel every other Englishman now spends his holidays on the Continent. Many new English words have been absorbed into the French language, such as *le teabreak, le walkout, l'establishment, le bore, le frightful bore,* etc. But, as successive French presidents have declared, a thousand years of history cannot be undone with a stroke of the pen. Pompidou's aside in an afterdinner speech ("Charlemagne spoke German to his horse, English to his valet, but French to his ministers and his mistress") caused much bad blood.

In Italy a popular-front government has come to power, and in Spain, too, following a long period of unrest after Franco's death, the Communists are now represented in the government. The Soviet leadership is not too happy about these developments. While advocating some radical domestic reforms, these Communist parties have demanded the withdrawal of all nonriparian navies from the Mediterranean. Both the Italian and the Spanish Communist parties have accepted the Common Market and have decided not to insist on the dissolution of NATO while the Warsaw Pact is still in existence.

The American military presence in Europe has been reduced to one and a half divisions, but American disengagement from Europe did not have the immediate dramatic consequences which were predicted by some Cassandras in Washington and London. The new Soviet leaders, headed by Shelest, Katiushev and Andropov, have accepted the fact that the establishment of a new European Security System (which some hostile critics used to call the Finlandization of Europe, but which is now commonly referred to as "Germanization") will be a long-drawn-out process lasting several decades. Their cautious policy has helped them to make significant progress: the countries of Western Europe have provided substantial credit loans and technological know-how to prop up the Soviet economy, supplying the Soviet consumer with cars, textiles, electrical appliances, etc. Critical comment on things Soviet is no longer openly voiced and most of the European countries have cut their defense spending.

The improved situation in Europe has made it possible for the Soviet Union to transfer to the Far East half of the forces stationed in Europe in

1971, so that by 1980 about three-quarters of the Soviet forces are concentrated along the Chinese border. The Soviet position in Eastern Europe has also improved: the new Yugoslav leadership, faced by a grave internal crisis after Tito's death, has drawn closer to Moscow; so have the Rumanians following a reshuffle in the Politburo in the middle seventies. The failure of another Polish uprising has finally convinced all would-be reformers in Eastern Europe that there is no hope for liberalization ("Socialism with a human face") unless—and until—there is a change or heart in the Kremlin. Political apathy has reigned in Eastern Europe for many years.

It was mistakenly assumed in the early seventies that as a result of the European Security Conference the doves in the Kremlin would gain the upper hand, and that consequently the East European countries would have greater freedom of maneuver. But the new Soviet leadership is convinced, not without reason, that while the Soviet Union should pursue a flexible and cautious line in foreign affairs, it cannot afford to make major concessions in its own empire. They have accepted the fact that the great majority of East Europeans continue to oppose Soviet control, but are confident that the future generations of Poles, Czechs and Hungarians will show less ingratitude. Inside the Soviet Union the standard of living has risen, though the gap separating it from European and American standards has hardly diminished. The main problem on the domestic scene is the spread of national feeling among the non-Russian peoples. Separatism has been contained by co-opting several Ukrainians, Azerbaijanis, Georgians and Uzbeks to leading positions in the state and party, and by exploiting the tensions between the national minorities. By and large, the population displays no interest in politics; the official doctrine is a mixture of Marxist, populist and nationalist components, with the leadership firmly in the saddle.

The fact that the Soviet Union has now emerged as the most powerful country in the world seems to have borne out the predictions of Lenin and Stalin. The latter has by now been almost completely rehabilitated, though his name is not frequently mentioned; certain minor political aberrations in the last few years of his life are explained by reference to his illness and consequent diminished responsibility.

The Chinese danger now looms larger than ever to the men in the Kremlin. A preemptive strike has repeatedly been discussed but was eventually rejected on the ground that a trustworthy regime in Peking could be installed and maintained only by stationing an occupation army in China, and this was dismissed as impractical. Soviet policymakers are almost wholly preoccupied with the threat constituted by China's growing military and economic might, its challenge to Soviet influence in the Third World and in the world Communist movement. Pravda now refers only infrequently and with sadness rather than anger to Western capitalism (which, after all, as Marx pointed out, at one time played a progressive role in history), in marked contrast to Sino-Fascism, the most dangerous enemy of proletarian internationalism and friendship between the peoples as practiced by the Soviet Union. This fear of China has prevented decisive Soviet action in Europe and in other parts of the world, despite the fact that the American retreat (the phrase, "a low profile," became discredited as the result of excessive use in the middle seventies) has opened unique opportunities.

Various national Communist regimes emerged in Southeast Asia following the end of the Vietnam war, but, totally absorbed in its internal affairs, this part of the globe has again become what it was before that war—a backwater of history. India's troubles were by no means over with the establishment of Bangla Desh. The civil war continued; the pro-Chinese forces gained ground and so did the movement in favor of a united Bengal. In the late seventies the pro-Chinese party in East Bengal won an electoral victory, seceded from India and has applied for U.N. membership. It may be joined by West Bengal, for the breakdown of India into five or six independent states on ethnic-linguistic lines seems now only a question of time. Mrs Indira Gandhi (still in power) has tried to stem the secessionist tide by granting the separatists a large measure of autonomy, but these concessions have been contemptuously rejected by the governments in Madras, Calcutta and the other capitals. Mrs. Gandhi's freedom of maneuver vis-à-vis Moscow is now compared unfavorably by her critics in the Lok Sabha with the position of the Nizam of Hyderabad vis-à-vis the British under the Raj.

Negotiations about a federal union between Iran and West Pakistan have so far been inconclusive. The new law discovered by a team of American political scientists at the University of Michigan has been widely acclaimed: It states that in the twentieth century nations always split, never unite for any length of time, unless, of course, held together by military force. (The law was the outcome of a seven-year project involving the use of the most modern computer techniques, financed by the Ford Foundation.)

In the Middle East the Arab-Israeli conflict has not been resolved. After thirty-eight peace missions and two more rounds of fighting (the second following the radical *coup* in Jordan in 1976), the borders are more or less what they were before. The peace parties in Israel and Egypt have grown in strength, but the attempts to find common ground have been unsuccessful, and it is generally assumed that another decade or two will pass before the uneasy armistice is replace by some more lasting arrangement. Sadat was overthrown by a group of fellow officers, who follow, broadly speaking, the same political line; Mohammed Heykal now acts as their spokesman and in a series of revealing articles has provided a scathing account from close at hand of the incredible incompetence shown by Sadat and his group. Soviet influence has grown stronger in Turkey, Iraq and Syria, but power is still in the hands of the military. Various reasons are adduced to explain the deep division in the world Communist movement. The one most frequently mentioned is the fact that Moscow no longer encourages the seizure of power by Communist parties unless it is itself in virtual control of the country.

The worst fears about the political fragmentation of Africa have not been realized; at one time it was believed that the continent would split up into 120 different states. According to a much publicized UNESCO study, a state is viable in the modern world if it has a television station, a police force of about a hundred, a national airline and a budget sufficient to assure the maintenance of a delegate at the U.N. Africa made some economic progress during the seventies, but it is as yet far from the "take-off stage."

Latin America has witnessed more revolutions, and in about half of the smaller countries pro-Communist groups or military juntas are now in power. But the nationalist component in these revolutions has proved to be much stronger than originally assumed. There has been considerable infighting between various left-wing groups, and while these new regimes have carried out some long overdue agrarian reforms, nationalized the banks and given a fresh boost to industrialization, their over-all record has not been impressive. Events in Latin America (with the possible exception of Mexico, Brazil and Argentina) now attract less and less interest even in the U.S., where they were originally followed with considerable apprehension.

## Scenario II, Or, the Burial of the Hatchet

Shortly after Mao's death, Brezhnev's serious illness and the resignation of Kosygin and Podgorny, the Presidium of the C.P.S.U. decided, upon the initiative of Katiushev, Poliansky and Andropov (the new troika) to normalize relations with China. The Kremlin watchers report that the attacks on Sino-Fascism in the Soviet press have suddenly ceased. The feelers put out by the Russians are at first treated with great caution in Peking. The People's Daily says that the Katiushev clique, the Brezhnev gang, and the fat old buffoon (Khrushchev) are all revisionist birds of one feather; they will not escape their just punishment at the hands of the toiling masses. After six months the Peking press and radio stop commenting on events in the Soviet Union altogether. There is a long and bitter dispute in the Chinese Politburo in which the anti-American party eventually prevails. The agreement reached between the two Communist superpowers opens (at Chinese insistence) with a public apology on the part of the Russians, who put most of the blame for the past misunderstandings on Trotsky, Beria and Khrushchev, an unprincipled deviationist from the teachings of Marx, Lenin, Stalin and Mao. The Russians promise extensive economic help—part loan, part reparations for the damage caused to the Chinese economy as a result of the sudden withdrawal of Soviet aid in the early 1960s.

The treaty of friendship and nonaggression emphasizes the sacred principle of absolute equality between all countries big and small. The high contracting parties undertake to refrain from intervention in each other's affairs as well as in those of third countries. A secret protocol contains a detailed outline of the division of the world into spheres of influence. The Soviet Union receives a free hand in Europe and the Middle East, while China's hegemony in Asia—including Japan and India—is conceded by the Russians. The future of Africa and Latin America is to be decided at a later stage. The pro-Soviet and pro-Chinese parties in these countries receive instructions to collaborate with each other.

The Sino-Soviet pact came as a great shock to the Western capitals, and created panic in New Delhi and Tokyo, but its effects were not immediately felt in Asia because China proceded more slowly and cautiously than its northern neighbor. The Japanese and Indian Governments were assured by Peking's special emissaries that the Asian co-prosperity sphere would be based on close economic cooperation and regular consultation on questions of foreign policy. The repercussions in Europe were more marked; following a new Middle East crisis which led to a Cuba in reverse (the Sixth Fleet was withdrawn from the Mediterranean), the Danish and Norwegian Governments, seconded by the Italians, proposed the transformation of NATO into a system of bilateral pacts on cultural and scientific exchanges. The West German Government, facing a Soviet ultimatum to end the Berlin agreement on the ground that Bonn had not lived up to the letter and spirit of the pact, declared its strict neutrality in any East-West conflict. Neutralism gathers momentum all over Western Europe and two years after the Sino-Soviet pact an all -European Neutrality Convention (E.N.C.) is signed in Prague. The Common Market countries invite Comecon to discuss a merger; the negotiations are successful and the Soviet Minister of Foreign Trade is unanimously elected Secretary General of the new organization. Soviet representatives in the European capitals explain that Moscow has no intention whatever of intervening in their internal affairs. It could not, of course, deal with parties or leaders who do not fully and sincerely accept the principles of the E.N.C.

Washington is assured by Moscow that the Soviet Union will scrupulously refrain from any interference in American domestic affairs, and in return expects America to abstain from meddling in European, Asian and African politics, since such intervention could only have the direst consequences for the United States. It is hoped (the note concludes) that closer economic relations will be established on the basis of this understanding.

### Scenario III, Or, Better Fifty Years of Europe than a Cycle of Cathay

The American domestic crisis continued throughout the seventies and the trend toward neo-isolationism persisted. At the same time, China, rent by bitter internal strife, again ceased to play an active role in world politics after Mao's death. The Soviet leadership, incapable of solving the country's economic problems, preoccupied with putting down unrest in the European satellites, and with appeasing the national minorities at home, faces the gravest internal crisis since 1920 and cannot pursue its foreign political aspirations with the necessary emphasis. Within the C.P.S.U. three factions have come into being; the split is no longer restricted to the Central Committee but divides the whole party. It has been reported from Moscow that in the elections to the 26th Party Congress there will be three lists of candidates.

In this state of affairs, two new centers of power emerge: Western Europe and Japan. They are not equal to the superpowers in military strength, but they have become active factors to be reckoned with in the new, highly complicated and forever changing global game of nations. It is the generally accepted view that America's misguided and futile attempts to avert the devaluation of the dollar, thus provoking a prolonged trade and currency war, helped to trigger off this process. However, in the last resort it was the decision to withdraw all but token military forces from Europe and the Far East which tipped the balance and led to Japan's rearmament and the creation of the European Defense Community. London and Paris pooled their nuclear resources in 1973, Germany and Italy made substantial financial contributions to the E.D.C. for improving its delivery systems, and by 1980 Western Europe as well as Japan have become virtually independent of the United States.

Japan, ruled by a nationalist-socialist coalition, pursues a delicate balancing act between China and the Soviet Union, trying to offend neither and to expand trade with both. As a token of good will the Soviet Union returned the Kuril Islands and Southern Sakhalin to Japan as part of a package deal envisaging the participation of Japanese capital in Siberia's industrial development. China countered by an agreement of similar magnitude with the Common Market countries.

Having regained its self-confidence and overcome its internal squabbles, Western Europe reasserts its position in the Middle East and Africa. Relations with the United States have again improved following the devaluation of the dollar and massive West European help to America to bring its balance of payments deficit under control.

## Scenario IV, Or, the Soviet Union Will Not Survive 1984

The Sino-American *rapprochement* continues and the Soviet Union fails to make further progress in Western Europe. It suffers further setbacks in the Middle East as President Sadat expels 20,000 Russian experts following the discovery of a conspiracy against him. Several more West European Communist parties dissociate themselves from Soviet policies. The performance of the Soviet economy deteriorates, Japanese steel production overtakes Soviet output in 1976. Irredentist movements sprout among the non-Russian peoples; high K.G.B. officials read Marcuse and Laing. An open crisis breaks out in Moscow following years of declining self-confidence among the top leadership. Backed by the military, Ustinov takes over power, only to be overthrown six months later by a rival faction headed by Katiushev. An uprising in Warsaw is followed by a revolt in Budapest and Prague. The Bulgarian Government offers to dispatch a parachutist division to restore order in Budapest; East German troops enter Poznan after Soviet troops disobey orders to put down the rebellion. The new Polish Government calls on the people to close ranks against the German invaders. The East German troops are withdrawn. The liberal faction in Moscow calls for the convocation of a Constituent Assembly in which all Socialist groups will be represented. Uzbekistan merges with Kazakhstan and declares its independence. The attempted secession is squashed, but "internal polycentrism" prevails in the Soviet Union and, preoccupied with their many internal problems, the new leaders decide to devote their energies mainly to consolidating their position at home.

China takes over the leadership of what remains of the Communist camp outside Europe (Outer Mongolia, North Korea, Southeast Asia, Latin America). The United States and Western Europe cut their defense budgets. Following the ouster of the Honnecker-Stoph group, the new East German Government suggests to Bonn immediate steps to reunify Germany. Greatly alarmed by this dramatic change in the European balance of power, the French and British Governments decide to rearm. President Kennedy sends Under Secretary of State Daniel Ellsberg on a fact-finding tour of London, Paris and Bonn. Ellsberg recommends

American intervention, but the Senate votes overwhelmingly against any American interference in European affairs.

## Scenario V, Or, Permanent Purge in China

After Mao's death Chou En-lai takes over. Mao's widow, a former Politburo member, is appointed assistant director of the local theater in Urumchi. Chou's rule is challenged by the Chinese Army under Chen Hsi-lien commander of the Shenyang military district. But another army group under Yeh Chien-ying comes out for Chou. Chou, suffering from insomnia, is given acupuncture treatment. His condition deteriorates, his deputy, Li Hsien-nien, takes over and moves to Canton. Following a local rebellion in Shanghai, Mrs. Mao's friends, supporters of the Cultural Revolution seize power, recall her from Urumchi. There are now three separate centers of power (Peking, Shanghai and Canton) and the struggle between army, party and Cultural Revolutionists affects all China. The head of state, Tung Pi-wu, aged 90, calls for unity but his appeal is not heeded. The Shanghai edition of the People's Daily quotes a saying of Mao: "Some old men are wise, others are foolish. Foolish old men should not talk in public."

Manchuria and Sinkiang gradually fall into the Soviet sphere of influence, Japan establishes close contacts with the Shanghai Government, whereas the United States promises its support to Canton. As a result of China's relapse into chaos the Soviet Union regains freedom of action in Europe and the Middle East, and becomes the predominant power in the Persian Gulf area, the Horn of Africa and the Indian subcontinent. For the sequel see Scenario II.

## Scenario VI, Or, the Collapse of the West

A new crisis in the Middle East, combined with a sudden wave of bankruptcies at home, causes a major slump in Wall Street. The American Government imposes new and higher tariff barriers; stringent economy measures are introduced. The Government convenes a meeting of the country's 80 leading economists; there are 84 different opinions as to how to tackle the crisis (Professor Galbraith offered four different views); Western Europe and Japan retaliate. America withdraws its troops from Western Europe and the Far East.

The quarrel between France and Germany on financial issues deepens, a new economic nationalism ("Everyone for himself") spreads in Western Europe with disastrous consequences for all concerned. A manifesto signed by Europe's 500 leading intellectuals warning against the wave of suicidal lunacy engulfing Europe is attacked in many newspapers both for lack of patriotism and for reflecting the "old cold war spirit." The number of unemployed in Britain reaches the two-million mark; the Labor party wins the general election under Jenkins (Clive, not Roy); the new progressive Prime Minister slashes the defense budget by half and decides to secede from the Common Market. Enoch Powell joins the Labor party and is appointed Foreign Secretary. France also suspends its membership in the Common Market, the last straw inducing Paris to break with the Ten being their unwillingness to make the study of Molière, Corneille and Racine obligatory in the upper forms of all European high schools.

In Norway and Denmark neutralist governments come to power; in Italy, Spain, Greece and Turkey popular fronts win the general elections. Russian-controlled military juntas take over in Iraq and Syria. Following years of civil war on the Indian subcontinent and a series of natural catastrophes, there is mass starvation, and disease takes its toll of tens of millions. Japan adjusts itself to the radical shift in the balance of power and asks American residents to leave the country. An isolationist coalition in Congress expresses satisfaction that at long last America has rediscovered its manifest destiny and freed itself from entangling alliances.

The first scenario described here seems to me the most likely by far. But all are possible on the assumption that, as Marx said, "It is not history as if she were a person apart that uses men as a means to work out her purposes, but history itself is nothing but the activity of men pursuing their purposes," and that human folly plays a frequently underrated part in this process.

*December 1971*

# The Next Ten Years

## A Review of History Yet to be Written

**Things Fell Apart—1974-1984: Ten Years That Shook The World,** by S. F. Richardson. United American Publishers.

Professor Richardson's competent and unemotional survey of world affairs in our time—published, moreover, at a reasonable price—is most welcome. The author takes the year before the flood, 1974, as his starting point: the year of Watergate, the Cyprus conflict, the Indian nuclear bomb, *Watership Down,* and *Once Is Not Enough.* The storm clouds were fully visible to all but the blind, yet the general inclination was to look the other way. The author compares the helplessness of Western governments in 1974-75 with their behavior in 1929-30. Such historical parallels seem a little far-fetched. The Great Depression of the Thirties came almost like a bolt out of the blue, whereas the arrival of the crisis of the Seventies was anything but sudden. It is not so much the intellectual failure or the lack of foresight in 1975 that seems so startling in retrospect but the paralysis of will and the absence of leadership. There was a surfeit of Cassandras, but their speeches and articles did not have the slightest impact on the conduct of policy.

On the basis of a quantitative analysis of the language used in ten American daily newspapers in 1974–75, the author reaches the conclusion that whereas up to the fall of 1974 the words *Haldeman, Ehrlichman, plumbers,* and *tapes* were more frequently used than any others on the front pages and in the headlines, subsequently there was a sudden switch to *Eurodollars, Roosa bonds, roll-over loan contracts, wage-push inflation, cost inflation, over-depreciation of exchange rates, overheating,* and *underheating.* One suspects that Professor Richardson could have made similar observations by a less circuitous route. For many months there had been a feeling of gloom and helplessness vaguely comparable to the *grand peur* just before the French Revolution. At the same time there was widespread feeling that a miracle was somehow bound to happen—that, for instance, the oil prices would return to their old level for purely economic reasons, without the application of political or military pressure on the part of the consumers.

When the dramatic events of 1975 took place, hyperinflation had been in full swing in many countries for more than a year; share prices in New York, London, and elsewhere had fallen more rapidly and extensively than in 1929; some banks had closed as far back as summer 1974. It is difficult to point to any specific date in the history of the world crisis comparable to Black Thursday in 1929, or to the collapse of the Kreditanstalt in May 1931. There was no sudden, startling denouement, except perhaps the crash in the Eurodollar market which led to the temporary closing of the stock exchanges in the world's financial centers. But this, too, had been expected for many months.

The crisis was precipitated by a combination of factors: violent fluctuations in world trade, the collapse of the credit-worthiness of countries such as Britain and Italy, the decline in commodity prices that came too late to stem the tide, the spiraling rise in domestic wages and in costs, the inability for the international banking system to absorb the oil producers' money. But there was not the slightest reason that these developments, which could have been brought under control, should also have caused a major political crisis. Prior to 1975 it had been the custom to argue that 1929 could not possibly happen again because certain lessons and new techniques had been mastered. But this was not really true. Instead of reflating, various governments tried to "tighten their belts" like Chancellor Brüning in Germany in 1930-32, and with almost equally fatal results.

The failure to take effective action was not economic but political and psychological in character. Most Western governments were too weak—or, to be precise, thought they were too weak—to control costs and wages; some of them, such as the American government, were afraid of "creeping socialism": the public, it was argued, would not stand for drastic measures. But as inflation worsened, the public was only too willing to accept almost any action. Instead, the Western governments pursued a beggar-my-neighbor policy, exporting unemployment to each other by trying to boost their own exports while cutting down on imports. This led, as could have been foreseen, to the rapid fall in world trade in 1975, to the introduction of various siege economies, to a fall in the standard of living and to more unemployment.

The United States (and the Soviet Union) were less affected by these events than the countries of Europe and Japan because their dependence on the volume of foreign trade was not that extensive. Even so, America had to face its gravest crisis since the Great Depression. In the last section of his book, Professor Richardson describes in painstaking detail the gradual recovery in the late Seventies and early Eighties, the ROWT conferences (Revival of World Trade) with their agonizingly slow progress, and the reestablishment of an international monetary system delayed for years and bickering and haggling.

The full blast of the political repercussions of the crisis was felt only in 1976. Dealing with the prehistory of the decade, Professor Richardson—rightly, in our view—mentions the Nixon scandal only in passing. It was predictable that a new school of revisionist historians would devote their energies to the rehabilitation of the thirty-seventh President, but their recent studies need hardly be discussed in this context. Watergate certainly played a negative role inasmuch as public attention was diverted from the coming crisis. On the other hand, it is not at all certain that but for Watergate there would have been more decisive action. Richardson's judgment on Kissinger is harsh and, everything considered, less than fair. The Secretary of State was exceedingly lucky, for when the edifice he had erected began to crumble he was no longer in office. Overpraised at the time, he has suffered of late from the regrettable tendency to write him off as little better than a humbug.

It should be recalled that what Richardson calls Kissinger's "great illusions" were shared by a majority of his compatriots and a great many people outside the United States. Furthermore, there is much reason to assume that the then Secretary of State was, in fact, more skeptical about the long-term prospects of his own policy than most latter-day historians tend to believe. Given the general trend of public opinion in the United States at the time, the disarray of the Atlantic Alliance, and other extenuating circumstances, Kissinger should be faulted not so much for what he did but for the great expectations he helped to raise. His memoirs, which passed almost unnoticed when published, should be read as a useful corrective to the hostile interpretations of his policy (of which *The Devil and Mr. Kissinger* is only the most recent example).

If Kissinger was not the greatest Secretary of State, as many thought at the time, he certainly was not the worst; if he does not rate higher than B−, what is one to say in retrospect about his successor, Mstislav Sceszinski, the brilliant political scientist who, in a series of articles during the Nixon administration, pioneered the custom of using college grades to rate the conduct of foreign policy? Sceszinski, who became Secretary of State after the victory of the Democrats in 1976, dazzled his subordinates with a superabundance of original ideas, approaches, and concepts—sometimes at the rate of two a day. Several were quite useful; others were correct but incompatible with each other. Unfortunately, he never quite understood that original ideas were about the last thing a Secretary of State needed.

Scezinski was succeeded by Phil ("Military power never counts")

Harmke, a profoundly decent man without guile or deception. Harmke had only one fault, albeit a fatal one: he failed to realize that not all other foreign politicians were equally truthful, altruistic, and peace-loving. Harmke persuaded the President to ban all covert activities on the part of the CIA, except those connected with environmental studies. The experiment lasted for a year and although there is no saying how it would have developed had it lasted longer, the new course of the CIA sparked off a crisis in détente. Ambassador Dobrynin, now in his twenty-third year in Washington, handed a protest note to the President. In it the Soviet leaders argued that there would be intelligence services and covert activities as long as there were nation-states and that, since no one this side of a lunatic asylum could possibly assume anything else, they must to their regret interpret the announced changes in the character of the CIA as a cynical, deliberate attempt to mislead world public opinion, a step therefore detrimental to U.S.-Soviet relations.

Mention has been made that America withstood the storms of the Seventies better than the other countries of the West—much to the surprise and chagrin of some prophets of doom. The country was rent by internal strife on the eve of the crisis, and the mood was one of dejection. But the United States had greater reserves, both material and moral, than Europe and Japan. The feeling of resignation had not affected America to the same degree; there was still far more dynamism and resolve. If in the end America emerged stronger from the crisis, it was not due to the superior quality of its leadership during the years under review; apart from some memorable phrases in the Roosevelt tradition concerning the danger of phobophobia ("The only thing we have to fear is fear itself"), it is difficult to think of any major contribution by its statesmen or politicians. They did not, however, hinder the process of American recovery, and this in itself has been their historical merit.

The second New Deal was originally sponsored by men of the right; the combination of right-of-center leaders and left-of-center policies which de Gaulle had advocated for his native country found its reincarnation in Washington. The idea of greater state intervention in the economy went, of course, very much against the American grain; it had to be introduced on a provisional basis and frequently through the back door. If America now has a mixed economic system, this has come about not as the result of the pressure of the Left, but because more and more industrialists and bankers asked the federal authorities for subsidies and thus, indirectly, for state intervention. The political leadership, with all its commitment to a laissez-faire system and its aversion to bureaucratic action, realized that but for state intervention its chance of reelection would be nonexistent. They could not afford mass unemployment, the bankruptcy of major firms, and chaos on the markets; as the old mechanisms ceased to function, the state had to step in, irrespective of past experience or of its predilections and aversions. The crisis helped public opinion in the United States to differentiate between major evils and minor shortcomings, between dangerous sicknesses and passing hypochondria. It helped to do away with some of the hysteria and the shrillness which had been a characteristic feature of the style of American politics for many years prior to the crisis. The syndrome is, of course, familiar to psychiatrists: individuals and nations facing real emergencies often tend to act maturely and responsibly—very much in contrast to their past record. Americans no longer automatically blame their leaders for each and every disaster in remote parts of the globe. There is a little less parochialism, and broader perspectives have prevailed. Most of the cultural fads of the Sixties and early Seventies have gone out of fashion—largely due to boredom. There is still much criticism about the failures of political leadership, the inequities of American society, and the shortcomings of the quality of life. Measured by absolute standards, these complaints are only too justified; compared with the state of most other countries they seem almost trivial.

### Neither Washington nor Moscow

Who would have anticipated in 1974,'' writes Richardson, ''that a freshman Senator from the Middle West, a regional party secretary from Chelyabinsk, and a major in the Chinese People's Liberation Army would be the world's three most powerful men ten years hence?'' The answer to this disingenuous question is, of course, ''No one,'' for in a time of crisis unknown men always arrive from nowhere, even from Chelyabinsk. But if the emergence of these new men could not have been foreseen, the major international developments of the past decade should not have come as a surprise.

As regards détente, we are now sadder and wiser men. Much heralded in the early Seventies as a world historical turning point, it was, of course, but simply another stage in East-West relations. It prevented a major confrontation between the two superpowers, but did not deter the Soviet Union from expanding its sphere of influence wherever it could. The heated debates on the meaning of détente, on SALT, and on East-West trade seem a little ridiculous in retrospect, a curious mixture of exaggerated fears and unwarranted expectations. If the United States had military superiority until, roughly, the late 1960s, there was ''rough parity'' from 1969 to 1979; since then the Soviet Union has had NDMS (nondecisive military superiority).

The last decade witnessed, as the author notes, some Soviet progress but not as much as the Communists hoped and the West had feared.

From Moscow, it seemed that the "general crisis of capitalism," so often prematurely announced, had at last arrived. The immediate causes, to be sure, were not exactly those that had been predicted by Marx and Lenin; there was nothing in *Das Kapital* about hyperinflation, let alone about Saudi Arabia and Abu Dhabi. But the West seemed at the end of its tether, and it was assumed that the new Soviet leadership would establish the hegemony of its state and social system once and for all.

What then went wrong from the Soviet point of view? Events during the last decade have shown what should, of course, have been known long ago: that a grave crisis will not necessarily cause revolution but may lead to a state of anarchy (as in India), and that the political pendulum may swing to right-wing populism, formerly called national socialism. True, state intervention and a planned economy have prevailed almost everywhere, though not always within a Soviet-style political framework. The Soviet Union has reestablished control over Romania and Yugoslavia, but the reaction among West European Communists has been unfavorable. The Greek, Italian, Spanish, and Portuguese Communists— all now represented in their respective governments—have established a new political axis, and are critical of the Russians. Their slogan is, *"Washington y Moscu—ni la una ni la otra";* Theodorakis has written an anthem for them. The Soviet Union has suppressed without undue difficulty the occasional stirrings of independence in Eastern Europe, but the feeling in Moscow is that not one of these countries can really be trusted—with the possible exception of East Germany. Even the faithful East Germans are not popular in the Soviet capital; their standard of living is now twice as high as that of the Soviet Union, but the Russians are tired of listening to the advice freely offered by Berlin ("If you would work only half as hard as we do . . .").

Inside the Soviet Union there has been economic progress and there is a good chance that per capita income will soon reach the Spanish level. Intellectual dissent, which at one time received so much attention, continues to exist but has been negligible as a political factor. Potentially more dangerous were the centrifugal tendencies among the non-Russian nationalities—which, taken together, now constitute the majority. U.N. old-timers vividly remember the day when the Soviet representative in the General Assembly fainted as he realized that the Ukrainian and Byelorussian representatives had not voted for his proposal.

## Turmoil in the East

If the Soviet Union has made some progress in Europe and the Middle East, its Asian experiences have been less rewarding. The Indians and the other South Asians are bitterly resentful and feel, justly or unjustly, that they were let down by the Russians. When they asked for $100 billion worth of wheat, computers, machinery, oil, phosphates, laser-guided bombs, bauxite, and general-purpose loans, Moscow referred them to Washington and Abu Dhabi. In the early Seventies the Soviet leadership had decided against a preemptive strike against China on the assumption (which seemed reasonable enough at the time) that Maoist rule was not nearly as firmly rooted as it appeared and that, in the chaos that would ensue after Mao's death, support for separatist tendencies in Northern and Western China would result in the creation of *cordon sanitaire* between the Soviet Union and China. The subsequent events are well known and need not be recapitulated in detail: we all remember how the Soviet Union was drawn into the Chinese conflict, how in the face of Russian intervention the warring Chinese factions rallied against the "state-capitalist white devils," how a halfhearted Soviet intervention almost ended in military disaster, how in the process the Soviet Union turned all Asian Communist parties against itself. The conflict in the Far East continues to this day, and its end is not in sight. The fact that South Vietnam, Laos, and Cambodia have become Communist hardly provided much consolation, for, as the Moscow political analysts have correctly —albeit somewhat belatedly—noted, "Asian Communism" constitutes a phenomenon that is *sui generis,* about as distant from Marxism-Leninism as laissez-faire capitalism. Asian Communism following the Chinese example has emerged as an independent force in world affairs. Nominally the Soviet camp still exists, but there has not been a Communist world conference for fifteen years.

The break-up of India (preceded by the civil war in Bangladesh) had been predicted for a long time, but the unfolding of the tragedy took longer than generally expected. The combined Indian-Afghan attack against Pakistan resulting in the division of that country caused a great patriotic upsurge in India, but the euphoria lasted only a few months—as in the case of Turkey after her victory over the Greek Cypriots. In the end, a series of bad harvests, famines, and epidemics led to the inevitable catastrophe. The writ of the central government no longer runs outside New Delhi and its vicinity. Uttar Pradesh is in a state of civil war; other states are ruled by warlords, pro-Chinese guerrillas, or former princes; some are not ruled at all.

Large stretches of Southeast Asia and Africa were swept by famine and disease; the help extended by the industrialized countries, hit by domestic crises, was quite inadequate to cope with disasters of such magnitude. To compensate for the losses in life, the World Population Conference in Algiers in 1978 overwhelmingly passed a resolution calling on the Third World countries to double their population growth rate; it argued that a massive effort was needed which more thinly populated countries would not be able to undertake.

Colonel Qaddafi bitterly attacked the West for its insufficient assistance to the hungry and proudly pointed to the Libyan initiative: 50 million copies of the Koran had been distributed in Asia and Africa. A few countries, such as Nigeria, escaped the general ruin; they have hermetically sealed themselves against their less fortunate neighbors.

Professor Richardson recalls that a mere ten years ago some prophets of doom predicted that the new Armageddon would be in the Middle East; indeed, at that time the Arab-Israeli conflict almost caused a world conflict, and even Cyprus provoked a major crisis. Blessed the year that saw two half-bankrupt countries coming to blows because of some miserable villages near Larnaca, Famagusta, Paphos, which no one had heard of before or since. Happy the days when an American Secretary of State could spend four weeks shuttling between various Middle Eastern capitals to help them reach agreement on whether a few hills near a place named Al-Kuneitra should belong to one side or the other. What better evidence that the world did not know real problems at the time?

A small Palestinian state came into being despite stubborn Israeli resistance, and with this (as the Palestinians had rightly feared), their movement lost its momentum. A struggle for power in the new state ensued over who was to be Mayor of Ramallah and postmaster in Nablus. Appeals for the continuation of the Palestinian revolution were in vain, and what was regarded as the first stage in the battle for the destruction of Israel was also the last. True, guerrilla warfare continued, but, in view of the greater crises elsewhere, it no longer attracted any publicity and petered out after a few years.

The Arab countries were more and more absorbed in the struggle between "moderates" and "radicals," and other internal problems. The civil war on the Arabian peninsula affecting what was once Saudi Arabia, the two Yemens, and Oman is now in its seventh year. The infusion of large quantities of arms led to military takeovers almost everywhere and to the overthrow of the existing regimes.

The situation in Arabia is utterly confused—in the Southeast. Chinese-style guerrillas are running the country. Aden has been taken over by the Russians operating from Somalia, elsewhere Arab nationalist army units and various Muslim sects have established little republics.[1]

The United Arab Emirates, to no one's great surprise, have been divided between the Iraqi People's Democracy and Iran. Iraq, to all intents and purposes, is now a Soviet satellite, but it has received special dispensation to avoid the word *Marxism* in view of the unfortunate racial antecedents of the creator of "scientific socialism." In Iran, as in Turkey, Soviet influence is now paramount, though, like Afghanistan, the country still has some freedom of maneuver in domestic affairs. The ambition of the late and lamented Shah to bring prosperity and stability to his country was laudable, but the time at his disposal was insufficient and the political base of the regime too narrow.

It is now generally understood in the Middle East that the influx of great riches in 1974-76, far from being a great blessing, only hastened the loss of its independence. The Western decision, made in consultation with India and other Third World countries, to use force, if necessary, to bring down oil prices, encountered great resistance at first. The Western oil lobby conjured up the specter of a new world war and argued that the problem should be solved in a spirit of goodwill and close cooperation. It was only after friendly persuasion had failed and all negotiations had broken down that agreement about common action among consumers was reached. The Middle East oil producers countered by approaching the Soviet Union with a request for military aid in the event of a military attack. The Soviet leaders made it known that such help would be given unconditionally—provided, of course, the oil producers would cooperate in establishing a Soviet-Arab prosperity sphere in the Middle East. Realizing the implications of the Soviet offer, the oil producers split into factions: Iraq, Libya, Kuwait (ruled by a popular front government) favored accepting it, the others claimed that the game was, in the words of an old Arab proverb, no longer worth the kerosene lamp. Meanwhile, after some hard bargaining, the Soviet Union and the West decided to divide the Middle East into spheres of influence, an arrangement which has worked, so far, tolerably well. Oil production still continues, albeit on a considerably reduced scale; as the global slump spread, world consumption dwindled. Alternative sources of energy have come into use and the day seems near when once-prosperous places will be ghost towns—similar to the medieval caravan cities which fell into disuse once the traditional overland routes were no longer frequented.


### The Old World Gets Older

The less said about Europe, the better. Unlike Asia, it has been spared the ravages of war, famine, and pestilence, nor has it been physically occupied by foreign powers. But most of Europe is now run by authoritarian regimes; some use left-wing populist slogans, others right-wing populist propaganda. The difference between the two is insignificant. As if by consensus, the countries of Europe have opted for a profile so low that the old continent has all but disappeared from view. The last sign of hope for European unity was the emergence of an anticolonialist, anti-imperialist movement in France, Britain, and Germany directed against the Arab and Iranian takeover. At one time oil producers acquired ICI, Unilever, Shell, Volkswagen, Montedison, all but a few private banks, the West End of London, the first and sixteenth arrondissements in Paris, half of Munich and Hamburg, the *London Times,* and *Le Monde.* They were negotiating for the transfer to Dubai of Windsor Castle and the Arc de Triomphe. The effort to repulse these encroachments seems to have exhausted European energies. The European press, radio, and television have adopted a system of self-censorship which works very well. This in accordance with so-called Palme Doctrine adopted by most European countries: political and social injustice may be condemned but only if they happen in small countries—or at a distance of at least 4,500 miles.

The military coup in Britain predicted by many in 1974-75 failed to take place. How could there be a coup in the absence of an army? As the Labor government convincingly argued in 1975, "In view of Britain's economic situation, there is no danger of invasion and occupation." The abolition of the army led to the secession of oil-rich Scotland, under the able leadership of Mrs. Margo MacDonald.

The sad story of Europe raises the question of what went wrong. There was not, as in Greek tragedy, an inexorable fate driving heroes to their destruction. There was only stupidity, inertia, and countless missed opportunities. Crises, Jean Monnet once wrote, are the great federators, and the experience of the years of the locusts may not have been in vain. But for a long time to come historians will look for plausible explanations for something that remains inexplicable—how people of not less than average intelligence, fortified by past experience, aware of the dangers facing them, could have acted with so little wisdom and resolution. For all one knows, the question may remain a mystery forever.

*December 1974*

**NOTE**

1. The Saudi Arabian royal family is now comfortably settled in the state of Florida, most of which they managed to acquire before their overthrow. On a fine spring afternoon the royal princes, with their horses and falcons, can be seen hunting on the outskirts of Orlando and Sarasota.

# Terrorism

# Karl Heinzen and the Origins of Modern Terrorism

Karl Heinzen is no longer remembered today except perhaps by the few experts exploring the highways and by-ways of certain minute German left-wing sects in the 1840s, and by the even smaller number of historians specializing in German-American politics in the third quarter of the last century.

Heinzen figures marginally in most Karl Marx biographies because of his contacts with the founder of "scientific socialism" in the period between 1844 and 1847. (He wrote for Marx's *Rheinische Zeitung.*) Later on he bitterly quarelled with Marx and Engles who attacked him in a series of articles and a brochure.[1] These are pieces which (unlike, for instance, the *Anti-Dühring*) are read these days, if at all, by professional Marxologists only. A little book by C.H. Huber on Heinzen's political thought was published in Switzerland in 1932, and a full-length study in the United States by Carl Wittke (*Against the Current,* 1945) who is also the author of a Weitling biography.[2] Neither deals with the one aspect of Heinzen's thought which is, in retrospect, the most interesting by far—that of his role as the first ideologist—and great visionary—of modern terrorism.

My interest in Heinzen arose while engaged in research on guerrilla warfare and terrorism,[3] and I soon saw it was a tradition which could, of course, be traced far back into history. But its doctrinal foundations were laid only in the early nineteenth century. Men like Chrzanowski and Stolzman, Carlo Bianco and Budini are even less known today than Karl Heinzen, but it is precisely in works of these forgotten Polish and Italian radical democrats of the 1830s and 1840s that guerrilla theory with most of its military and political implications was first described and analysed in quite surprising detail—one hundred years before Mao Tse-tung. Most of these men were personally known to each other, meeting as they did in one or another of Mazzini's pan-European "secret societies." Their writings were forgotten for the simple reason that they were never tried

out in practice. Italy was eventually united and Poland became independent, but it was not as the result of guerrilla warfare.

Bakunin and Nechayev are commonly regarded nowadays as the
pioneers of the concept of systematic terrorism. Bakunin's pamphlets of
1869 and the famous *Catechism*, are reprinted to this day all over the
globe. ("I no longer adhere to all of Nechayev's revolutionary
catechism", George Jackson reported in the 1960s from San Quentin
prison about his Black Power doctrines.) Bakunin and Nechayev strongly influenced later generations of Russian terrorists; and since Russian
terrorism had its admirers and imitators in America, India, Western
Europe, and elsewhere, their fame spread throughout the world. There is
no denying that the impact of the writings of Bakunin and Nechayev was
greater than that of all other apostles of terrorism. But there is another
earlier tradition of terrorist thought, which antedates it by several
decades; it was in many respects more detailed and, in retrospect, more
prophetic.

Its best known proponent was Johann (John) Most, the German Social
democratic leader who settled in the United States in the early 1880s.
Having been converted to anarchism (and violence) in London, he continued to edit *Freiheit*, the most outspoken and radical anarchist
newspaper of the day. He had a devoted group of followers among recent immigrants from Central and Eastern Europe. Johann Most has
never been quite forgotten; an *Anarchist Cookbook* published in the
militant 1960s is derived from his *Revolutionare Kriegswissenschaft* of
the 1880s, and there has been in recent years in his native Germany a
Most revival on a modest scale following the New Left's search for
ideological roots. But upon closer inspection of Most's writings it appears that he was not really the *fons et origo* of the Western theory of
systematic terrorism—many of his ideas on the subject were derived
from Karl Heinzen, by four decades his senior. The two never met:
Heinzen died in Boston shortly before Most set foot on American soil.
But Most acknowledged his intellectual debt to Heinzen, and at least on
one occasion Heinzen served as an alibi for him. After the murder of
President McKinley (in 1901) *Freiheit* published an unsigned article in
justification of the murder of tyrants. When Most was brought to trial, it
was the American socialist leader Morris Hillquit who defended him, and
he claimed that the article had actually been written by Karl Heinzen fifty
years earlier and that it was directed against European monarchs rather
than American Presidents.[4] The judge was not, however, impressed and
Most had to take enforced residence on Blackwell's Island for about a
year.

Karl Heinzen was born in Grevenbroich, Westphalia in 1809, lost his
mother at an early age, and was (according to all accounts) a difficult,

irascible child. He did not get along with his teachers, and was thrown out of Bonn University after a year. He then joined the Dutch colonial army, but a few weeks service in the Dutch East Indies sufficed to persuade him that he had made a mistake, and with some difficulty, he succeeded in getting himself released. Upon his return to Germany he became a minor state official. His experiences in the bureaucracy induced him to publish, in the early 1840s, various articles, pamphlets, and books highly critical of the existing order which led to his resignation, and subsequently in 1844, to his emigration from Germany.

When Heinzen first went to the USA in 1847 he already had the reputation of one of Germany's most extreme republicans. For a while he had been on close personal terms with Karl Marx. The reasons for their ideological dispute, as seen by Heinzen, were given in a little book entitled *The Heroes of German Communism (Die Helden des teutschen Communismus*) published in 1848 in Switzerland. For Marx and Engels he was "ruffian", a "scoundrel", a "wretch", intellectually inferior in every respect—a fool, moron, ass, imbecile, clown. But this, after all, was the usual tenor of polemics between rival groups in the German emigration. There is no denying that Heinzen was not much of a philospher, and he admitted himself that his knowledge of economics was non-existent. But he had no rival at the time as far as the use of invective was concerned, and no contemporary has written in his autobiography so savagely, indeed so vulgarly if you wish, about Marx's character. Marx could be equally vulgar in his *ad hominem* attacks, but he usually kept the grosser expressions of contempt and displeasure for private correspondence: Heinzen, on the other hand, knew no such inhibitions. But the quarrels between these two are part of another story, and so is Heinzen's role in the revolution of 1848. He immediately returned to Germany, when the news of the uprisings in various European capitals had reached America. Once the uprisings had been put down he fled to Switzerland, where his activities as a publicist annoyed and embarrassed the Swiss so much that they offered him an *ex gratia* payment of 1200 francs if only he would leave Swiss soil. He went next to London where he had lodgings near Leicester Square (and later in what is now Westbourne Grove) from September 1849 for about a year.

In November 1849 he wrote two articles in a London German-language newspaper which were subsequently published as a pamphlet. He suggested, *inter alia,* that in the next Revolution a few million reactionaries would have to be killed.[5] This led a writer in *The Times* to demand that individuals disseminating such hellish doctrines should be deported with 24 hours.[6] But the authorities took no notice and Friedrich Engles' letter to the *Northern Star,* dissociating himself from Heinzen was, in retrospect, quite unnecessary. Engels argued that Heinzen did not belong to the Social Democratic party, that he had never hurt a single countryman, and that it was an insult to the British nation to assume that such a man could conceivably cause any damage to the mighty British Empire.[7] Heinzen left London of his own free will in late 1850 and settled in the United States—editing German-language newspapers in New York, Cincinnati, Louisville and ultimately in Boston ("the only civilised city in the United States").

My case for regarding Heinzen as the pioneer of modern terrorist doctrine rests on two articles entitled "Der Mord" (published in a small German emigré newspaper in Switzerland, *Die Evolution*, in January and February 1849)[8] *Die Evolution* was published in Biel by August Becker, a fellow-radical who also settled subsequently in the United States; its original title should have been *Die Revolution*, but this was not acceptable to the Swiss authorities; and as a compromise, it was decided to drop the "R". An expanded and rewritten version was published in London in 1850; it first appeared in English (*Murder and Liberty*) in New York in 1853—with the somewhat mysterious by-line, "A Contribution for the 'Peace League' of Geneva." There were subsequent reprints and I shall be quoting in the following from an edition by H. Lieber (Indianapolis 1881).

Heinzen's argument runs briefly as follows. The destruction of human life is always unjust and barbarous; humanity absolutely condemns all killing. But precisely because the endeavor is to abolish murder, humanity is compelled to draw the sword and to become murderers of the murderers: "If one man is permitted to murder, all must be permitted to do so."[9] Murder on the most colossal scale has been, and still is, the chief means of historical development—stupid weakness and sentimental lamentations should not be allowed to obscure this fact. Having surveyed, in some detail, certain instances of mass murder throughout history, Heinzen reaches the conclusion that a Revolution which shuns the responsibility for killing all reactionaries is only committing suicide. The French Revolution was buried by the emigration:

> Let it be attended to that next time there can be no emigration, unless it can be stowed away in some remote corners of the world.

Since the reactionaries murder to maintain their rule, the revolutionaries must murder to be free. The victor is always right: there is no room for moral scruples.

The greatest of all follies is the belief that it is possible to commit a crime against despots and their accomplices. A "crime" against them is not just a right, it is self-defense; and it is a duty. The road to humanity leads over the summit of cruelty—nothing less than this is the inexorable law of necessity dictated by the reactionary forces. Not to accept this obvious fact is to renounce a better future for mankind; if one wants to accomplish the end, one must not flinch from the means.

Heinzen rejected with contempts the argument of the "genteel revolutionists" who claimed that certain things should be done but not openly proclaimed. This, according to Heinzen was mere cowardice:

> "What you dare not proclaim, you should also not permit to be done. What is right should be proclaimed openly, before all the world."

In his articles written in late 1848 Heinzen stated that "we must become more energetic, more desperate." This led him into speculations about the use of arms of mass destruction; for the greater strength, training, and discipline of the forces of repression could be counterbalanced only by weapons that could be employed by a few people and that would wreak great havoc. These weapons, according to Heinzen, could not on the other hand be used by regular armies against a few individual fighters. He mentioned, in passing, the use of poison gas, of ballistic missiles (Congreve missiles, in nineteenth-century military parlance), and mines which could destroy whole cities with 100,000 inhabitants.

The key to the Revolution was in modern technology, such as new, more powerful explosives and new means of food poisoning. In his brochure, published in 1853, he was already far more specific and provided several scenarios for doing away with the

> preponderance of the engines of mass destruction by means of the homeopathic use of powerful destructive substances which would cost little to furnish and might be obtained or prepared with little risk of discovery.

He confessed that he was "neither soldier, nor chemist, nor engineer." Therefore, he left it to "professional men" to "use the following hints for further inventions."

The first hint Heinzen attributed to the *Augsburg General Gazette:*

> Yesterday afternoon the most terrible, most lamentable event of modern history transpired. When the illustrious crowned heads of Germany, who had assembled at the congress of monarchs at Vienna made an excursion by railroad, a fearful explosion was heard at a place where the road passes a precipice a hundred feet high. At the same time, the locomotive and the entire train darted over the precipice. All the monarchs broke their necks, and only two

mistresses escaped with their lives, so that, at present, Germany is without monarchs. An investigation showed that a revolutionary monster had laid upon the rails a small case of the size of a thimble filled with fulminating silver, which exploded on the first contact with the wheel of the locomotive and hurled the whole train from the track. A similar accident is said to have overtaken the Czar of Russia in the vicinity of Warsaw.

The second hint was supposed to derive from the *Vienna Gazette:*

The guerrillas of the Baconyan Forest now use the following fearful weapon, which is calculated to render individual men terrible to organised masses. They have guns of double ordinary thinkness. These are first charged with a strong charge of powder, and on top of this with an iron capsule fitting the barrel exactly, about four inches long, and conical at the upper end. Inside this capsule there is another smaller one filled with powder which is closed at the upper point with an easily explosive percussion-cap, and the space between the inner and outer capsule is filled with poisoned iron shot. Whenever this charge is shot against some object, the capsule explodes and scatters a shower of poisoned shot, each grain of which may destroy a human life. In this way a single man, *omnia secum portans,* may become dangerous to a hundred opponents. Lately such a charge was fired from the forest upon a battalion of imperial chasseurs, and wounded sixty men of whom on the next day fifty had died.

From the *Prussian State Gazette* which Heinzen took the trouble to inform us was "now published in Potsdam" came a third hint:

Unfortunately General Wrangel failed entirely in reconquering the city of Berlin, which is now wholly in possession of the revolutionists. He was foiled by a desperate mode of defence by which the rebels demoralised the troops completely. At first they fired iron tubes filled with melted lead, which scattered a deathly shower on the advancing battalions. Nevertheless the gallant soldiers, incited by the Prince of Prussia with the prospect of pillaging the city and of executing all the revolutionists on the spot, penetrated into several avenues. But here they were cut down in companies by explosive bombs which suddenly burst forth from the pavement of the street, and which did such terrible execution, that even the most gallant soldiers could not be induced to proceed further, since at every step they had to fear a fresh explosion. It is said that these explosive bombs consist of shells filled with powder and furnished with a percussion hammer, which are buried beneath the pavement in places which the enemy cannot discover, in such a way that the hammer acts as soon as foot steps on the stone placed over it. It is said the revolutionists have laid in every avenue such a number of similar bombs, that the capture of the city would cost the lives of 100,000 soldiers. It seems that the men of the revolution no longer deem it necessary to imperil their lives in a useless martyrdom, if mere machines can assure their success. A significant sign of the times! As soon as our present mode of warfare is overthrown and disorganized, the army and the monarchs are lost.

The fourth hint came in this passage from the *Milanese Gazette:*

The party of despair has now recourse to truly diabolical means. Every one who is of any value for the order and morality of society, must tremble day and night for his life. *Poison* is the universal watchword of the revolutionists, since they are deprived of all other weapons. Cases of poisoning the victuals, the water, the tobacco, etc. for the soldiers, we have previously reported. But the hellish invention has gone farther. Every knife, every dagger, every pin that is drawn against the men of order, is now poisoned. For this purpose they use strychnine, prussic acid, etc, nay, even the blood of corpses.

With unexampled refinement of cruelty, they use a poison even the pus of revolutionists who rotted to death in dungeons, and direct the weapons so poisoned against the most sacred lives. Thus the general of the Jesuits and two cardinals were wounded lately in this fashion; they will die within three days; and His Holiness escaped a similar fate only by the cushion of fat in which the arrow lodged.

For the poisoning of bullets, the revolutionists, who are now everywhere zealously engaged in the study of physics and chemistry, use only poisons that are not too readily volatilised by heat. They also use glass bullets filled with quicksilver and even with prussic acid, which, of course, kill without fail, if their contents come into contact with the blood. In filling hollow metal balls with less refractory poison, they mix these first with wax or tallow, in order to avoid their volatilisation as much as possible.

From windows, cellars, holes in walls, etc. they usually discharge their poisoned missiles from airguns, so that no explosion is heard. But since several of these weapons, too, have been discovered, the monsters use simple trunks or pipe-stems, one or two feet long, made of tin or wood, nay, even macaroni-tubes, from which they blow against their victims everywhere, even in churches, peas and small arrows with poisoned harbed points. They need only scratch the skin, in order to produce a deadly effect and the discovery of the perpetrator is rarely possible.

Our whole art of war and all our cannons are powerless against this homeopathic war of a diabolical party. It is a terrible task in these times to be a man of order. Even loyal men express the doubt that order has been carried too far. But how is it possible to moderate in order? We must now murder all, or we shall be murdered. Merciful Providence! do not abandon us!

As for the fifth hint, Heinzen tells us that a correspondent of "La France" vouched for the following communication:

The ingenuity of the men of the revolution in the production of new means of destruction is equalled by the caution practised in the organisation and disposition of their agents. At the head of their assassins, whom they call liberators, is a single person, whose name has not been mentioned yet in the revolutionary would but who, on account of his reliability and astuteness, enjoys the full confidence of the principal leaders. This person continually receives considerable sums of money, without his knowing whence they come. It is his principal task to have new means of destruction invented and manufactured, and to engage reliable agents that use them. These assistants, fanatical men of extreme determination and reliability, exist under all possible characters, do not know each other, and converse singly with their chief who visits them in their residences, and whose domicile they do not know. It is said that in France and Italy alone there are several hundred of these agents. It is so much the more difficult to escape them, since, if an especially important person is the victim, they are all directed at the same time against him. If one of these should be discovered and arrested, he could not betray the others, even if he should wish to do so, and these others are at once busy to take his place and to avenge him.

This organisation of assassins is wholly independent. But besides there is the great revolutionary organisation ready to embrace at once the opportunity for seizing control, if the victim that obstructed its path should have fallen.

His Majesty has not been able to leave the Tuileries during the past few weeks, because his life was threatened on all sides, although no one knows how and by whom.

Finally, there was this from the *"Moniteur"*:

His Majesty the Emperor Louis Napoleon and the palace of the Tuileries are no more. The palace was last night suddenly blown up by a terrible explosion, and buried under its ruins the emperor and the entire court, that was just assembled around him. A fearful *coup d'état*. The explosion was brought about by a few copper balls about the size of a man's head. These balls had been made by some revolutionist and placed in a lower story by a soldier. The greater part of each ball was filled with nitro-glycerine or, as some maintain, with carbonic acid which, as is well known, has far more explosive power than powder, and which explodes by a simple elevation of temperature. (Its efficiency is greatly increased if the carbonic acid is first liquified by compression.)[10] In order to effect the heating of the gas in the ball, the latter had been furnished with works whose index ignited a small quantity of phosphorus and powder by rapid friction, half an hour after the placing of the balls. In order to avoid the elevation of temperature from the outside and, consequently, a premature explosion, the balls were encased in ice, and, to avoid ignition by some shock on rolling them into the cellar, the whole was covered with a coat of India rubber. Such effective means only the revolutionists could use. But the time for lamenting is over, and a new era begins. The revolution has conquered; and the victor is right. The *Moniteur* always serves the conqueror. *Vae victis!*

Heinzen had, in his articles of 1849, envisaged the blowing up "if necessary" of half a continent.[11] But his subsequent career was not devoted to the practical application of his theories. In the United States he became a staunch fighter for Women's Rights, and one of the most extreme spokesmen of the Abolitionists, a collaborator of William Lloyd Garrison, Horace Greeley, Wendell Phillips, and many other leading anti Negro slavery radicals of the day. He gave Abraham Lincoln what is known as critical support; and at one time he had the chief advocate for the abolition of the presidency in order to make America more democratic. He continued his polemics against Marx all along the columns of his *Pioneer*—Communism, as he saw it, would merely lead to a new form of slavery. In a Communist America, as Heinzen once wrote, he would not be permitted to travel from Boston to New York to make a speech in favour of Communism without having official permission to do so.

Having moved from New York's Bowery to Boston in 1857, Heinzen became something of an establishment figure in radical circles—"the sage of Roxbury." His seventieth birthday was a major social event and he was serenaded by an assembled choir. He cultivated the German gymnasts (the *Turnerbund*), at the time a force in German-American politics, Heinzen was a staunch opponent of Bismark, and after 1870, on many occasions castigated the militaristic and chauvinistic tendencies he detected in Imperial Germany. This was not a popular line at the time; and, but for Mrs. Heinzen's millinery shop, the *Pionier* would hardly have lasted as long as it did.

Heinzen's style was repetitive and inelegant; the continuous use of the strongest invective he could think of was bound to repel all but his most loyal readers. The most interesting part of the *Pioneer* was the literary *feuilleton*: he published *avant-garde* French and Spanish writers; Heinzen's own poems, novels, and plays, on the other hand, were mediocre, to say the least. He had a small but faithful group of admirers all over the United States, and his funeral in 1880 was one of the largest Boston had witnessed for a long time. The speeches made at the graveside were subsequently published in a book to commemorate the event.

One day last spring I visited Forest Hill cemetery in South Boston where Karl Heinzen is buried. It is the biggest cemetery I have ever seen, but it is one of the best kept, and Heinzen's grave was not too difficult to find. On a little hill there was a statue with Heinzen's bust, nine feet high. On it there were two inscriptions. One is in German:

> *Die Freiheit war's die mir den Geist beschwingte, die Wahrheit war's die mir das Herz verjüngte* (Freedom inspired my spirit, Truth rejuvenated my heart).

And the second is in English:

> *His Life Work—the Elevation of Mankind.*

*August 1977*

## NOTES

1. *Die moralisierende Kritik und die kritisierende Moral* (Brussels, 1847).
2. See Melvin J. Lasky, "Wilhelm Weitling", in *Encounter* (March).
3. See my *Guerrilla* and *Terrorism* (both published by Weidenfeld and Little Brown, 1977) and *The Guerrilla Reader* (New American Library, 1977).
4. This argument, repeated in Hillquit's autobiography (*Loose Leaves,* 1934), was actually not quite true. The article published in *Freiheit* was a paraphrase rather than a literal reprint of Heinzen's article 1849 (on which more below).

5. *Deutsche Londoner Zeitung,* 9 and 16 November 1848. This newspaper—in which the year before the *Communist Manifesto* had been published—was financed incidentally by Karl, Duke of Brunswick.
6. "Anti-Socialist", *The Times,* 23 November 1849.
7. *Northern Star,* 1 December 1849.
8. This periodical is now virtually unobtainable; I am obliged to the Swiss State Archives for having provided a copy. Heinzen's original article appears in English translation in my *Terrorism Reader.* The expanded English version has come into my hands only recently.
9. Some of the more eccentric formulations of the 1849 articles were deleted in the English version. This refers, for instance, to the observation that murder might well be a "physical necessity" inasmuch as the atmosphere or the soil of the earth needed a certain quantity of blood. *Blut und Boden,* indeed!
10. The explosive properties of nitro-glycerine were already known in the 1850s but it was only in the next decade, following Alfred Nobel's experiments that it was put to practical use.
11. Marx commented in a letter to his disciple Wedemeyer in New York: "Heinzen wants to become a martyr by threatening to devour hundreds of thousands of millions of men for breakfast. . . ."

# The Futility of Terrorism

## I

A few days before Christmas a group of terrorists broke into the OPEC building in Vienna; the rest of the story is still fresh in the memory and need not be retold. Coming so soon after the attacks of the South Moluccan separatists in the Netherlands, the incident occasioned a great hand-wringing and tooth-grinding among editorialists all over the globe with dire comments about the power concentrated in the hands of a few determined individuals and harrowing predictions as to what all this could mean for the future. Because the significance of terrorism is not yet widely understood, such a nine days' wonder could be regarded as an action of world-shaking political consequence. Yet, when the shooting was over, when the terrorists had vanished from the headlines and the small screen, it appeared that they were by no means nearer to their aims. It was not even clear what they had wanted. Their operation in Vienna had been meticulously prepared, but they seemed to have only the haziest notion of what they intended to achieve. They broadcast a document which, dealing with an obscure subject and written in left-wing sectarian language, might just as well have been broadcast in Chinese as far as the average Austrian listener was concerned.

The Vienna terrorists claimed to be acting on behalf of the Palestinian revolution, but only some of them were Arabs and it is not certain that there was a single Palestinian among them. Their leader was the notorious "Carlos," a Venezuelan trained in Moscow and supported by Cuban intelligence in Paris—a branch of the Soviet KGB. Yet the operation, according to the Egyptian press, was paid for by Colonel Qaddafi. The working of modern transnational terrorism with its ties to Moscow and Havana, its connections with Libya and Algeria, resemble those of a multinational corporation; whenever multinational corporations sponsor patriotic causes, the greatest of caution is called for.

Similar caution is required if one is to avoid exaggerating the importance of terrorism today. It is true that no modern state can guarantee

101

the life and the safety of all of its citizens all of the time, but is it not true that terrorists somehow acquire "enormous power" (to quote our editorialists) if they kidnap a few dozen citizens, as in Holland, or even a dozen oil ministers, as in Vienna. If a mass murder had happened in Vienna on that Sunday before Christmas, long obituaries of Sheik Yamani and his colleagues would have been published—and within twenty-four hours, ambitious and competent men in Tehran and Caracas, in Baghdad and in Kuwait, would have replaced them. Terrorists and newspapermen share the naive assumption that those whose names make the headlines have power, that getting one's name on the front page is a major political achievement. This assumption typifies the prevailing muddled thinking on the subject of terrorism.

In recent years urban terrorism has superseded guerrilla warfare in various parts of the world. As decolonization came to an end there was a general decline in guerrilla activity. Furthermore, rural guerrillas learned by bitter experience that the "encirclement of the city by the country-side" (the universal remedy advocated by the Chinese ten years ago) was of doubtful value if four-fifths (or more) of the population are city dwellers, as happens to be the case in most Western industrialized countries—and quite a few Latin-American countries too. With the transfer of operations from the countryside to the cities, the age of the "urban guerrilla" dawned. But the very term "urban guerrilla" is problematical. There have been revolutions, civil wars, insurrections, and coup d'etat in the cities, but hardly ever guerrilla warfare. That occurs in towns only if public order has completely collapsed, and if armed bands roam freely. Such a state of affairs is rare, and it never lasts longer than a few hours, at most a few days. Either the insurgents overthrow the government in a frontal assault, or they are defeated. The title "urban guerrilla" is in fact a public-relations term for terrorism; terrorists usually dislike being called terrorists, preferring the more romantic guerrilla image.

There are basic differences between the rural guerrilla and the urban terrorist: mobility and hiding are the essence of guerrilla warfare, and this is impossible in towns. It is not true that the slums (and the rich quarters) of the big cities provide equally good sanctuaries. Rural guerrillas operate in large units and gradually transform themselves into battalions, regiments, and even divisions. They carry out political and social reforms in "liberated zones," openly propagandize, and build up their organizational network. In towns, where this cannot be done, urban terrorists operate in units of three, four, or five; the whole "movement" consists of a few hundred, often only a few dozen, members. This is the source of their operational strength and their political weakness. For while it is difficult to detect small groups, and while they can cause a great deal of damage, politically they are impotent. A year or two ago anxious newspaper readers in the Western world were led to believe that the German Baader Meinhof group, the Japanese Red Army, the Symbionese Liberation Army, and the British Angry Brigade were mass movements that ought to be taken very seriously indeed. Their "communiqués" were published in the mass media; there were earnest sociological and psychological studies on the background of their members; their "ideology" was analyzed in tedious details. Yet these were groups of between five and fifty members. Their only victories were in the area of publicity.

*Terrorist Myths*

The current terrorist epidemic has mystified a great many people, and various explanations have been offered—most of them quite wrong. Only a few will be mentioned here:

**Political terror is a new and unprecedented phenomenon.** It is as old as the hills, only the manifestations of terror have changed. The present epidemic is mild compared with previous outbreaks. There were more assassinations of leading statesmen in the 1890s in both America and Europe, when terrorism had more supporters, than at the present time. Nor is terrorist doctrine a novelty. In 1884 Johannes Most, a German Social Democrat turned anarchist, published in New York a manual, *Revolutionary (Urban) Warfare,* with the subtitle "A Handbook of Instruction Regarding the Use and Manufacture of Nitroglycerine, Dynamite, Guncotton, Fulminiating Mercury, Bombs, Arsons, Poisons etc." Most pioneered the idea of the letter bomb and argued that the liquidation of "pigs" was not murder because murder was the willful killing of a human being, whereas policemen did not belong in this category.

It is sometimes argued that guerrilla and terrorist movements in past ages were sporadic and essentially apolitical. But this is not so; the Russian anarchists of the last century were as well organized as any contemporary movement, and their ideological and political sophistication was, if anything, higher. The same goes for the guerrilla wars of the nineteenth century. The guerrilla literature published in Europe in the 1830s and 1840s is truly modern in almost every respect. It refers to "bases," "liberated areas," "protracted war" as well as the gradual transformation of guerrilla units into a regular army. The basic ideas of Mao and Castro all appeared at least 100 years earlier.

**Terrorism is left-wing and revolutionary in character.** Terrorists do not believe in liberty or fraternity or egality. Historically, they are elitists, contemptuous of the masses, believing in the historical mission of a tiny minority. It was said about the Tupamaros that one had to be a Ph.D. to be a member. This was an exaggeration but not by very much. Their manifestos may be phrased in left-wing language, but previous generations of terrorists proclaimed Fascist ideas. Nineteenth-century European partisans and guerrillas fighting Napoleon were certainly right wing. The Spanish guerrilleros wanted to reintroduce the Inquisition, the Italian burned the houses of all citizens suspected of left-wing ideas. Closer to our own period, the IRA and the Macedonian IMRO at various times in their history had connections with Fascism and Communism. The ideology of terrorist movements such as the Stern gang and the Popular Front for the Liberation of Palestine encompasses elements of the extreme Left and Right. Slogans change with intellectual fashions and should not be taken too seriously. The real inspiration underlying terrorism is a free-floating activism that can with equal ease turn right and left. It is the action that counts.

**Terrorism appears whenever people have genuine, legitimate grievances. Remove the grievance and terror will cease.** The prescription seems plausible enough, but experience does not bear it out. On the level of abstract reasoning it is, of course, true that there would be no violence if no one had a grievance or felt frustration. But in practice there will always be disaffected, alienated, and highly aggressive people claiming that the present state of affairs is intolerable and that only violence will bring a change. Some of their causes may even be real and legitimate — but unfulfillable. This applies to the separatist demands of minorities, which, if acceded to, would result in the emergence of nonviable states and the crippling of society. It is always the fashion to blame the state or the "system" for every existing injustice. But some of the problems may simply be insoluble, at least in the short run. No state or social system can be better than the individuals constituting it.

It is ultimately the perception of grievance that matters, not the grievance itself. At one time a major grievance may be fatalistically accepted, whereas at another time (or elsewhere) a minor grievance may produce the most violent reaction. A comparison of terrorist activities over the last century shows, beyond any shadow of doubt, that violent protest movements do not appear where despotism is worst but, on the contrary, in permissive democratic societies or ineffective authoritarian regimes. There were no terrorist movements in Nazi Germany, nor in Fascist Italy, nor in any of the Communist countries. The Kurdish insurgents were defeated by the Iraqi government in early 1975 with the greatest of ease, whereas terrorism in Ulster continues for many years now and the end is not in sight. The Iraqis succeeded not because they satisfied the grievances of the Kurds but simply because they could not care less about public opinion abroad.

**Terror is highly effective.** Terror is noisy, it catches the headlines. Its melodrama inspires horror and fascination. But seen in historical perspective, it has hardly ever had a lasting effect. Guerrilla wars have been successful only against colonial rule, and the age of colonialism is over. Terrorism did have a limited effect at a time of general war, but only in one instance (Cuba) has a guerrilla movement prevailed in peacetime. But the constellation in Cuba was unique and, contrary to Castro's expectations, there were no repeat performances elsewhere in Latin America. The Vietnam war in its decisive phase was no longer guerrilla in character. There is no known case in modern history of a terrorist movement seizing political power, although terror has been used on the tactical level by radical political parties. Society will tolerate terrorism as long as it is no more than a nuisance. Once insecurity spreads and terror becomes a real danger, the authorities are no longer blamed for disregarding human rights in their struggle against it. On the contrary, the cry goes up for more repressive measures, irrespective of the price that has to be paid in human rights. The state is always so much stronger than the terrorists, whose only hope for success is to prevent the authorities from using their full powers. If the terrorist is the fish—following Mao Tse-tung's parable—the permissiveness and the inefficiency of liberal society is the water. As Regis Debray, apostle of the Latin-American guerrillas, wrote about the Tupamaros: "By digging the grave of liberal Uruguay, they dug their own grave."

**The importance of terrorism will grow enormously in the years to come as the destructive power of its weapons increases.** This danger does indeed exist, with the increasing availability of missiles, nuclear material, and highly effective poisons. But it is part of a wider problem, that of individuals blackmailing society. To engage in nuclear ransom, a "terrorist movement" is not needed; a small group of madmen or criminals, or just one person, could be equally effective—perhaps even more so. The smaller the group, the more difficult it would be to identify and combat.

**Political terrorists are more intelligent and less cruel than "ordinary" criminals.** Most political terrorists in modern times have been of middle- or upper-class origin, and many of them have had a higher education. Nevertheless, they have rarely shown intelligence, let alone political sophistication. Larger issues and future perspectives are of little interest to them, and they are quite easily manipulated by foreign intelligence services. As for cruelty, the "ordinary" criminal, unlike the terrorist, does not believe in indiscriminate killing. He may torture a victim, but this will be the exception, not the rule, for he is motivated by material gain and not by fanaticism. The motivation of the political terrorist is altogether different. Since, in his eyes, everyone but himself is guilty, restraints do not exist. Political terror therefore tends to be less humane than the variety practiced by "ordinary" criminals. The Palestinian terrorists have specialized in killing children, while the Provisional IRA has concentrated its attacks against Protestant workers, and this despite their professions of "proletarian internationalism." It is the terrorists' aim not just to kill their opponents but to spread confusion and fear. It is part of the terrorist indoctrination to kill the humanity of the terrorist—all this, of course, for a more humane and just world order.

**Terrorists are poor, hungry, and desperate human beings.** Terrorist groups without powerful protectors are indeed poor. But modern transnational terrorism is, more often than not, big business. According to a spokesman of the Palestine "Rejection Front" in an interview with the Madrid newspaper *Platforma,* the income of the PLO is as great as that of certain Arab countries, such as Jordan, with payments by the oil countries on the order of $150 million to $200 million. Officials of the organizations are paid $5,000 a month and more, and everyone gets a car as a matter of course; they have acquired chalets and bank accounts in Switzerland. But the "Rejection Front," financed by Iraq, Libya, and Algeria is not kept on a starvation diet either. The Argentine ERP and the Montoneros have amassed many millions of dollars through bank robberies and extortion. Various Middle Eastern and East European governments give millions to terrorist movements from Ulster to the Philippines. This abundance of funds makes it possible to engage in all kinds of costly operations, to bribe officials, and to purchase sophisticated weapons. At the same time, the surfeit of money breeds corruption. The terrorists are no longer lean and hungry after prolonged exposure to life in Hilton hotels. They are still capable of carrying out gangster-style operations of short duration, but they become useless for long campaigns involving hardships and privation.

All this is not to say that political terror is always reprehensible or could never be effective. The assassination of Hitler or Stalin in the 1920s or 1930s would not only have changed the course of history, it would have saved the lives of millions of people. Terrorism is morally justified whenever there is no other remedy for an intolerable situation. Yet it seldom occurs, and virtually never succeeds, where tyranny is harshest.

*The terrorist's friends*

Events in recent years offer certain obvious lessons to terrorists. These lessons run against the terrorist grain, and have not yet been generally accepted. For example, terror is always far more popular against foreigners than against one's own countrymen. The only terrorists in our time who have had any success at all are those identifying themselves with a religious or national minority. It is sectarian-chauvinist support that counts, not drab, quasirevolutionary phraseology; Irish, Basques, Arabs, and the rest have found this out by trial and error. The media are a terrorist's best friend. The terrorist's act by itself is nothing. Publicity is all. Castro was the great master of the public-relations technique, from whom all terrorists should learn; with less than 300 men he created the impression of having a force of overwhelming strength at his disposal. But the media are a fickle friend, constantly in need of diversity and new angles. Terrorists will always have to be innovative; they are the super-entertainers of our time. Seen in this light the abduction of the OPEC ministers rates high marks.

The timing of the operation is also of paramount importance, for if it clashes with other important events, such as a major sports events or a natural disaster, the impact will be greatly reduced. Whenever terrorists blackmail governments, it is of great importance to press realistic demands. Democratic authorities will instinctively give in to blackmail—but only up to a point. The demand for money or the release of a few terrorist prisoners is a realistic demand, but there are limits beyond which no government can go, as various terrorist groups have found out to their detriment.

Psychiatrists, social workers, and clergymen are the terrorist's next-best friends. They are eager to advise, to assuage, and to mediate, and their offer to help should always be accepted by the terrorist. These men and women of goodwill think they know more than others about the mysteries of the human soul and that they have the compassion required for understanding the feelings of "desperate men." But a detailed study of the human psyche is hardly needed to understand the terrorist phenomenon; its basic techniques have been known to every self-respecting gangster throughout history. It is the former terrorist, the renegade, who has traditionally been the terrorist's most dangerous opponent. Once again, the terrorist should never forget that he exists only because the authorities are prevented by public opinion at home and abroad from exercising their full power against him. If a terrorist wishes to survive, he should not create the impression that he could be a real menace, unless, of course, he has sanctuaries in a foreign country and strong support from a neighboring power. In this case political terrorism turns into surrogate warfare and changes its character, and then there is always the danger that it may lead to real, full-scale war.

Recent terrorist experience offers some lessons to governments too. If governments did not give in to terrorist demands, there would be no terror, or it would be very much reduced in scale. The attitude of Chancellor Bruno Kreisky and his minister of the interior, who virtually shook the terrorist's hands, is not only aesthetically displeasing, it is also counterproductive. It may save a few human lives in the short run, but it is an invitation to further such acts and greater bloodshed. However, it would be unrealistic to expect determined action from democratic governments in present conditions. In wartime these governments will sacrifice whole armies without a moment's hesitation. In peace they will argue that one should not be generous with other people's lives. Western politicians and editorialists still proclaim that terrorism is condemned "by the whole civilized world," forgetting that the "civilized world" covers no more than about one-fifth of the population of the globe. Many countries train, equip, and finance terrorists, and a few sympathetic governments will always provide sanctuary. Western security services may occasionally arrest and sentence foreign terrorists, but only with the greatest reluctance, for they know that sooner or later one of their aircraft will be hijacked or one of their politicians abducted. Ilyich Ramírez Sánchez ("Carlos"), the Venezuelan terrorist, is wanted in Britain for attempted murder, yet Scotland Yard decided last December not to press for his extradition from Algiers. For, in the words of the London *Daily Telegraph* "the trial of an international terrorist could lead to political repercussions and acts of terrorist reprisals." A good case could be made for not arresting foreign terrorists in the first place but simply deporting them. The European governments on a West German initiative have had some urgent deliberations in recent weeks as to how to collaborate in combating terror. But, according to past experience, it is doubtful whether international cooperation will be of much help unless it is worldwide.

These observations do not, of course, refer to the South Moluccans, the Kurds, and other such groups in the world of terrorism. They fight only for national independence; they are on their own because they fulfill no useful political function as far as the Russians and the Cubans are concerned. The Libyans and Algerians will not support them because they belong to the wrong religion or ethnic group, and even South Yemen will not give them shelter. They are the proletariat of the terrorist world.

Terrorism is, of course, a danger, but magnifying its importance is even more dangerous. Modern society may be vulnerable to attack, but it is also exceedingly resilient. A plane is hijacked, but all others continue to fly. A bank is robbed, but the rest continue to function. All oil ministers are abducted, and yet not a single barrel of oil is lost.

Describing the military exploits of his Bedouin warriors, Lawrence of Arabia once noted that they were on the whole good soldiers, but for their unfortunate belief that a weapon was dangerous in proportion to the noise it created. Present-day attitudes towards terrorism in the Western world are strikingly similar. Terrorism creates tremendous noise. It will continue to cause destruction and the loss of human life. It will always attract much publicity but, politically, it tends to be ineffective. Compared with other dangers threatening mankind it is almost irrelevant.

*March 1976*

## II

It is part of the conventional wisdom of our time that terrorism is one of the crucial problems facing mankind. If repetition made an argument correct, this one surely would be. I have dealt with some of the myths about terrorism in a previous article; the present essay tackles a few more without, unfortunately, great hope of exhausting the topic. How much terrorism is there, and is it really increasing? Around the globe over the past decade perhaps some 10,000 people have been killed by terrorist actions; this includes both domestic and international terrorism, Latin America, Ulster, and the Middle East as well as Colonel Qaddafi's multinational flying circus. Such a figure obscures an immeasurable amount of tragedy and pain, but it is also true that as many people were killed in the Lebanese civil war in three months or perished in a few weeks in the Cambodian purge or in the Colombian *violencia*. More important, for the past three or four years the number of terrorist operations has shown a marked decline, most dramatically perhaps in the case of hijacking. There were more than fifty cases in 1970, whereas during the past year there have been only four or five.

Terrorism occurs in cycles; the most recent one reached its apex in the early 1970s and has been on the decline. The major terrorist groups of the late 1960s and early 1970s, such as the Tupamaros in Uruguay, the Brazilian ALN, the Canadian FLQ, the Weathermen, and the various European, North American, and Japanese groups have been defeated. The Argentinian ERP and the Montoneros, who seemed so near to success only a few months ago, have suffered a setback from which they will probably not recover. The number of terrorist operations carried out by the Palestinian organizations had substantially decreased even before the Lebanese civil war. Dozens of books and thousands or articles have been written about the subject of Palestinian terrorism, but the number of Israelis killed in 1975 was about fifty—less than the number of victims in one night in Beirut.

There has been a minor resurgence of terrorism in Spain and Mexico, but, seen on a global scale, the downward trend is quite unmistakable. American commentators have referred to the "stupendous cost" of such countermeasures as guarding American embassies abroad. Yet a little probing shows that the sum involved amounts to a mere $40 million, less than the projected cost of one B-1 plane. And as it has long been customary to guard embassies in any case—against thieves, for instance, or stray dogs—even if there is no terrorist danger, the real cost is probably much lower yet.

All this is not to say that terrorism will soon disappear. It has powerful international patrons and in the more distant future there is of course the danger of the use of unconventional weapons by terrorists. Even at the present stage, international (as distinct from domestic) terrorism could lead to limited war, but this has not happened. At present, terrorism is on the decline. The question remaining to be asked is, Why has this fact not yet registered?

*The publicity campaign*

The media act as a selective magnifying glass: terrorism always exerts a strange fascination, especially from a safe distance. It has all the ingredients of a good story—mystery, quick action, tension, drama. It seems natural, therefore, that the media should give terrorism inordinate publicity. The vital importance of publicity has been realized by generations of terrorists all over the world: the terrorist act alone is nothing; publicity is all. The Algerian rebels of the 1950s quite deliberately transferred their struggle from the countryside to the capital, even though they suspected that they could not possibly win the battle for the capital. As one of them wrote, if ten enemies are killed in the *djebel,* no one will take notice, but even a small incident in Algiers will be picked up by the American press and prominently featured the next day in New York. He was quite right—the Algerians were beaten in the struggle for the capital, but they won the fight for publicity, which, in long run, was the decisive battle. What is news, certainly in the Western world, depends upon the presence of newspapermen and TV cameras. The case of Israel is most instructive in this respect. A massacre or a mass execution in a Third World country will rate at most a few paragraphs. However, if ten schoolgirls burn a tire in Bethlehem, all hell will break loose, for in Israel there is one of the heaviest concentrations of newpapermen on earth. This is partly because their editors believe that everything happening in Israel is most important and that world peace depends on it, and partly because Israel is one of only three or four countries left outside Europe, Japan, and North America in which journalists can move about freely. Let them try to cover terrorists training in Libya or an execution in Sudan, let them try to probe deeply into the struggle between terrorists and the army in Argentina, and they will soon find themselves in very serious trouble indeed. There is no such danger in Israel, and for this and other reasons the Israelis, however much they protest, will be overexposed for years to come.

Selective publicity, then, is one of the sources of misconception about terrorism: another is the vagueness—indeed, the utter carelessness—with which the term is used, not only in the media but also in government announcements and by academic students of the subject. Terrorism is used as a synonym for rebellion, street battles, civil strife, insurrection, rural guerrilla war, coups d'etat, and a dozen other things. The indiscriminate use of the term not only inflates the statistics, it makes understanding the specific character of terrorism and how to cope with it more difficult.

Terrorism grew out of the time-honored tradition of tyrannicide; Brutus was a sort of terrorist; so were Wilhelm Tell and Charlotte Corday. The question of whether tyrannicide is permitted in certain circumstances has preoccupied generations of philosophers and theologians, and the general consensus is now that one cannot unconditionally condemn it except perhaps on the basis of a total, Gandhian commitment to nonviolence. For there are obviously cases in which there is no redress against tyranny, in which murder is no crime but a liberating act. Every terrorist would claim to be Wilhelm Tell fighting unspeakable despotism and cruelty, but, as a rule of thumb, one learns more about a terrorist group by looking at its victims that at its manifestos.

Contemporary terrorism has definitely changed its character: before the first world war systematic terrorism was on the whole limited to the Tsarist and Ottoman empires, which, by the exacting standards of that period, were about the most despotic regimes in the world. Today terrorism occurs only in democratic societies and in halfhearted authoritarian regimes; it no longer dares to challenge an effective dictatorship. As the character of terrorism has changed, so has the character of those practicing it. Even the bitterest foes of the Russian revolutionaries of the 1880s recognized their integrity, courage, and selfless devotion. Even to compare a Sofia Perovska (or an Emma Goldman) with the heroines of the 1970s—Patty Hearst, Bernardine Dohrn, or the late Ulrike Meinhof—is to invite ridicule.

Terrorism's strange fascination preoccupies many people, metaphysicians as well as popular novelists. Yet there is no more clarity about the phenomenon than there was eighty years ago, when a wave of assassinations, mainly involving freewheeling anarchists, shocked Europe and America. In the 1890s the behavioral sciences were in their infancy; all kinds of strange theories were bandied about: cranial measures of captured terrorists were taken, and a connection between terrorism and lunar phases was detected. Cesare Lombroso, the most distinguished criminologist of his day, found both a medical and a climatological explanation: terrorism, like pellagra and some other diseases, was caused by certain vitamin deficiencies, hence its prevalence among the maize-eating people of Southern Europe. He also found that the further north one went the less terrorism there was; Lombroso did not quite reach the North Pole in his investigations.

It is easy to poke fun at Lombroso's theory of vitamin deficiency, but the basic idea underlying it was not all that outlandish. For terrorists are usually angry and aggressive people, and it has long been known that there are some internal violence-generating factors and that some people have a lower violence threshold than others. Neurophysiologists have studied the correlation between aggressive behavior on one hand, and abnormal showings in electroencephalography, the function of adrenaline and thyroid secretion, the role of endocrinological disorders, and enzyme deficiencies causing hypoglycemia on the other. Their research has been inconclusive so far.

Political science has not made that much progress either since the early days. Large-scale cross-national investigations into the incidence of political violence have been undertaken in American universities for fifteen years; the correlations between terrorism and caloric intake, newspaper circulation, and the number of physicians have also been studied. A frustration and relative deprivation index has been established, using factor analysis, multiple regression, and other sophisticated statistical methods. Employment has been found for many doctoral students feeding facts and figures into computers. Only a few years ago hints were dropped about striking findings, and the general feeling in the profession was that a major breakthrough was just around the corner. Such optimism is no longer widespread, even though the computers are kept going. Suddenly people realized that the scales and models were not applicable to Communist countries, and perhaps not to Third World military dictatorships either. Doubt began to spread about whether it is always frustration that causes terrorism, and whether, even if it does, it can be measured. Statistical methods, in short, are of little help if underlying them there is confusion. Sweeping theories of the "terrorist personality" developed in the past have only contributed to this confusion.

Connections between terrorism and economic trends are at best tenuous. Terrorism in Uruguay and Argentina reached its peak at a time of stagnation and economic crisis, but in Brazil it came at a time of rapid economic development. In Latin America it has occurred in the countries with the highest living standards, such as Cuba, Uruguay, and Venezuela, but also in those with the lowest. Nationalist terrorism has been rampant in Ulster, which is one of the poorest regions of the United Kingdom, and in relatively deprived Quebec. But it has also occurred in Euzkadi (the country of the Basques) and Croatia, which are among the most developed and prosperous parts of Spain and Yugoslavia. In short, the search for a magic formula and a comprehensive theory of terrorism is illusory. Terrorism can be understood only by studying historical and political experience and by taking into account the specifics of each situation, not by feeding into computers ten years of news items from the files of the *New York Times.*

*More repression, less terrorism*

We may be able to do without a general theory of terrorism but greater clarity is needed to cope with concrete situations such as hijacking, the taking of hostages, et cetera. In this respect a great deal of emotion has been engendered, and there is no denying that dealing with terrorists does indeed involve real dilemmas. This takes us back to the question of the origins of terrorism which occurs, some argue, wherever people have legitimate grievances. Remove the grievances, remove poverty, inequality, injustice, and lack of political participation, and terrorism will cease. These sentiments are shared by all men and women of goodwill but as a cure for terrorism they are of little value. Given the complexity of the world, concessions to one national group will almost invariably result in injustice to another. Latin-American terrorists maintain that they fight for greater political freedom and social justice; there is no reason to disbelieve their claims. Yet what little one knows about the personalities leading these groups does not inspire confidence, for these would-be *caudillos* are elitists, not radical democrats.

If any lesson can be drawn from the experience of several decades of terrorism, it is the uncomfortable and indeed shocking conclusion that the more the injustice and repression, the less terrorism there is. In other words, terrorism succeeds only against nonterrorists, namely groups or governments which refrain from responding to indiscriminate murder with equally indiscriminate repression. Terrorism continues in Ulster not because the terrorists are invincible but because the British government treats the violent men of both sides decently, unlike the Brazilians or Iranians, Russians or Yugoslavs. A professor of law in testimony to a Congressional committee said recently that he was not sure whether deterrence against terrorism worked. He could not have been more mistaken: the problem, alas, is not whether terrorism can be stamped out; even fifth-rate dictatorships have managed to achieve this. The real issue is, of course, the price that has to be paid to eradicate terrorism.

The nonconcession policy of the present administration, as stated both publicly and informally, has been bitterly attacked by critics in the Foreign Service, among whom demoralization is said to have spread. They understandably fear their fate if they should have the misfortune of becoming hostages one day. Their criticism is based on arguments which are by now familiar: they do not know if deterrence really works; being beastly to the terrorists will not solve the problem.

One can certainly sympathize with the concern shown by members of the Foreign Service and their spokesmen. When around the turn of the century an anarchist took a few shots at Umberto I, the king of Italy said that this was an inevitable professional hazard. It would be unrealistic to expect such philosophical resignation (or sense of duty) in our day and age, and a first secretary at an embassy will rightly argue that he is not a king. Nevertheless, an individual's concern for his own survival does not necessarily add conviction to his arguments.

Each terrorist action is different, and there may indeed be cases in which concessions may be advisable—not because the victim is very prominent but because there is no reason to assume that appeasement will encourage further terrorist attacks. This means in practical terms greater leniency in dealing with groups that are not particularly dangerous, such as the South Moluccans, but firmness toward those that are. This applies in particular to the new brand of international terrorism; it is quite unrealistic to suggest "drastic action" against terrorists after they have retired to the coffeehouses of Tripoli or Benghazi. It is equally unrealistic to call for action from the United Nations, such as the establishment of an international court dealing with terrorist activities. Various international conventions exist with the purpose of combating terrorism; they may be of interest to lawyers and insurance companies, but they have not the slightest practical importance. Bilateral pacts (such as the agreement between the United States and Cuba) may be of some help, but hoping for cooperation on a global scale is quite unprofitable. The Sixth Committee of the General Assembly of the United Nations has been debating the subject for several years, and it has been even less successful than the old and much ridiculed League of Nations. These discussions will no doubt go on for many years to reach an utterly predictable result.

Appeasing terrorism does not offer a solution, and as the danger of the use of nonconventional weapons moves nearer it is no longer even a short-term palliative. Prof. Bernard Feld, the distinguished physicist, once discussed the nightmarish consequences of the disappearance of twenty pounds of plutonium from government stocks. What if the mayor of Boston received a note to the effect that a terrorist group had placed a nuclear bomb somewhere in central Boston, accompanied by a crude diagram which showed that the bomb would work? Would the scientist not have to advise the mayor to surrender to blackmail rather than risk the destruction of his hometown? But one successful case of blackmail leads to another, and what would our scientist's advice be if faced with contradictory threats by extreme left-wing and right-wing, or nationalist-separatist groups? A policy of surrender would lead to constant tyranny by small groups of people or, more likely, to anarchy and destruction, unless of course society learns to live with blackmail.

There is the danger of overreacting to terrorism, of focusing one's attention and marshaling one's efforts against a minor irritation which, for all one knows, may never outgrow the nuisance stage. Paradoxically, while terrorism is on a small scale, it is not really that important what kind of approach is taken. Once a society faces a determined terrorist onslaught it will choose a hard-line policy anyway, as shown, for instance, by Turkey and Iran, by Israel and Egypt—not to mention Latin America. For terrorism is blackmail, and the victim of blackmail is less likely to forget and to forgive than the victim of almost any other crime: he feels a special sense of outrage because it is not just his life or property that has been affected. He has been humiliated; his elementary human rights, his dignity and self-respect have been violated. To argue that this counts for little, to maintain that one should always be guided by expediency, is asking too much of human nature, especially if the expediency is really no more than the rationalization of surrender.

Terrorism, to summarize, is no more than a nuisance at present. One day mankind may be threatened by the weapons of superviolence, but, if these should ever be used, it is of course at least as likely that this will be done by governments or, in the case of chemical or biological agents, perhaps by individuals. There is the certainty that society will not be able to satisfy the demands, justified or unjustified, of all its members. There is equally the certainty that some individuals will at some future date have the skill and the determination to dictate their wishes to society. Such action would, of course, be irrational, leading sooner or later to destruction without precedent. It is not certain, unfortunately, whether this perspective will deter individuals or small groups of people convinced that society or the whole world ought to be punished if their demands are not met. These are the disquieting prospects for the more distant future. For all one knows, they may never materialize, but, if they do, the peril will have to be faced without panic and hysteria. It is for this reason more than any other that the muddled thinking on terrorism, the myths and the humbug, could be one day a source of great danger.

*November 1976*

# Second Thoughts on Terrorism

## I

I finished writing *Terrorism* (Boston: Little Brown, 1978) in the spring of 1977; little did I know how greatly terrorism would preoccupy us during the second half of that year and in 1978. In my book I had said that terrorism usually occurs in waves and that the terrorist wave (with some notable exceptions) seemed to be on the decline. I still think this to be true, at least in a global perspective, for if there has been a temporary resurgence of terrorism in West Germany and a more lasting one in Italy and Turkey, it is also true that in most other parts of the world where terrorism had been rampant only a few years ago, it has decreased. This refers, for instance, to the Middle East, to Latin America, and even to Northern Ireland. But all predictions about the occurrence of terrorism are risky, as indeed I had noted, simply because terrorism is not a mass movement, but carried out by very small groups of people. There is no accounting for the acts of 50, or even 500, people in a society of 50 million: terrorism is possible at any time, in all free or semifree societies. It is perhaps more likely in some conditions than in others, and these conditions certainly deserve to be investigated, but accident undoubtedly plays a great role.

It has been argued that terrorism in our time occurs above all in the countries which were on the losing side in the Second World War, and far-reaching conclusions have been drawn from this fact (which is at best half-true). It could be argued with equal justice that there is a connection between terrorism and soccer, for the four countries which finished on top in the world championships of 1978 were all affected by terrorism (Argentina, Brazil, Holland, Italy). To regard the "objective conditions" the key for the understanding of the occurrence of terrorism in our time is to chase a chimera. Native terrorism has not occurred, and is not likely to occur, in certain countries, such as, Scandinavia. This may be connected with the fact that there is no tradition of political violence in these societies, but then it is also a fact that terrorism (except that of

117

the nationalist-separatist kind) has seldom occurred in small countries or in small towns for the obvious reason that it is far more difficult to hide in such places than in the anonymity of the big city.

Recent manifestations of terrorism have shown some interesting innovations. Until recently, terrorist movements took pride in elaborate ideological justification, but this is no longer so. One looks in vain for a terrorist doctrine in political terms among German or Italian or Japanese terrorists similar to that of the *Narodnaya Volya* or the anarchists. Perhaps contemporary terrorists believe that no such ideology is now needed, or perhaps they are unable to formulate their strategy in a coherent manner. Events in recent years have also made it clear that terrorism is increasingly guided by remote control. This is not, of course, to say that all terrorist groups receive foreign help, or are guided by outside powers, nor is the phenomenon altogether novel: fascist Italy supported the Croatian Ustasha and other such groups in the 1930s. But of late, warfare by proxy has become more widespread, even if great care is obviously taken by the governments concerned not to leave any traces. Terrorists are men and women on the run. Without outside help they could not have possibly displayed such coordination and logistical sophistication, not to mention the problem of finances and the supply of arms, as they did, for example, in the kidnappings and murders of Schleyer and Moro. Such remote control may be difficult to prove in a court of law, and the countries affected may be reluctant in any case to make such charges against governments that are important oil producers or whose military power commands respect.

Lastly, there is the question of sympathizers, which has been a bone of contention, above all, in West Germany. It is ridiculous to cast aspersions on elderly poetesses and well-known novelists. In the same way it is reprehensible to brand as a sympathizer everyone who stands for political and social change. But there *are* sympathizers. When Rosa Luxemburg and Karl Liebknecht were killed in 1919, and again when Walter Rathenau was assassinated by terrorists of the extreme right a few years later, the German left quite properly pointed out that the murderers had not come from nowhere, that their actions should be viewed against the climate of violence that had been instigated by their intellectual mentors. The same is true today. Those who have been advocating "progressive violence" against "repressive toleration" did not envisage the indiscriminate killing of innocent people, and they can always argue that they should not be held responsible for the actions of the *terrible simplificateurs* who misunderstood their teachings. And yet. .

## II

There has been an upsurge in terrorism during the last year in Italy, Spain, Turkey, and a few other countries. The resurgence of Italian terrorism has been widely reported all over the world following the spectacular abduction and subsequent murder of Aldo Moro, the leading Italian politician. Italy's main terrorist groups, the Brigate Rosse (Red Brigade) and the NAP are believed to count no more than a few hundred members, and the "hitmen" among them may be no more than twenty. But they have shown a great deal of efficiency, the number of their supporters may be numbered in the thousands, and the fact that several police reports were found in a Rome flat abandoned by Brigade members shows that they have infiltrated the police and probably also the judiciary. The Italian terrorist scene is of interest furthermore because of the international connections between the terrorists and their sympathizers abroad, and the difficulties to document these ties in detail. As far as the background of the terrorist groups is concerned and the reason for their success, Italy presents few riddles; many if not most terrorist cadres belonged originally to Communist youth organizations and left the party because it was not activist enough. The success of terrorism in Italy on the other hand is quite obviously connected with the general crisis of Italian politics and society and the resulting weakness of the state.

Nor are the origins of Spanish terrorism shrouded in mystery. It is now almost entirely restricted to the Basque region and while its practitioners use extreme Marxist verbiage, their inspiration, their inspiration is quite obviously nationalist. The particular violence of ETA can perhaps be explained against the background of specific Basque fears of losing their national identity; Basques probably now constitute a minority in their historical provinces. On the other hand, as the recent elections have shown, the terrorists are a small minority in the nationalist camp. The feeling of isolation and of a race against time may have contributed to the intensification of the terrorist struggle.

Terrorism in Turkey where some 250 persons were killed during the first half of 1978 again presents unique features—it is conducted mainly between activists of the extreme left and the far right. The former specialize largely in abductions and armed robberies, the latter in individual assassination. The terrorists of the far left are predominantly of middle-class origin, those of the extreme right are to a large extent of proletarian origin; the extreme left dismisses them as "Lumpenproletariat militants" but this is of not much help in understanding their social background. The situation is further complicated because the "right-wing" propaganda stresses the need to combat social injustice and, generally speaking, propagates a national socialist (but not fascist) line, and these happen to be also propaganda slogans of the extreme left. More than in Italy, and far more than in Spain, the universities have become the main battle scene of the terrorist stuggle.

Terrorism in Argentina has been largely stamped out during the last two years in a wave of bloody repression in which not only many terrorists lost their lives, but also many people who had nothing to do whatsoever with terrorism. Less attention has been paid to the fact that terrorism in Argentina (as in Brazil, but not in Uruguay) has been distinguished from the very beginning by exceptional cruelty. Thus, the terrorists have seldom hesitated to kill innocent bystanders who happened to witness the preparation of one of their attacks, owners of cars that were seized for their operations, or even their own wounded comrades—for fear that they would talk when arrested. Today the once Trotskyite ERP has virtually ceased to exist, and the remnants of the left-wing Peronist Montoneros have transferred their activities to Rome, and, to a lesser extent, to Paris.

Palestinian terrorism, despite some spectacular exploits, has been on the wane during the last few years. In fact, there has been more internecine killing between Arabs than attempts to hit at Israel (the killing of the editor of *Al Ahram* in Nicosia, the murder of a cabinet minister at Abu Dhabi airport, the assassination of the North Yemen president and the PLO representative in London, and other such incidents). It remains to be seen to what extent this has been the result of the Lebanese civil war and the growing tensions within the Arab world, or whether the terrorists have been discouraged by the fact that attacks against Israeli targets have shown diminishing political returns. While nationalist-separatist terrorism in Ulster seems to be on the decline at least as far as the number of victims is concerned, there has been an upsurge in France, mainly on the part of Corsican and Breton militant groups.

### III

This short and incomplete survey of terrorist activities shows the great differences in the character of the terrorist struggle and the fortunes of the terrorist groups. In the United States there has been relatively little terrorist activity but a great deal of discussion—though not remotely as much as in Germany. But these debates have not been very productive, partly because there has been a great deal of confusion on the very topic of discussion. Books have been published in which Robespierre, Hitler, and Lenin appear side by side with Yaser Arafat and Carlos, in which every possible kind of political violence from above and from below is described and analyzed without much discrimination. Reviewing one such study, Conor Cruise O'Brien has noted that the author affixed the terrorist label to all those he disliked, a practice for which one may feel sympathy, but which hardly produces a better understanding of modern terrorism. On the other hand, some overzealous political scientists have claimed that unless there is agreement on a foolproof, "scientific" definition of terrorism there can be no meaningful discussion of the subject; but is it likely that there ever will be such a comprehensive definition? The lack of discrimination in analyzing terrorist activities has unfortunate consequences inasmuch as statistics are concerned—to give but one example, what is the value of figures in which aircraft hijacking carried out by "bona fide terrorists" are lumped together with hijackings by armed men or women who are not members of a terrorist organization but were merely trying to escape from a police state—or even the actions of lunatics? A CIA report published in July 1976 flatly states that "more incidents were recorded [last year] than ever before." But the fact that more were recorded does not mean that more such incidents have actually occurred.

If the criteria used are, as admitted, quite arbitrary, the results will be equally arbitrary and comparisons, both on the historical level and between various regions, become quite meaningless. The study of terrorism in America will have to find its way between the Scylla of vagueness and confusion and the Charybdis of a sterile, purist fixation on definitions to make any progress at all. The West German experience has shown that computers may be of great value in apprehending terrorists, but they are of no help in understanding the mainsprings and the motivation of terrorism unless there is, in the first place, a minimum of conceptual clarity. And this, by and large, is not yet the case.

## IV

We have to turn to Germany for the most extensive and in some ways most interesting discussions about the character of modern terrorism. There have been few terrorist operations in the *Bundesrepublik:* two citizens were killed in 1974, three in 1957, one in 1976, twelve in 1977, none so far in 1978. Many terrorist activists have been apprehended. But the terrorist phenomenon has occupied not only German politicians, but also historians, sociologists, political scientists, and educators, not to mention theologians and philosophers.[1] Some results are trivial, such as the insight that there are no monocausal explanations; some simply translate well-known questions into professional jargon without enhancing our knowledge; some are manifestly wrong; some sound doubtful—this refers, for instance, to studies which claim that political violence appears predominantly in countries where fantasies of cleanliness are frequent.[2]

There is a widespread belief that above all we need a general theory of terrorism—and that such a theory is possible. But even though at the end of the day we shall not be nearer to such a theory, certain suggestions have emerged which certainly warrant further examination. The neo-Marxist critique of terrorism is well known. As Herbert Marcuse recently put it: "The terrorist compromise the struggle for socialism which after all, is also their own. Their methods are not those of liberation. . ."[3] But if, according to Marcuse, the struggle against "repressive toleration" is a categorical imperative, it is not that obvious that one should reject terrorist operations, except perhaps for tactical reasons. If terrorism is rejected, and not just for tactical reasons, why assume that only the "methods" of the terrorists are not those of liberation? There is a strong totalitarian component in terrorism as Bracher has shown and in the "terrorist personality." Only if socialism is equated with the nationalization of the means of production, only if all the democratic, humanitarian, and libertarian aspirations of socialism are ignored, can the German terrorists attachment to "socialism" be taken at face value. Bassam Tibi, a left-wing Arab political scientist teaching at a German university, has suggested that while terrorism in a democratic state is "criminal," this is not so in societies in which fundamental human rights do not exist.[4] This proposition seems at first sight irrefutable but Tibi's version seems somewhat impaired as he singles out Iran, Chile, and South Africa as the main (or only) bastions of such repression. One can easily think of far bigger and more powerful countries in which elementary human rights do not exist. Is terrorism permissible there? Marcuse, for one, has been aware of the problem ("a very delicate one") but has so far found no satisfactory answer apart from claiming that terrorism in Franco Spain (the assassination of Carrero Blanco) was justified, whereas in East Germany it is not.[5]

Problematical in a different way are attempts from the other end of the political spectrum to interpret the origins of terrorism. Wilhelm Kasch, a professor of theology, has explained terrorism as the urge to destroy—the self and others—born out of radical despair, a new form of a "disease unto death" (shades of Kierkegaard and Heidegger), which manifests itself by way of the inability to make common cause with others *(Gemeinschaftsunfaehigkeit)*, the loss of the capacity to understand reality, aimlessness, and even the deterioration in the quality of language used. This seems a fair enough description but Kasch then proceeds to postulate terrorism as an imminent part of a society without God, the consequence of "methodological atheism."[6] Of course, the basic concept is not new, but, on one hand, the decline of religion has gone on for centuries without leading towards terrorism, and, on the other, it would be only too easy to point to the incidence of terrorism in many lands in the Middle Ages precisely among religious sectarians and fanatics. Fanaticism, in other words, is not a monopoly of atheists.

According to Gerhard Schmidtchen and Hermann Luebbe the roots of terrorism have to be traced to the general disorganization (of the society and the individual alike), to the decline of morality, and the loss of democratic legitimacy and of the authority of democratic institutions.[7] There is little to quarrel with in such broad propositions but they apply to most modern societies including many in which there has been no terrorism. On the extreme left a critique of this kind will be viewed as putting things on their head, for general disorganization and the decline in morality, the "legitimacy crisis" (and also terrorism) are in its view only secondary manifestations of the general crisis of capitalism. In the case of Germany the specific German fate, the lack of German identity, and the *unbewaeltigte Vergangenheit* (the past that has not yet been mastered) are frequently invoked in this context—and not only on the left. This also refers to the fact that the purge of Nazism has been incomplete and the rejection of the fascist legacy not consistent, and to the difficulty of the younger generation to respect parents who were Nazis—or who failed to resist. If so, Austria should be a hotbed of terrorism. Austrian identity is even more dubious; pro-Nazi enthusiasm was, if anything, greater in Hitler's native country, and former Nazis, with perhaps a handful of exceptions, suffered no lasting harm in Austria after 1945.[8] Yet there is no terrorism in Austria—and thus the theory collapses. Social and individual psychologists have enumerated a number of features characteristic for many terrorists: at the beginning there is always political and social engagement, or in popular language "idealism." But the future terrorist fails to accept the inevitable frustration involved in growing up, the discrepancy between the ideals and the ugly realities which he faces in late puberty is too great—something in him gives way. This is accompanied by a disturbed relationship towards authority on one hand and his own emotions on the other (the fear of love) and thus he drifts towards terrorism—the only apparent alternative to drinking or taking drugs. Those suffering from individual problems transfer them on society and see the cure for their hangups in violent action and the overthrow of institutions.

The problems of adolescence are, of course, well known, but how much does such analysis contribute to an understanding of terrorism? How to explain that 99.99 percent of adolescents—even young radicals—react differently? The only plausible answer is that potential terrorists always exist, but that a variety of circumstances such as the cohesion of society, the strength of the state, and the general political situation determine whether they will actually proceed to terrorist action. Psychological interpretation could perhaps be of some help in explaining the high proportion of women among German terrorists; the explanation, one suspects, may not be that complicated but it remains to be studied in detail.

Most of the interpretations that have been mentioned so far contain a kernel of truth, even though it is sometimes a minute one. But what they have to offer about the motivation of terrorism in Germany has no bearing on terrorism in other countries—least of all on nationalist-separatist terrorism, which is the most frequent form in our age. In many ways they try to explain too much. World historical processes such as the cultural crisis, the crisis of legitimacy, or the crisis of "late capitalism" are invoked to explain the behavior of a few dozen people.

The contribution of criminology to the study of terrorism has been neglected so far but it is precisely in this direction that some advance seems most likely. There has been a notable reluctance to look at the criminological evidence, partly no doubt because the motives of the terrorists differ from those of the common criminal. But criminology has been preoccupied for a long time with issues such as aggression and the problem of causality in crime; it knows that people are more likely to kill in a group than individually, that the psychological obstacles to killing are reduced when the distance between the killer and the victim is increased. All this and other observations are of considerable relevance to terrorism. Above all, criminologists have known for a long time what students of terrorism are now learning from trial and error—that human beings are not arithmetical units that can be added up and divided in order to find a median, the "average terrorist."[9] As Thomas Aquinas wrote, *Individuum est incommunicabile.*

A great deal of work remains to be done on, for instance, the importance of ideology in terrorism and about the interaction between individual psychological motives and objective, i.e., political and social conditions. The serious study of terrorism is only beginning, but there should be no illusions about what it will be able to achieve. The issues involved are, in part, straightforward, obvious, and easily explicable. But there are also other aspects of terrorism which may forever remain beyond our comprehension.

## NOTES

1. Their publications include Sepp Binder, *Terrorismus,* Bonn, 1978; M. Funke (ed.) *Terrorismus. Untersuchungen zur Struktur and Strategie revolutionaerer Gewaltpolitik,* Kronberg, 1977; H. Luebbe, *Endstation Terror,* Stuttgart, 1978; Bergedorfer Gespreaechskreis, *Terrorismus in der demokratischen Gesellschaft,* Hamburg, 1978; H. Geissler (ed.), *Der Weg in die Gewalt,* - Muenchen, 1978; H. Glaser, *Die Diskussion ueber den Terrorismus (Aus Politik und Zeitgeschichte,* June 24, 1978).

2. Robert S. Frank, *The Prediction of Political Violence from Objective and Subjective Social Indicators.* International Psychoanalytical Congress, Edinburgh, 1976.
3. *Die Zeit,* September 16, 1977.
4. *Die Neue Gesellschaft,* 7, 1978.
5. J. Habermas et al., *Gespraeche mit Herbert Marcuse,* Frankfurt, 1978, p. 150.
6. H. Geissler (ed.), *Der Weg in die Gewalt,* Munchen, 1978, p. 65.
7. G. Schmidtchen, *Bewaffnete Heilslehren* in Geissler, loc. cit., p. 39; H. Luebbe, *Endstation Terror,* Stuttgart 1978, passim.
8. The case of Bernhard Vesper is frequently mentioned in this context. The former husband of Gudrun Ensslin committed suicide in a psychiatric clinic in 1971, and wrote an autobiographical novel *(Die Reise,* published posthumously in 1977) in which his relationship with his father, a literary luminary of the Third Reich, is described in detail. There has been no Vesper case in Austria.
9. W. Middendorff, in Geissler, loc. cit., p. 182.

# World Affairs and U.S. Foreign Policy

# The Psychology
# of Appeasement

Every historical situation is unique, but now and then an event recalls
the past with such force that comparisons become inevitable. Thus,
Robert J. Kane, president of the American Olympic Committee, answer-
ing appeals to boycott the Olympic games in Moscow in 1980, has recently objected to what he calls "the intrusion of politics in the Olympics."
"We view the current issue of human rights as one of a political nature,
not one of sports." Mr. Kane's main interest, one assumes, is athletics,
and it would be unfair to make heavy weather of his statement. Indeed,
there is something to be said for his view. For the Soviet leadership,
human rights *are* a political issue (although so, for that matter, are
sports). If we were to begin applying political criteria, moreover, U.S.
athletes would have to withdraw from most international competitions.
Then too, although Mr. Kane did not say so, from a strictly political
point of view there may actually be arguments, albeit not very strong
ones, *in favor* of U.S. participation in the Moscow games.

The whole issue is of considerable interest because more than forty
years ago the very same debate took place, and the same arguments were
used, based on the same misconceptions. In 1931 it was decided that
Berlin would be the venue of the Olympic games of 1936. But then Hitler
came to power and it was said that neither German nor foreign Jews
would be permitted to participate. American sports organizers and also
some Europeans put pressure on the Nazis, who then announced that
they would waive restrictions on "non-Aryans." Eventually one Jew, an
ice-hockey player, was permitted to represent Germany in the winter
Olympics in Garmisch, and a fencer, Helene Mayer, in the summer
games. According to the Nuremberg laws, Miss Mayer was "half-
Aryan" anyway. A former Olympic champion (Amsterdam, 1928), she
was also a great patriot who was, she said, proud to fence for her country
again. Still, she had to be satisfied with a bronze medal; a Hungarian
Jewish girl named Ilona Schacherer took the gold.

These German concessions were not deemed sufficient by many

leading figures in American sports. For even if the Nazis incorporated a Jew (and a half) in their team to prove their good will, it could hardly be claimed that they were living up to their obligations to conform with the Olympic spirit ("a school of moral nobility and purity") and the Olympic code, with its emphasis on the spirit of chivalry and fair play. How could a Jewish athlete possibly prepare for a competition of such magnitude if all the race tracks of Germany, all the swimming pools, all the playing fields were closed to him, not to mention the fact that he might be denied the use of public transport, attacked in the street, or perhaps even put into a concentration camp? And to top it all off, the Nazis had made it abundantly clear that they considered sports an integral part of the Nazi ideology and practice, and especially of propaganda—to show the superiority of the Third Reich over the decadent West.

Among the Americans who suggested that their country should boycott the Olympics were leaders of the American Federation of Labor; such figures as Damon Runyon, Paul Gallico, and Westbrook Pegler; civic leaders like Al Smith and Hugh Johnson; and many important athletes of the day. Their chief was Judge Jeremiah T. Mahoney, a pugnacious Irishman and president of the influential Amateur Athletic Union, who noted, quite correctly, that not only Jews but also Protestants and Catholic sportsmen were discriminated against in Germany and that the Nazis, generally speaking, were engaged in the Nazification of the Olympic games on a large scale. These opponents established the "Committee for Fair Play in Sports."

The counterattack was led by Avery Brundage, a wealthy Chicago builder who at the time was president of the American Olympic Committee and was subsequently for many years president of the International Olympic Committee. He was ably assisted by Charles Sherill, a one-star general, who, as a Yale sophomore, had been credited with inventing the crouched start in track races. Brundage and Sherrill argued that there *was* fair play in Germany—Brundage had been to Germany for a few days and seen no evil. Sherrill claimed that anyway there had never in history been a prominent Jewish athlete; he saw his task as getting at least one Jew on the German Olympic team, and with that his job was finished. As for the alleged obstacles placed in the way of Jewish athletes trying to reach Olympic stature, he had no business discussing that in Germany, for this would be a blatant case of political interference. Brundage and Sherrill said that it was all "merely a question of sports." Those proposing a boycott were in their opinion Jews or Communists, or both. They warned there would be a wave of anti-Semitism in America if a small minority succeeded in dictating to the majority. Sherrill also averred that Mussolini was a great man, a man of courage in a world of pussyfooters; Brundage, more cautiously, spoke of the contributions made by the Olympic games toward the moral betterment of the human race.

The great confrontation took place at the Amateur Athletic Union convention in Pittsburgh in November 1935. Brundage and Sherrill had a narrow majority, and with this the movement to boycott the games collapsed. In other countries the story was more or less the same. There was some opposition in France and Britain but it was not very determined, and on the other hand some prominent Jewish sportsmen such as the British sprint champion Harold Abrahams actively lobbied for participation at Berlin.

And thus in August 1936 the greatest, best-organized, most successful games got under way in the wonderful new Olympic stadium. These games have entered history as the Nazi Olympics. In an editorial published in November 1935 the New York *Times* had predicted that "if the Olympic games come off in Berlin as arranged, the event will be hailed as a wonderful Nazi demonstration and triumph." It *was* a triumph, an enormous success from the Nazi point of view. German athletes did better than those of any other nation; the prestige of the Third Reich soared at home and abroad. Thousands of visitors were deeply impressed by the spectacle of so many young Germans marching through the streets of Berlin—a demonstration of discipline, of joy, of peaceful competition. For some (as for Muhammad Ali when he met Brezhnev forty years later) it was the greatest hour of their lives. As Beverly Nichols, the British writer, recently reminisced: "This was Hitler's most spectacular exercise in his campaign to present the acceptable face of fascism. It was the biggest window-dressing operation in history. Berlin was *en fête,* beflagged and beribboned. . . . We were all dazzled—all of us—whether we were politically Right, Left, or Center. Even I, a fanatical peace-at-any-price pacifist, was almost ensnared. . . ."

What are the lessons of 1936? It is easy in retrospect to find mitigating circumstances for the decision to go to Berlin: Germany would have gone to war in 1939 in any case, and the Nazi Olympics were not of much consequence in the moral and political build-up toward this aim. Forty years have passed, a new generation of American (and French and British) innocents has grown up, and again there are mitigating circumstances: today's Russians cannot compete with yesterday's Germans as organzers, and for achievement in athletics they will have to depend heavily on the state amateurs from Cuba and East Germany. Among their own sportsmen it will be difficult to find political enthusiasts, and it is unlikely that visitors from abroad, except the most naive, will return persuaded that they have seen the future and that it works. Like the Helsinki Final Act, the 1980 Olympic games are a window-dressing operation.

Nevertheless, whether people from the West should give their hand to a basically fraudulent operation of this kind is a different question altogether. The practice of the games has deviated so much from the original idea promoted by Baron Coubertin that they have become little *but* occasions for making political points, and (where the media are concerned) for making money. As Brian Glanville, the British novelist and sportswriter, has recently noted, the Olympic movement, which was supposed to foster the amateur spirit and "comity," has in fact fostered dishonesty, nationalistic fervor, drug addiction, and the exploitation of the very young. In addition, most sportsmen are quite indifferent to human rights and similar issues. If they regarded the murder of dozens of Mexican students on the eve of the 1968 games as no more than an annoying interference with their preparations, there is no reason to assume that their feelings will be different with regard to the cause of freedom in the Soviet Union. In Mr. Glanville's opinion, the Olympic games and the Soviet Union deserve one another.

It has been said that the presence of many thousands of foreigners in the Soviet capital will have a liberalizing influence. Yet in 1936 the arrival of so many foreigners in Berlin did not make the slightest difference as far as the local population was concerned. In any case, German citizens were still freely permitted to travel abroad at that time; Soviet citizens have no such privileges. True, the forces of law and order in Moscow will have to work overtime for a few weeks, and there is always the danger that there may be some minor mishaps, but it would be wrong to attribute major political importance to the Western appearance in Moscow. The tourists will come and go; the KGB remains.

By now there are many vested interests involved in the 1980 Olympics —political, financial, and bureaucratic—and each has its own reason for justifying the charade. And so the runners and the swimmers will compete in Moscow, the Soviet dissidents will continue to be reeducated in the camps, and men of good intention will go on warning us against the intrusion of politics into sports. But that is why, every so often, it may be useful to remind ourselves that there is a word to describe such easy rationalizations for accepting the view of reality which our enemies offer us. That word is appeasement.

Since World War II the term "appeasement" has acquired an exclusively bad connotation—principally through being associated with the conduct of England and France toward Germany during the period of Hitler's rise to power, and especially with the 1938 Munich agreement between Neville Chamberlain and Hitler. Yet prior to that time the term was merely neutral—meaning, to quote one historian, "the reduction of international tension by the methodical removal of the principal causes of friction among nations." Even at the time of the Munich agreement, the London *Times* could write: "The policy of international appeasement must of course be pressed forward.'' It was only later that the term acquired a different significance—so different, in fact, that an authority on the subject (W. N. Medlicott) could write by 1961 that "appeasement should now be added to imperialism on the list of words no scholar uses.'' A case could be made for adding "détente" to the list.

Appeasement has been practiced since time immemorial in relations among nations and states, principally by small and weak countries against their powerful neighbors. Sometimes the practice has met with success, sometimes not, depending always on the general situation and the appetites and ambitions of the powerful neighbors in question. The policy of Prussia vis-à-vis Napoleon up to 1806 was a blatant case of appeasement; so too was Sweden's policy vis-à-vis Nazi Germany in the early years of World War II. In all such cases it is legitimate to ask whether some other policy would have been advisable or indeed possible. For it cannot be argued that appeasement of an aggressor *never* pays; again, Sweden in World War II is a good example.

But if is wrong simply to dismiss a policy of appeasement without considering its chances of success, it is equally wrong to ignore the truth that there is always in appeasement a tendency toward the rationalization of weakness, toward wishful thinking. This inclination may be rooted in altogether honorable motives—such as a deepseated longing for peace—or in an (equally sincere) naiveté, or, less creditably, in a basic defeatism (as in pre-war France). The policy conducted by Chamberlain cannot be reasonably condemned as morally wrong, except in its last stages; rather, it was shortsighted and politically wrong, based on false premises. When Halifax wrote in 1938 that the German people longed for détente he was probably correct, but it was an irrelevant statement, for German foreign policy in 1938 was not being made by the German people. In the Third Republic, by contrast, the general political decay, was such that a defeatist attitude could lead in some cases to active and enthusiastic collaboration with the Nazis.

Some policies of appeasement are rooted in dire necessity, others in shortsightedness, confusion, or even cowardice. The last kind, far from pacifying and resolving conflict, often only serves to postpone the inevitable confrontation, and so aggravates tensions and actually increases the danger of war. As dictatorships become accustomed to the retreat of democracies, they naturally assume that things will remain this way. If the democracies then decide to make a stand—as they usually do at the worst possible moment and under the worst possible conditions—the shock at this sudden display of "unreasonableness" may prevent compromise and help set the stage for a major world crisis. Western Europe faced a situation of just this kind in the late 1930s.

What does all this have to do with relations between the United States and the Soviet Union today? Is détente turning out to be just another version of appeasement, both in fact and in name? One thing that can be said with assurance is that just as a policy of appeasement can only be judged by taking into account the objective circumstances involved, so détente—and by implication, its supposed opposite, cold war—must be placed in historical perspective.

Here we immediately come upon a paradox. If we were to depict the ups and downs of U.S.-Soviet relations in the form of a diagram, the curve would reach its lowest point in the years 1948-52, the years of Stalin's greatest animosity toward the West, and its upper limit in 1971-72, when Nixon and Brezhnev met and showered on another with the rhetoric of peaceable intentions. Yet the fact is that during the "dangerous" years of the 1950s and 1960s, Soviet arms-spending did not increase as steeply as it has done in the 1970s, the years of "détente." According to data recently published by the Arms Control Agency, headed by Paul Warnke, Soviet military spending rose from $80 billion in 1967—adjusted for inflation—to $121 billion in 1976. (American military spending fell during this period from $120 billion to $87 billion.) Again: the years in which Soviet foreign policy was most pacific were the years immediately after Stalin's death; the closer we come to the present period of "relaxation of tensions," the more tension there seems to be—the Cuban and Berlin crises, the Yom Kippur War, several African wars and coups in Asia, and the end is not yet in sight.

Détente, in other words, seems to be nothing but the continuation of the cold war by other means, and sometimes by the same means. This is not to say that it has nothing to recommend it as a policy, especially from the Soviet point of view. As far as the Russians are concerned, their foreign policy has always made greater progress when they have taken a "soft" line toward the outside world than during periods when a harsher line prevailed (such as during the "third period" of the Comintern in the late 1920s or the late Stalin period). In this connection, Sir William Hayter, a former British ambassador to Moscow, has invoked the Aesopian fable about the bet between the sun and wind over the best way to get a man's cloak off: the more the wind huffs and puffs, the tighter the man clasps his cloak around him; the sun need but smile, and the man removes his cloak of his own volition. "Détente," Sir William has observed, "is an alternative way of getting the West to take its cloak off."

Détente may also have its advantages for the West, but what is important to remember in this context is that "détente" and "cold war" are only two sides of the same coin. One side may have been cleaned and polished, but only an inexperienced collector would be willing to pay a higher price on that account alone. This point is worth stressing if only because the idea has gained ground in the United States that cold war and détente are diametrically opposed strategies. Thus, there is now in some circles a great fear of a "return to the cold war," which, it is believed, will somehow lead directly out of the present situation ("détente") to a catastrophic future. And out of this fear there arises the impulse to appeasement.

Underlying the appeasement of the 1930s was a trauma, that of World War I, the many hundreds of thousands of soldiers killed at Paschendaele and the Somme. Underlying the appeasement of the 1970s is the trauma of Vietnam. Democracies, with rare exceptions, always incline to pacifism, and they find it difficult to understand those who do not share this predisposition: how can anyone be so unreasonable as to consider war an instrument for the solution of conflicts? Having met individual Germans in the 1930s, many Englishmen and Frenchmen reached the conclusion that these were not fanatics but eminently sensible people, people like themselves; surely they would not want to go to war.

Today there cannot possibly be more than a handful of people in America who have any sympathy for the Soviet political system, the attractiveness of which is clearly limited to the world's most backward countries, from Afghanistan to South Yemen and Ethiopia. There are, however, others who think that American politics are evil and American society is sinful, and that for this reason America has no right to play an active part in world affairs—except perhaps to share its riches with less fortunate countries. Some of these people will welcome further American setbacks, or at the very least will view with misgiving any improvement in America's position, which in their opinion would lead only to the strengthening of reactionary forces.

Supporters of the kind of détente that is indistinguishable from appeasement see themselves as rational, moderate, and open-minded—"liberals," in short—in contrast to "hawks," whose views are said to be based on a pathological distrust of Soviet motives, on aggressive impulses, on a dangerous, primitive patriotism, and in some cases on crude self-interest—"conservatives," in short. The advocates of détente/appeasement sees the Soviet Union as a giant country beset by major internal problems with which its aged leaders are unable to cope. These internal difficulties, the argument continues, make any major foreign-political adventure highly unlikely. By and large, the Soviet Union is a status-quo power, or in the process of becoming one. American conflicts with Russia are largely based on misunderstandings which, with patience and good will, can be resolved. The movement toward greater freedom in the Soviet Union is inexorable; the West has a historical opportunity to expedite this development by following a

moderate policy and thus assisting the doves in the Kremlin.[1] To influence events in Moscow, we ought to expand our contacts in every
field—intensify economic relations, strengthen cultural ties, build
bridges of every kind, and, generally speaking, develop systematically a
climate of trust and friendship. For unless there is such a web of close
relations, the Russians will have no major stake in détente and the West
little leverage over them.

The appeaser is not much alarmed by Soviet advances in Asia, Africa,
the Middle East, or elsewhere; he is alarmed by the climate of "hysteria"
which he believes these advances have engendered in the United States.
The Soviet Union, he holds, cannot afford to expand its sphere of influence any further without grave risk; events in Africa have shown that
the Russians are as likely as not to be expelled from countries in which
they have gained a temporary foothold. All in all, he believes, Soviet advances should not be exaggerated: nowhere have Soviet soldiers been involved, and as for the Cubans, no one can say for certain whether they
have not been acting largely on their own.

Similar arguments are used in the field of defense. The Russians,
deeply shocked by their traumatic experiences in World War II, are said
to have learned the obvious lesson: always be prepared. But their
strength is purely (or mainly) defensive in nature, and if they have out-
paced the West in arms, one should not forget that they do face potential
enemies—both West and East. The appeaser is not unduly worried by
reports about Western military inferiority, because, even if true, such
analyses are meaningless. In the nuclear age, military force can no longer
be translated into political influence.

The appeaser sympathizes with Soviet dissidents but regards them as a
nuisance; he is concerned, rather, with the "obsessive and crusading"
approach of President Carter toward human rights in the USSR, and the
general overreaction to Soviet dissent in the West. With all one's good
will toward this handful of brave people, their complaints should never
be allowed to obstruct the wider attempts at reconciliation between West
and East. The dissenters are isolated politically, and in the long run the
cause of freedom in the Soviet Union will be helped more by a climate of
détente and relaxation of tensions than by the futile and pathetic
demonstrations of the dissenters. The appeaser severely denounces
Brzezinski; commends Secretary of State Vance; and distrusts President
Carter for his undue emphasis on human rights. According to the appeaser, the President ought to refrain from any statement or action that
might be considered provocative by the Soviet leadership.

Lastly, and most decisively, there is the issue of SALT. This affects the
security of the United States, indeed its very existence, and the peace of
the world. It should therefore, according to the appeaser, be treated dif-

ferently from all other subjects and addressed on a continuing basis with the highest priority. Indeed, the urgency of concluding an accord with the Soviets in this area is now greater than ever. For whereas it was once claimed that in the field of nuclear weapons the Soviet Union aimed at no more than parity with the West, most people who held this view are now willing to admit that they were mistaken. But for the appeaser, the fact of growing Soviet superiority only underlines the need for conciliatory gestures, since any other course would lead to confrontation. Some supporters of appeasement say that they themselves are ready to take action to catch up with the Soviet military effort, but the American people are unwilling to assume the necessary financial and political burden; others insist that the United States should simply accept the fact that it will no longer be number one in the world—in their view, a healthy development in any case.

Appeasement is a powerfully attractive position for many sectors of the population in a democratic society, but some have embraced it more enthusiastically than others, Diplomats, it goes without saying, are professionally inclined toward appeasement; unless they pursue it to excess, they should perhaps not be charged with actually sinning in this regard. Most diplomats—Secretary Vance's colleagues among them—would no doubt argue that while Soviet behavior has been tiresome, our side is not blameless either, and that quiet diplomacy is far more effective than harsh words and defiant gestures. And when quiet diplomacy shows no results—it hardly ever does, except on matters of no political consequence—there is always some excuse.

Big business, despite Leninist mythology to the contrary, is usually found in the front line of appeasement. Profitable deals depend on peace and calm; a political crisis always has a detrimental effect on business. A few may benefit from rearmament, but most do not. Thus, when the Moscow representative of International Harvester was arrested by the KGB on some minor trumped-up charge, he was dropped by his colleagues like a leper, and gained the support of his own firm only after some delay. This too is an old story. Writing on Chamberlain, Harold Nicolson noted that it was not the descendants of the old governing classes who displayed the greatest enthusiasm for him but the descendants of the industrial revolution: "Mr. Chamberlain is the idol of the businessmen." And A. L. Rowse, the historian, added, "These men were essentially middle-class, not aristocrats. They did not have the hereditary sense of the security of the state, unlike Churchill, Eden, and the Cecils." The point should not be stretched too far (there is no aristocracy in America), but it is certainly true that big business in the U.S. has no "hereditary sense of the security of the state." It wants protection for its operations abroad, but it is quite reluctant to pay for it. It wants business and politics to be kept strictly apart.

The churches (and for good measure, the synagogues) are an important segment of the appeasement camp, for reasons that need hardly be elaborated in detail. British appeasement in the 1930s owed much to Nonconformism; Sir Nevile Henderson, the arch-appeaser, noted in his autobiography that he had been "selected by Providence for the definite mission of helping to preserve the peace of the world." The fact that, historically, the church has not always lived up to its peaceful mission— one need only cite its record in Nazi Germany and in Fascist Italy—makes many contemporary churchmen doubly anxious to have a spotless attitude. "We are not the policemen of the world" thus becomes a modern version of Cain's protestation of non-responsibility for Abel in Genesis 4:9—incidentally, the text of one of Chamberlain's most famous speeches in 1938. Other churchmen have veered toward a curious form of radicalism, supporting all kinds of spurious liberation fronts, attacking democratic countries, turning a blind eye to oppressive dictatorships.

American media have a bias toward appeasement; the same was true of most British and French newspapers in the 1930s. Some editorialists and columnists in our age pontificate like bishops, taking for granted their moral right and intellectual qualifications to do so. As keepers of the liberal conscience, they harp on guilt feelings the way the appeasers of the 1930s harped on the "injustice" done to Germany in the Versailles peace treaty. They know, in any case, that it is the task of the media to criticize one's own government, not the government of others.

Lastly, the universities. Dozens of books, thousands of articles have been published over the last fifteen years to the effect that the outbreak of the cold war was predominantly the fault of Truman, Dulles, and their acolytes, that the United States is the spearhead of world reaction and imperialism, that its policy has been counterrevolutionary all along, that Soviet totalitarianism is a figment of the imagination, and that the Western democracies have been moving steadily towards fascism. Stalin and his successors are presented in this literature either as harmless social reformers or as conservative status-quo politicians. This brand of revisionism has been taught for years and has entered college textbooks; one of its saving graces may be that it contains the seed of its own destruction, as a new generation must inevitably come along to revise the revisers, but for the moment it is still going strong. One must be careful, of course, to dissociate the academic foreign-policy establishment from views like these, but even in the establishment, appeasement has many influential proponents—just as it had them on both the Left and the Right in the 1930s, from Toynbee to Trevelyan and Charles Beard.

Appeasement, in short, has been "in" for a long time, and opposition to it strictly unfashionable. There are signs that this may now be changing. But why should it have gone on for so long? The politics of appeasement are the *Fleurs du mal* of a more widespread political decadence—a decadence highly visible in both England and France in the 1930s, and especially in France, where society seemed to have lost its instinct for national self-preservation. There are in America at the present time elements of decadence, which are based not on a cosmic despair but, to the contrary, on a belief that the country is so secure that no outside danger can possibly threaten it. Daladier complained in 1938 that France was being represented abroad as a "drab country frightened about her future, concerned only with material interests." Actually, as subsequent events were to show, this was a fairly accurate description. But present-day America does not really resemble pre-war France; there is, if anything, a similarity with pre-war Britain, a country adrift, confused, and misguided, whose people, good-humored and peace-loving, are willing to be pushed around and lied to both at home and on the international scene.[2] But in Britain in the 1930s there was a limit beyond which this process could not go, for the British were not masochists, and they did not believe that the future belonged to the dictators. At the moment of truth, the remaining diehard defeatists disappeared without a trace, like the ships of the Spanish Armada.

Is America nearing such a moment of truth today? It is certainly the case that a turning point is at hand in U.S.-Soviet relations. Even in the camp of the appeasers there is a new lack of confidence in "détente"— brought about not so much by the force of counter-argument, of which there has been, of late, a considerable amount, as by the disillusioning actions of the Soviet Union. Soviet rearmament has proceeded at a steady rate over the years, and the Russians, while making no secret of their desire to receive a maximum amount of economic and technological aid from the West, have also made no secret of their intention to continue the ideological struggle, i.e., confrontation. This does not, for them, refer to philosophical debates over the merits of the respective social systems but to real political struggle which may well involve limited military operations. It means, for all practical purposes, the extension of the Soviet sphere of influence.

The sudden realization that the West has fallen behind has led to a sense of danger and even of crisis. It is still true that the immediate danger is less than it was in the 1930s: the Soviet Union, unlike Nazi Germany, is under no constraint to go to war, and even if there were such a temptation, there is always the nuclear deterrent. But if the nuclear bomb will prevent global war, it will not forestall local wars outside Europe. And this means, as everyone must know by now, the end of the old-style détente.

A process of gradual reorientation has thus begun. It would be unwise to hasten this process, for the illusions of the early 1970s will not die easily, and there are still a great many people ready to give détente (as they understand it) yet another chance. Indeed, it is still claimed by some that détente was never given a first chance. Thus, in a recently published symposium Samuel Pisar and David Riesman argued that linkage of the human-rights issue to normalization of relations with the USSR "undermines the remnants of détente": others, such as Stephen Cohen of Princeton and Donald Kendall of Pepsi Cola, have maintained that increased trade could do much to cement relations with the Russians and that workable coexistence is threatened by resolutions such as the Jackson-Vanik Amendment.[3] These arguments, however, do not survive critical examination: disillusionment with détente in the West set in well before the human-rights issue ever became topical, and there is no reason to assume that more trade or even more aid would have an effect either on Soviet arms-spending or on the active pursuit of Soviet foreign-policy aims in Africa, Asia, and elsewhere.

About East-West trade in general it can be truly said that seldom in history has so much been written by so many about so little. The amount of such commerce is small by any standards, and Soviet policy holds that it should not grow beyond a certain, limited percentage of overall Soviet foreign trade. The development of U.S.-Soviet commercial dealings has been hampered not so much by American restrictions as by Soviet lack of hard currency. The outstanding hard currency debt of the Russians is now nearing $20 billion; the debt of the Communist bloc as a whole is well beyond $50 billion. Thus, when the Soviets warn the West that they intend to divert their trade to countries which do not practice credit restrictions, this is merely another way of saying that they wish to reallocate their debts. Such threats should be faced with equanimity in the West, yet in certain circles they still create a condition of near-panic. Thus, a Washington *Post* writer recently urged that the U.S. help Russia alleviate its oil crisis, for unless it did so the Russians might be in an ugly mood, and this could have, *inter alia,* regrettable consequences for Israel.

Messrs. Pisar, Cohen, and Kendall also suggest that détente should be founded on a mutual understanding of the two superpowers' national interest. Détente could indeed be saved if the national interest of the United States were defined as pertaining to North America alone, with a much more liberal view taken of Soviet national interest—covering Europe and Asia, and, for good measure, perhaps also Africa. But it is doubtful whether this kind of "symmetry" would appeal to many Americans, and it is certain that in a long-range view it is not in America's best interest.

Thus, the process of disenchantment will go on. Intellectually, it must be said, the case for appeasement was never particularly impressive; it rested not so much on an objective political analysis as on a mood, a set of hopes and fears. There is no denying that the aspirations involved were often praiseworthy, but a policy arising from such aspirations can only succeed if there is at least a minimum of reciprocity from the other side. The Soviets, alas, are not in a reciprocating mood, and they have pulled the rug out from under the appeasers. (Still, it is doubtful that a single Western diplomat or columnist will have to look for a new job as the result of having been persistently wrong.)

But what, it will be asked, could possibly, replace détente? The answer, quite obviously, is more détente. But it must be a retreat (or an advance) from appeasement to true détente. The game must no longer be played according to one-sided rules; there must be fewer unilateral concessions. Soviet views on the continuation of the ideological (i.e., political) struggle should be taken seriously in Washington, and America should do some reciprocal struggling of its own. Whether those who now direct U.S. foreign policy would be capable of pursuing a more effective policy is not certain, but this is not the decisive issue. For once it were accepted that true détente has to be based on mutual benefit, there would be irresistible pressure for policy change—under the present management if possible, under a new one if necessary. There would be pained outcries, not only from Moscow but also from nearer home, invoking the dangers of "confrontation." But these would be rearguard actions which would not affect the generally more healthy direction of U.S.-Soviet relations.

*October 1978*

## NOTES

1. Any student of the Nazi era will have come across dozens of newspaper columns and diplomatic memoranda calling upon Western leaders to support the "moderate" Hitler against the extremist Ribbentrop or the bellicose Hess or the aggressive German generals. Halifax to Henderson, British Ambassador in Berlin, August 5, 1938: Hitler fears Britain and France as much as Britain and France fear him; his mass demonstrations of military might are reactive in nature, sparked by the predictions of German intelligence that the Western powers intend to launch a preventive war against Germany.
2. This is perhaps a good place to note that although I have limited myself here to examples of appeasement of Germany (and Italy) in the 1930s, and of the Soviet Union more recently, instances abound elsewhere as well. Of late, both Western Europe and, to a lesser extent, the United States have had to swallow many a bitter pill dispensed by the oil-producing countries of the Middle East and North Africa.
3. *Common Sense in U.S.-Soviet Relations,* edited by Carl Marcy, American Committee on East-West Accord, Washington, 1978.

# The World
# and President Carter

Among the more engaging features of the American political system is the custom of extending wide indulgence to every incoming administration, both in foreign policy and domestic affairs. For its part, every new administration also observes certain time-honored rituals, chief among them being the promise that under its dispensation all things will be different. Thus, it seemed only natural for President Carter upon assuming office to announce a "new American foreign policy for a new world" and for the new Secretary of State to proclaim a radical reversal of his predecessor's foreign policy ("highly compartmentalized and essentially static détente") as well as an end to what Mr. Brzezinski called "ideological warfare." The new administration in fact not only promised new solutions but also uncovered new problems and promised to solve them as well. The old conflicts (we were told) had become less acute, and there was a need to turn away from them and face the future.

Not all these pronouncements were purely ritualistic in origin. Many of the men and women who came to Washington in January of last year had been genuinely critical of U.S. foreign policy for years and were sincerely convinced that, given the opportunity, they could improve it. And this they still seem to feel themselves capable of doing. If at the end of his first year in office the President expressed surprise at the "intransigence and complexity" of a number of international problems, there have been as yet few similar admissions by his aides, most of whom seem to be satisfied with their policies and reasonably happy with their own performance.

Their enthusiasm is not, however, shared by the majority of the American people, 52 percent of whom, according to a recent Harris poll, have taken a negative view of the new administration's foreign policy. There have been growing complaints, most of them justified, about quick diplomatic successes that turn out to be spurious, about policies that show more consideration for America's enemies than for its allies, about a retreat from the high idealism of the early days to an aimless and inconsistent pragmatism.

143

The human-rights issue is as good an example as any of this kind of retreat. The President mentioned human rights no fewer than three times in his inaugural address, and soon thereafter he affirmed in a letter to Andrei Sakharov that "Human rights is a central concern of my administration. . . . We shall use our good offices to seek the release of prisoners of conscience." An Office of Coordinator for Human Rights and Humanitarian Affairs was set up, with a staff of some thirty people. Thus far, the office has been involved mainly in lodging complaints with various Latin American governments and the government of South Korea, and in advising cuts in assistance to countries like South Africa, Uruguay, Ethiopia, and Argentina. As far as they go, these are worthwhile efforts. But the real problem is not how to deal with South Korea; it is how to deal with countries like Uganda or Cambodia, in which there are no "prisoners of conscience" because the government simply murders its opponents, and with countries like the Soviet Union and some of its allies, in which the violation of human rights is an integral part of the political system.

That the human-rights policy would cause displeasure in the Kremlin was clear from the start. But it has also aroused opposition here at home from those who said that the new policy carried with it the risk of endangering détente, and that nothing was worth that risk. Thus, in one widely reprinted speech, David Riesman warned that an emphasis on human rights would inevitably revive the cold-war mentality, and all the dangers to humanity therein entailed. For this reason, much as he admired the courage of the Soviet dissidents, and much as he shared the values that inspired a man like Sakharov, Riesman said, he had consistently refused to sign petitions or to lend his name to any manifestation of protest in behalf of Russian dissenters.[1] Similar views, albeit more cautiously phrased, have been expressed by others, among them leading members of the administration, all of whom share the basic assumption that an emphasis on human rights in U.S. foreign policy must somehow make a nuclear conflict more likely.

If this assumption were correct, the case of these critics would be unassailable, since human survival should obviously take precedence over other considerations. But the assumption happens to be wrong. The Soviet leaders do not regard the American human-rights policy as a form of warmongering, but simply as a counter-attack in the ongoing ideological struggle, and one that is quite inconvenient from their point of view, putting them, as it does, on the defensive. Soviet leaders have said countless times that, détente or no détente, ideological warfare with the West will continue unabated, but they regard this struggle as a one-way street: while they have the right, and indeed the duty, to attack the political and social system of the West, the West has no right to respond in kind, for its arguments are by definition mendacious and demagogic. American critics of a strong U.S. posture on human rights have tacitly accepted the Soviet interpretation of détente and simply refuse to recognize that a lasting understanding between the superpowers (as opposed to the short-term measures now envisaged) will become possible only after the Soviet political system has become more open. No one can say with confidence whether this will happen in our time, but it certainly will not be brought about by giving back to the Soviets their monopoly in the conduct of ideological warfare.

Critics of the administration's early emphasis on human rights were concerned not only with the supposed threat it posed to détente, but also with the supposed disruption it would cause in the balance of power within the Kremlin itself. Brezhnev, so the argument went, might soon be forced out of office by his illness, thereby giving more power to other, harder-line factions in the Soviet military-industrial complex. But the fact is that Brezhnev will not last forever in any case, and even if he should be replaced by a less moderate faction, there is not reason to assume that his successors would feel bound by earlier agreements. Moreover, although there are, to be sure, certain tactical differences among contending parties in the Kremlin, these differences do not affect essential Soviet policy. One can think of a great many arguments for or against stressing human rights in foreign policy, but to make one's stand depend on the state of Brezhnev's health, or on hypothetical power shifts in the Kremlin, is to reduce political debate to the kindergarten level.

The United States, in any case, has retreated very far from its original position on the human-rights question—this, despite the fact that European governments, after an initial half-heartedness, showed themselves quite willing to cooperate with President Carter's initiatives, and despite the fact too that public opinion throughout Europe was sympathetic to the human-rights issue from the very beginning. No one expected the new policy to produce quick results, and no one demanded that human rights be made the one and only condition of dealing with foreign governments. But some foresight and consistency, not to mention a bit more courage, could have been expected.

What, then, has been achieved so far? In a recent interview with *U.S. News and World Report,* Secretary of State Vance maintained that "anybody who has watched and seen what we have done and what the results have been—particularly in Latin America—would recognize that very substantial progress has been made." But has it? It is true that the lot of a handful of individuals imprisoned in a few countries has been alleviated, and that the new Office of Human Rights helped stall a loan to El Salvador until that regime moderated some of its practices. But these achievements have been purchased at a price that far outweighs the good they may have done.

No great courage is needed to denounce the crimes committed by South Africa—the United Nations does it once a week. But wherever the slightest risk has been involved, and occasionally also when the risk involved has been small or non-existent, the administration has tended to retreat from its declared purpose. The Shcharansky case is a good example. Once President Carter had formally denied the allegation that Shcharansky was a CIA agent, there was nothing to prevent the U.S. from taking a strong stand against the Soviet treatment of this dissident, for instance by threatening not to participate in the Belgrade talks over the Helsinki accords; there is no doubt that the Soviet authorities would have retreated. Instead, the Russians were given to understand that American public opinion would not tolerate a *severe* sentence for Shcharansky, and the decision was made to proceed with the Belgrade charade. The administration was tested, and it failed the test. As a result, there have been more arrests in the Soviet Union, and the situation of political prisoners has actually deteriorated. The Soviet Union has learned that the United States is not really serious about human rights.

If the balance sheet on human rights after Carter's first year in office is thus far negative, what about the larger question of U.S.-Soviet relations in general?

From their first days in office. President Carter and his advisers declared that too much time and energy had been expended by past administrations on East-West relations. By now, however, there are clear signs that the administration recognizes that U.S.-Soviet relations impinge on most aspects of world affairs, and that the old problems will not vanish simply because a new set of officials would like them to. Thus, Washington is once more preoccupied with issues which have become, if anything, even more highly charged than they were previously.

One such problem, which can no longer be overlooked, is that of arms control and the Soviet military build-up. As the most recent Brookings Institution study on the subject puts it—in a tone of genuine bewilderment—"With each passing year it has become more difficult to explain the continuing momentum in the Soviet defense build-up." Indeed, the Soviet build-up *is* impossible to explain, at least on the basis of assumptions cherished by the *Bulletin of the Atomic Scientists* or the Harvard-MIT arms-control seminar—namely, that there is no such thing as superiority in the arms race, and that the Russians, in any case, are not seeking it. To this day, the Secretary of State continues to maintain that the Soviets merely want nothing more than strategic parity—a view echoed by Professor George Kistiakowsky in a recent article in the New York *Times Magazine,* in which he warned that the baseless nightmares of the

Committee on the Present Danger and other "hardliners" about Soviet intentions were leading the country into great peril. Professor Kistiakowsky urged the U.S. not to take too seriously the writings of Russian military experts about a winnable nuclear war, and advised the administration not to deploy new weapons systems lest they destabilize the situation and make mutual monitoring impossible. Instead, the highest priority should be given to a total nuclear test ban.

The weakness of this argument is that the Russians simply have not shown much interest in reducing their nuclear arsenal, as was demonstrated last March by their brusque reaction to President Carter's suggestions for mutual arms reductions. Nor have the Russians been troubled by the possible consequences of destabilizations; whenever they could do so, they have introduced new weapons systems into the picture. In short, if some rough equilibrium of forces still exists between the U.S. and the Soviet Union, it is based not on Soviet actions, but rather on American technological superiority. If a new treaty were to be arrived at, permitting the Soviet Union to maintain its growing advantage, the resulting asymmetry would not only be immediately disadvantageous to the U.S., it would also make future arms agreements that much more difficult to obtain.

After the Soviet rejection of the original Carter plan last spring, the administration came up with a more modest formula calling for much smaller reductions in the arms ceilings, prohibition of mobile missiles for a three-year period, and a limitation over the next three years on the cruise missile, the one weapons system in which the U.S. still has a significant advantage and which is vital to the security of Europe. This new proposal was leaked to the press, thus causing a violent outcry on the part of the administration and some Senators and Congressmen—a curious response since the leaks, after all, did not involve national security but concerned matters that would soon be made public in any case. Those who complained most loudly, moreover, were the very people who only a short time before had been the sharpest critics of government secrecy, and the most passionate upholders of the public's right to know. What they apparently feared was that premature release of the new proposals would provoke opposition, and this in fact was exactly what happened.

For once, the opposition was not restricted to the United States, nor could it be attributed solely to the allegedly dubious motives of American hardliners. In Britain, especially, reaction to the news of a proposed limitation on cruise missiles was sharp. Thus the *Economist* wrote on September 24:

The U.S. is in the position of many great powers before it: it has to choose

> between an accomodation with its adversary and the confidence of its
> allies. It can stand ready to share the cruise missile, or it can run the very
> real risk of damaging the alliance on which its own security, as well as
> Europe's, depends.

And again even more emphatically on October 22:

> If this treaty results in a Russian missile strength not very different from
> what it probably would have been without any agreement at all (which is
> what the figures suggest) at the price of starting to unravel the Atlantic
> alliance, then the treaty will not be bad, but disastrous.

The London *Times* wrote on December 10:

> What is important at the moment is that Soviet-American negotiations
> should not preempt decisions which deeply affect European interests and
> require European participation. This has not happened yet, but it could
> happen in the future. . . . They [the Europeans] have good reason for being
> unsure.

Professor Lawrence Martin, one of Britain's leading military experts,
said in an article last October that

> West Europeans should note that many Americans pushing for a complete
> ban really want to "denuclearize" U.S. alliance policy, limiting any use of
> nuclear weapons only to deter direct aggression against the United States.
> And Americans eager for nonproliferation should ponder what their allies
> might do for protection if American guarantees weakened.

And lastly, Lord Kennet, a Labor peer, in a letter to the London *Times*
(December 15):

> [Western Europe, Israel, Japan, India, etc.] are threatened by a class of
> weapons which does not threaten the U.S. If the United States does not
> choose to upset Russia by talking about the matter, we had better do so
> ourselves.

Similar voices were heard in other European countries, all expressing
unease (to put it mildly) about the direction U.S. policy was taking.

The administration, in its turn, tried to reassure its allies and urge
them not to overreact. Thus Leslie Gelb, director of political-military affairs at the State Department, warned that "If you paint the Russians as
ten feet tall, you have acomplished the basic purpose of Soviet foreign
policy without their having to lift a finger." This is good advice as far as
it goes, but beyond the issue of how Soviet might is perceived, there is,
alas, the issue of hard facts and figures. When due allowance has been
made for exaggeration and "worst-case analysis" on the part of the ad-

ministration's critics, it is still true that in the last few years the Soviet Union has achieved advantages over the U.S. in throw-weight, megatonnage, and numbers of missiles and bombers; that in 1977 they gained advantages in equivalent weapons; and that under the SALT II proposals, the last U.S. advantage (in number of total warheads) would pass to them within no more than five or six years' time. To talk of the need for recognizing "the legitimate security interests of the Soviet Union" under these circumstances is pure anachronism; the Soviet Union's security interests were taken care of a long time ago, unless of course one happens to believe that the Soviet Union will not feel secure until it has a clear superiority all along the line. There can be no question about the desirability of a strategic arms agreement, but the administration, in its wish to conclude a treaty as quickly as possible, seems to have made concessions which serve neither American interests nor, for that matter, the cause of arms control.

It has been said, and not without some truth, that mistakes in the field of defense planning need not be fatal; the consequences of such mistakes will not be felt for a number of years, and there may well be a chance to correct them somewhere along the way. The decisive issues in U.S.-Soviet relations are not, however, the purely technical ones described above. Rather, they concern our basic assessment of Soviet policies and intentions. Confusion in these areas is potentially far more dangerous; and some recent statements by administration spokesmen tend to confirm the impression that there is indeed a great deal of such confusion.

Take, for instance, two recent statements by Marshall Shulman, who is both special adviser on Soviet affairs to the Secretary of State and head of President Carter's Interagency Committee on Soviet policy, and whose pronouncements therefore must be taken as a key to thinking in the White House and the administration. In an article in *Foreign Affairs* published in 1976, Professor Shulman provided advice on "Learning to Live with Authoritarian Regimes." The article was not, as one might have supposed from its title, devoted to Afghanistan or Morocco, but rather to the Soviet Union. It is hard to believe that this blurring of the enormous difference between authoritarian and totalitarian regimes was an accident, or that it was unconnected with the general drift of the Carter administration's position in world affairs. A more recent policy statement by Professor Shulman before the House International Relations Committee (October 31, 1977), though couched in more cautious terms, included assumptions about our relations with the Soviets that simply will not survive critical analysis:

> At the philosophical level, we believe that there can be a useful dialogue between societies that start from the needs of the society and emphasize the

fulfillment of material needs, and those that start from the dignity and worth of the individual and emphasize the fulfillment of political rights.

Now, there may indeed be room for agreement on any number of matters between the two superpowers. But can it seriously be maintained that a "dialogue" is at all feasible between two societies, one of which is open and the other closed? Professor Shulman may meet with Dr. Arbatov or some other spokesman of the Soviet dictatorship at Pugwash or some other place, and may indeed have a discussion with him over issues of policy, but no dialogue is possible between the two societies, since Soviet *society* cannot freely express itself. It is ironic that a few weeks after Professor Shulman's statement, U.S. diplomats in Moscow were instructed by the State Department to limit their contacts with Soviet citizens so as not to endanger overall diplomatic relations. So much, then, for the famous "dialogue." Still more dangerous is Professor Shulman's contrasting of individual human rights and "economic" rights as though the two were mutually exclusive. Democratic government, by definition, cannot possibly neglect the "needs of the society," whereas a dictatorship can do so with impunity. It would be interesting to know what the result would be if Soviet society were given the choice between missiles and consumer goods—but unfortunately Soviet society is not consulted about its "needs."

To belittle the crucial differences between a free society and an unfree society is a serious matter. The Soviet Union may be weaker than we think, it may even be less aggressive, or its economic performance may be stronger than we think, but it certainly is not more open than we think. Politicians may ignore the views of their advisers, they may even sometimes reach correct conclusions on the basis of false premises (just as a mysterious force sometimes protects sleepwalkers). But to build a policy based on misconceptions about the Soviet political system is bound to cause trouble.

European misgivings about the future of the Atlantic alliance stem from the belief that sooner or later the defense of Europe will have to be based on the cruise missile and that Washington seems either to ignore this fact or not to care. Some of these fears were dispelled, temporarily at least, by the Secretary of Defense on his trip to Europe last November, but uncertainties still remain about American economic polities. Indeed, economic issues are among the most urgent problems facing the U.S. in its relations with allies. Concluding his economic summit meeting last May in London, President Carter reported complete unanimity between himself and European leaders. No such unanimity would be possible today, with the dollar having dropped some 11 percent in proportion to the Deutsche mark and about twice as much in comparison with the yen during the last year.

Although this drop does not concern them overly since it facilitates American exports, administration spokesmen have offered various explanations for it. The fall of the dollar, they say, is the result of speculation; the yen and the mark were undervalued; Japan and West Germany, in contrast to the U.S., have not done enough to reflate the world economy. Some of these arguments contain a grain of truth, but the American policy of "malign neglect" (to quote unkind critics) has also been quite shortsighted and irresponsible. The upward valuation of the mark and the yen can hardly contribute toward a reflation of the world economy. What it can do is help reduce American losses caused by the growing U.S. trade deficit (about $30 billion at present), which is itself the result of still increasing oil imports. Indeed, continuing American dependence on these imports is an unmitigated disaster whose effects are bound to be felt abroad no less than at home. Such dependence has made it more difficult to freeze the price of oil; if the value of the dollar falls even further, and if the price of oil goes up, the countries mainly affected will be the ones least able to afford it.

What if the European banks, having supported the dollar in the past, were to use their holdings to buy up American corporations? Such a development might be welcomed by some in the U.S., but it would surely be resented by many others, and it would certainly cause further complications in relations between the U.S. and its allies. The policy, in other words, of viewing the depreciation of the dollar as an "offshore problem" can perhaps be justified as a short-term palliative; but if this policy is maintained for any length of time, it is bound to create a worldwide currency crisis with incalculable economic and political consequences.

There are legitimate conflicts of interest between America and its main trading partners which will not be easily resolved, if in fact they can be resolved at all. But so far, the attempt has not even been made—the dangers of protectionism and a shrinking in world trade have simply been ignored. President Carter has recently promised intervention to prevent a further decline in the value of the dollar. It remains to be seen whether this declaration will be followed up by determined action.

Turning from Europe to the Middle East, one cannot deny that American freedom of action there has been rather severely curtailed. But even granting the limitations built into the Middle East situation, the performance of the administration must be judged as gravely wanting.

While the Middle East situation is certainly dangerous, and bound to remain so for a long time, this is only in part because of the Arab-Israeli conflict. On the other hand, it has been obvious for quite a while that there is no imminent danger of war in the Middle East except perhaps at the fringes, between Algeria and Morocco, say, or in the unlikely event of direct Soviet intervention. The Carter administration must be aware of this, yet official Washington has nevertheless relentlessly turned out speeches, declarations, and admonitions to the effect that the Arab-Israeli conflict is the most burning issue on the international scene (in a speech in California not to long ago, President Carter even put it ahead of the SALT talks in his list of priorities). And all this at a time when a real war was under way in Africa, and when there was a danger of political changes in Europe having far graver potential consequences than anything that could conceivably happen in the Middle East.

This single-minded concentration on the Arab-Israeli conflict at the expense of all other problems did not, of course, begin with President Carter, but his administration has approached the conflict with even greater zeal and more glaring misconceptions than those of its predecessors. Though it should have been clear that the step-by-step approach chosen, perhaps instinctively, by Henry Kissinger was the only way to reduce tensions in the area, the new administration, under the compulsion to come up with novel approaches, opted for a policy which would at best have led to an impasse, and at worst to disaster. Geneva was the worst possible forum for peacemaking in the Middle East; the inevitable failure there would almost certainly have increased tensions in the area.

If the road to peace does not lead through Geneva, it has been clear for a long time that there was a chance to break the deadlock if Israel were able to reach a *modus vivendi* with one Arab country; and it was equally clear that, given the weakness of Jordan, this country could only be Egypt.[2] It is perhaps regrettable that the initiative came from Cairo rather than Jerusalem, but perhaps—again—it could not have been otherwise. This is not to say for a certainty that the present negotiations will prove successful, or that, even if they do, the Arab-Israeli conflict will be resolved. But even if the present talks should fail or be sabotaged, they surely indicate the proper direction for future peace-making efforts in the Middle East.

As for bringing the Soviet Union into the process (a step for which no one in Washington seems at present eager to claim credit), this remains altogether incomprehensible, even with the benefit of hindsight. A comprehensive and lasting peace in the Middle East may well be impossible without the Soviet Union, but since the Soviet Union has no interest whatsoever in any such peace, except perhaps on terms that would be unacceptable not only to Israel but also to the other main participants, including the United States, what point could there have been in reintroducing the Soviets into the situation? If nothing else, the Soviet reaction to President Sadat's recent peace initiative (comparing him, among other things, to Hitler) should have provided a salutary lesson. The Soviet leaders may have suffered a temporary setback in the Middle East, but at least they, in contrast to Washington's Arabists, have mastered the elementary lesson of politics: to support one's friends, rather than trying to be on good terms with all the participants in a conflict.

Why did the administration assume that the Russians would be "helpful"? Why did it fail to realize that the overall aim of U.S. policy in the Middle East should have been the prevention of war, rather than the pursuit of a goal which, under present circumstances, was a mere chimera? At the moment these questions may be purely academic, which makes them no less disturbing. For what is at stake are not just some tactical errors of judgment but a basic misreading of the Middle Eastern situation. To be sure, there have been signs of a more realistic approach in U.S. policy in the Middle East in the form of a new understanding that since the Rejection Front does not want a peaceful settlement in any case, no time should be wasted in futile efforts to gain its good will. But not everyone in Washington has arrived at this new understanding, and backsliding is still possible.

If the Carter administration's Middle East policy has suffered from a surfeit of misguided activism, its policy in the Far East seems to have suffered from the opposite. The charge of having neglected Japan, made by Zbigniew Brzezinski and other members of the Trilateral Commission against the former administration, can be made with equal validity against the Carter administration in its first year in office. If anything, unease in Japan has actually increased under the present administration, following President Carter's decision to withdraw all American ground forces from Korea over the next few years. The impending withdrawal is regarded not only as the possible prelude to another Far Eastern war, but also as the beginning of an American retreat from the Western Pacific— a policy which, whether deliberate or not, is bound to lead to a realignment of forces in the Far East, with Japan moving into either the Soviet or the Chinese orbit, or perhaps opting for heavily armed neutrality.

Such scarcely trifling consequences have not, however, been sufficient to deflect the advocates of withdrawal from their course; if "most Koreans" are seeking a peaceful, reunited Korea, the arguement goes, who are we to insist on a divided Korea? The fact that "reunification" is unlikely to be peaceful has not often been mentioned. More recently, the administration's Far East experts seem to have accepted what should have been obvious from the beginning—namely, that even a neo-isolationist policy like the proposed U.S. withdrawal requires an overall strategy, and that more is required for the accomplishment of an orderly retreat—in both the military and political arenas—than a bit of tinkering here and there.

U.S. policy toward China has similarly suffered from an absence of clear guidelines. Yes (it was said), recognition of Peking is our aim, but not an urgent one, and yes, we also have a commitment to Taiwan. Secretary Vance journeyed to Peking, but the purpose of his trip is not quite clear to this day—it certainly has not contributed to an improvement in relations between the two countries, or even to a clarification of the issues under dispute. To the thorny issue of Taiwan there is admittedly no easy answer, but Taiwan, so far as the Chinese are concerned, can wait; they are far more interested in U.S. policy toward the Soviet Union, about which there has thus far been no meetings of minds. According to U.S. envoys, the Chinese take, or pretend to take, the Soviet "threat" far too seriously. The Chinese, on the other hand, as they made clear to subsequent visitors, believe that the makers of American foreign policy are either not very bright or not very brave, and that little will be gained by establishing closer relations with the United States—with the possible exception of the economic field.

If has been said that the greatest changes in U.S. policy during the Carter administration have taken place in Africa, but this is an exaggeration, for present American policy in Africa was first outlined in Kissinger's Lusaka address in April 1976, in which he criticized South Africa and declared the Rhodesian government to be illegal. To be sure, this African policy has been further elaborated under the present administration. It is now maintained that Africa should be supported as a whole rather than allowed to break into fragments, and that Africa should be left alone to solve its own problems. These are both desirable prescriptions, but, unfortunately, African nationalism *is* fragmented—the Afras, for instance, are even now turning against the Issas (and this despite the fact that no one had heard of either one until last year). Nor is the decision to leave Africa alone solely in our hands. In the existing power vacuum, the pressure of a few hundred, let alone a few thousand, foreign "experts" or soldiers can make a world of difference, as was shown by the case of Angola. Zaire, too, in the absence of American support, might well have been taken over but for the decision of the French and the Moroccans to step in. Meanwhile, there has been fairly massive Soviet involvement in the Horn of Africa, and the Cubans show every indication of staying where they are.

We have been told by Andrew Young not to get paranoid about a few Communists, but how few are few? According to Ambassador Young, their number in Angola was at one time around 50,000, which by Chinese standards may not be many, but by the standards of warfare in Africa is a massive force. We were assured that the Soviet Union would not reap major gains in Africa but would, on the contrary, get trapped in a quagmire as the U.S. had done in Vietnam. Moreover, to cite Ambassador Young again, once the fighting stopped and the trading began, we would be the beneficiaries, for many African countries would them move from the Soviet Union toward the United States. Some of this has in a sense come to pass: since the Soviet Union cannot provide the economic and technical assistance many of its African clients need, they are only too eager to obtain it from the United States, presumably with Soviet blessing. But if talk of "Marxism" in Africa is foolish, so is the idea that the Soviets have suffered any setbacks there. Rather, the Soviet Union—because it has had no hesitation about engaging in intervention by proxy—has considerably strengthened its position in many parts of Africa whereas the United States, except where South Africa is concerned, has adhered to a strict policy of nonintervention. It is one thing to argue that America's policy of passivity in Africa has been unavoidable, given the mood of Congress and the predictable outcries in the media. But to claim that this policy has been a huge success is fatuous nonsense.

So far as policy toward Cuba itself is concerned, one can express little but bewilderment. If a reasonably persuasive case could have been made for recognizing Cuba and renewing trade (a euphemism for subsidizing the Cuban economy and alleviating the Soviet burden) before Cuba decided to intervene in Africa or was commissioned to do so, no such case can be made now—or so it would seem. Yet amazement must be recorded at the administration's continued willingness to normalize relations with Cuba even after the massive involvement in Angola was under way. It took several months before policy-makers reluctantly accepted the fact that little progress could be expected on the diplomatic front so long as the military intervention continued. Meanwhile, the U.S. delegation in the United Nations has worked closely with the Cubans in preparing a resolution condemning Chile for various human-rights violations. Such condemnation may well be deserved, but it issues forth rather strangely from Cuba, a country with more political prisoners, and less freedom, than even Chile can boast. Which takes us back to where we began—the assertion by Secretary of State Vance of "very substantial" progress on human rights, especially in Latin America. . . .

Can anything be said to the credit of the administration's record in foreign policy? The obvious answer is that the world cannot be changed in a year, and that certain of the Carter initiatives—like the Panama Canal treaty, for instance—ought to be welcomed. The administration has been on the right track in trying to slow down nuclear proliferation and the arms trade and cannot fairly be faulted if these attempts have not been successful. Nor can the State Department or the White House be held responsible for all the setbacks in foreign affairs. While Congress may have saved the administration from making mistakes on the SALT negotiations, its inability to agree on an energy program, combined with the pressure of the protectionist lobby, has certainly weakened the U.S.

posture abroad. A measure of blame, too, for certain policy failures undoubtedly lies with America's allies who still are not pulling their weight in the economic field (Japan) and in defense (Western Europe). Finally, despite setbacks, NATO is in slightly better shape now than it has been in years past. There is even a growing awareness in Washington that the Soviet Union will only agree to halt its military build-up when it realizes the other side is determined to match it.

And yet there remains reason for concern, for thus far, at least, it is difficult to discern any clear idea of America's role in world affairs. In fact, what makes it so difficult to comment now about U.S. foreign policy is the absence of any clear concept; instead one faces vague trends and contradictory statements at frequent intervals, a source of bewilderment to friend and foe alike. Though neo-isolationism seems to have fallen out of fashion in recent days, there is a great deal of confusion as to what America is legitimately entitled to do in defense of its vital interests.

A new generation is making its presence felt in the upper and middle echelons in Washington—the generation whose outlook was largely formed by the experience of the Vietnam war. While many of these young policy-makers have come to realize that the world is different from Senator McGovern's vision of it, others have not yet achieved such wisdom. It is not so much the lack of intellectual brilliance or original ideas which is worrisome, though these qualities do not seem to be in very ample supply. The problem lies elsewhere—in a kind of crisis of adaptation, one might say. The dead hand of Vietnam still weighs heavily on the American memory, and the fear of involvement in some dubious foreign adventure still clouds much of the thinking of official Washington. It is the old story of the cat which, once burned, never approached a stove again.

Apart from the Vietnam trauma, a curious parochialism seems to be in the American air, a tendency to analyze world problems solely in terms of the American experience which ends up muddying rather than clarifying the issues. The dividing line is no longer between hardliners and doves, between "interventionists" and those opposed to intervention. Rather, it is between the acceptance and the rejection of political reality as the basis for political action. One can only hope that something short of a major crisis will bring a sense of political reality into play for those who still need to learn a proper respect for its intractable force.

*February 1978*

### NOTES

1. Quoted from *Commonweal,* November 11, 1977.
2. This argument was developed in my article "Peace with Egypt?" *Commentary,* March 1974.

# America and the World: The Next Four Years, Confronting the Problems

"Critical" is one of those adjectives whose value has been severely depreciated by overuse, yet in speaking of the importance of future developments in American foreign policy no other word will do. For a long time now the United States has been so preoccupied with internal problems that foreign policy has seemed an unwelcome intrusion. The world, however, has not been able to wait patiently for the United States to sort out its domestic difficulties. In the past few years there has been a marked deterioration in the position of both America and its allies—politically, militarily, and economically—and new problems have by now emerged on top of the old familiar ones which still remain unresolved. Thus the Carter administration has come into office at—precisely —a critical moment, and the question arises as to how well it is equipped to cope. Although in certain areas it has made what appear to be bold moves, it remains to be seen how much of this is rhetoric and how much is real, and whether what is real is of value. The truth is that the setbacks suffered in recent years have caused the margin for experiment to shrink considerably, and the apprenticeship of the new administration is therefore likely to be either very short or very costly; one hopes it will not be both.

To start with the most obvious case, the Middle East: although the idea that a comprehensive peace settlement is possible there in the near future belongs to the realm of fantasy, all the signs indicate that the push for just such a settlement is to be given high priority, simply because everyone says the time for it has come. This, indeed, is one of the few issues on which Moscow and London, liberals and conservatives, oil companies and Arabs and Trotskyites agree. I have already argued at length in these pages that a resolution of the conflict between Israel and the Arab states, itself an unlikely prospect, would in any case not necessarily bring peace to the Middle East, which contains plenty of other volatile elements in addition to the Arab-Israeli confrontation. If, moreover, some of the planners have their way, and a new Palestinian state is established on the West Bank, the situation is liable to deteriorate even further. It is said that unless there is some movement toward de-fusing the Arab-Israeli conflict there may well be a new war two or three years hence. This is quite possible, but the establishment of what is sure to be a non-viable and therefore irredentist state in Palestine would lead to a new war with even greater certainty. There remains the hope that a fresh impetus may coax the two sides out of the present impasse and that this may eventually result in Palestinian autonomy within a wider framework, such as a federation with Jordan. But a Geneva-type con-ference aiming at a comprehensive settlement is the approach perhaps least conducive to progress toward this end. The most one can reasonably aim for at this juncture is a beginning in a process that will take many years to unfold. Any attempt to force a lasting, comprehen-sive settlement here and now is bound to end in breakdown.

Moreover, to concentrate on that comprehensive, lasting, but elusive peace settlement—something the Carter administration shows every sign of intending to do—is to ignore another urgent Middle Eastern problem which has far more serious implications: the price of OPEC oil. The large-scale indebtedness that has resulted from the price of OPEC oil is an infinitely more acute danger to world prosperity and stability, and thus to world peace, than the Arab-Israeli conflict. Were it not for oil, indeed, the Arab-Israeli conflict would be just another of the irritants disturbing world peace. What magnifies the danger in Western eyes is the fear that a new Arab-Israeli war may lead to another oil embargo and thus to the economic ruin of the importing nations. Yet quite irrespective of the Arab-Israeli conflict, the economies of many countries cannot af-ford oil at the current price levels. And despite the optimistic talk one hears in certain circles, financial collapse on a global scale remains a very real threat. The riots in Egypt earlier this year are just a first indication of the coming storms in the countries most affected.

Saudi Arabia was praised last December for its statesmanlike restraint in deciding to increase the price of oil by only five percent instead of fif-teen percent. But since the United States, West Germany, and Japan are already financing the oil imports of the insolvent countries—OPEC's contribution being insignificant—and since there is little prospect that these debts will be paid back, it is difficult to see what the general jubila-tion was all about. Although there is no easy way to solve the problem, there are many ways to reduce the pressure (and the price), ranging from conservation measures and the development of alternative sources of energy to eliminating the oil companies as intermediaries and creating conditions in which the cartel might break up. It is precisely in this direc-tion that American initiatives at home and leadership abroad will be needed to avert disaster.

Relations with the Soviet Union remain one of the central issues facing the new administration. President Carter has been urged by ex-ambassadors (from George Kennan to Charles Yost) and business interests (from Coca Cola to El Paso Oil) to put an end to the "neglect" of relations with Russia. What in their view is needed, as a recent statement by the American Committee on U.S.-Soviet Relations puts it, is "a resolute abandonment of the stale slogans and reflexes of the cold war, a recognition that this is a new era, with different problems and possibilities, and a determination not to be governed by the compulsions of military competition." There is little to quarrel with in sentiments of this kind, but how they are to be translated into the terms of arms control, of economic cooperation, and of political management is another matter.

The general feeling among experts is that the race to control strategic arms is being lost.[1] Of course the only sure way to "win" this race is to break down national boundaries—something no country is at present willing to do. Another, less far-reaching, and probably not entirely foolproof way is massive and unhampered on-site inspection, but this has been emphatically rejected by the Soviet Union. All other suggestions, however ingenious, become irrelevant with the progress of technology. There is no known procedure, except perhaps on-site inspection, to verify whether a cruise missile, for example, has a range of 600 or 3,000 kilometers. Nor is verification always useful even where it can be carried out.

As to the present state of the arms race: in the SALT-I negotiations, American policy-makers accepted unequal ceilings for intercontinental ballistic missiles (ICBM's)—1,054 for the U.S., 1,618 for the Soviet Union. The assumption in Washington was that the Russians could not be expected to negotiate from a position of inferiority, but once they had drawn even with the U.S., they would no longer be interested in building new missiles and effective arms-limitation talks could at last be held. (It was on this ground that the New York *Times* recently welcomed the successful Soviet testing of a submarine-launched ballistic missile.) Unfortunately the impeccable logic of this analysis has been lost on the Soviet Union, which has continued to forge ahead; the terms "parity," "sufficiency," and "destabilization" do not exist in Soviet strategic doctrine. In retrospect, it seems almost certain that the arms race could at least have been slowed down if the United States had made it crystal clear that every ICBM deployed by the Russians over and above 1,000 would be matched. But such a course of action was considered hawkish or unnecessary—"[What], in the name of God, is strategic superiority? . . . What do you do with it?" asked Secretary of State Kissinger. As a result, present-day ceilings are far higher than they need have been.

While extolling the virtues of fruitful cooperation among nations and attacking the reactionary circles in the imperialist countries for spending too much on defense, the Soviet leaders have produced new weapons systems in almost every field, built a big fleet, deployed new generations of ballistic missiles, and, generally speaking, spent between two and three times more per capita on defense than the U.S.[2]

In spite of various efforts to ignore or belittle this Russian push forward (the *Times* continues to insist that the Russians have only been "running hard to overtake an American lead"), the contradiction between Soviet words and deeds has begun to register. Attention has been focused on it by groups like the Committee on the Present Danger and the task force of outside experts ("Team B") called in to review the CIA estimate of Soviet military capability. Reports of the Soviet build-up have even been described as "ominous," or at the very least "impressive," in circles which would have brushed such information aside not very long ago. The section on defense in this year's Brookings Institution study, *Setting National Priorities,* for instance, warns that the American decline in real defense spending must not be continued.

The constant and rapid growth of Soviet power over and above what could be explained away even by the most charitable observers as needed for the defense fo Russia has also caused disenchantment among some arms controllers who used to believe that once a low level of deterrence is assured there is no longer any connection between military strength and political influence. This illusion—and several others as well—also figured in the debate in the 1930s over German rearmament, as can be seen from the recently published fifth volume of Martin Gilbert's excellent biography of Churchill. Looking back on the years when he was warning his countrymen—without great effect—against German rearmament, Churchill said in 1938: "Four years ago, when I asked that the airforce should be doubled and redoubled . . . Lord Samuel thought my judgment so defective that he likened me to a Malay running amok. It would have been well for him and his persecuted race if my advice had been taken. They would not be where they are now and we should not be where we are not." The task of playing Cassandra was a thankless one; there was not a day when Churchill was not accused of being a warmonger, a reckless man, utterly devoid of judgment, wanting to plunge his country into a holocaust, and this at a time (to quote the stock phrases used against him) when there was a real chance that Europe could free itself from the nightmare haunting it, and from an expenditure on arms that was beggaring it.

In retrospect, one can discern four distinct stages in public reaction to Churchill's constant warnings. In stage one (1933-34), it was claimed that the reports about German rearmament were grossly exaggerated or altogether untrue. In stage two (1935), it was admitted that Germany was investing vast resources in rearmament, but not that Germany was catching up with Britain. Some said that Germany was big but inefficient, others claimed that it was not as big as it looked, and others used both arguments at the same time. In stage three (1936-37), it was conceded that Germany had reached parity or had even overtaken Britain but it was also contended that such superiority was meaningless in military terms, that the specific geopolitical situation of Germany had to be taken into account (the need to "defend" itself against potential enemies in the West as well as in the East), and that there was no reason to assume that Germany wanted war. Eventually, the full extent of German superiority could no longer be denied, but it was precisely because the Germans were so much stronger that the counsels of appeasement prevailed in stage four. Survival, it was then said, had to be the overriding consideration, Britain would never be ready to fight in view of its vulnerable position, a "moribund people such as ours is not equipped to deal with a totalitarian state" (Lord Rothermere). Hence Chamberlain's policy of trying gradually to remove "hostility between nations until they felt they could disregard their weapons."

All this will sound eerily familiar to anyone who has followed the debate in America in recent years over Soviet military capabilities and intentions. The historical context changes, but the psychology of appeasement remains fairly constant. Nor is this psychology the monopoly of any one section of the political spectrum. The idea, for example, that determination in foreign policy and defense is part of right-wing ideology is historically mistaken; in the 1930s the leading appeasers in Britain and France were on the Right (though they were helped along by elements on the Left as well). Today appeasement is stronger on the Left, but again there is considerable support from the other side (i.e., right-wing isolationism). Appeasement, in any case, has a momentum and logic of its own, and once it has proceeded beyond a certain stage, it no longer matters whether the original inspiration came from the Left or the Right. There is the famous case of Marcel Deat, a leading French socialist, who persuaded himself that it was not worthwhile dying for Danzig and then became a leading collaborationist of the Nazis.

There is, of course, one basic difference between the 1930s and the situation today—which is that nuclear weapons have made a major war far less likely. The aggressors in the 1930s could hope for a quick and easy victory, but this is no longer so today (provided, of course, the West does not invite aggression by neglecting its defenses, both strategic and conventional). Hitler wanted war; the Soviet leaders do not. But precisely because the military issues are no longer that straightforward, confusion tends to be even more widespread than in the 1930s. Not only have the arguments and illusions of the 1930s returned in full force, but they have been compounded by others suitable to the nuclear age. Thus we hear it said that the Soviets are slow learners who have not as yet mastered the essentials of strategy in the nuclear age and are merely squandering money and resources on arms that cannot possibly give them a military or political advantage. Others in a more familiar spirit point to Russia's geopolitical situation and its feeling of insecurity because it has to defend itself on two fronts. Still others stress tradition and culture—the Russians have always been great believers in quantity.

It is useful to keep the historical parallels in mind at this moment when the pressure to sign another SALT treaty is becoming so strong. That pressure is coming from Washington as well as from Moscow. On the Soviet side, the policy has all along been to weaken the American position slowly and to avoid sudden shocks. Soviet leaders know from bitter experience that the U.S., once threatened or challenged, is still capable of gigantic efforts, such as happened after the launching of Sputnik-1 and on several other occasions. Hence the urgency with which Brezhnev—mindful of the growing realism in the U.S. over the Soviet build-up—now insists on the completion of the SALT talks. On the American side, some say that even a meaningless treaty is better than no treaty, or that this is the last chance before the moderate Brezhnev is succeeded by younger leaders believing in a winnable war. The logic is curious: after all, if such leaders should materialize, they would obviously not feel bound by agreements entered into by their predecessors. Those who warn that the race to control strategic arms is being lost admit that their own cures are "complex, messy, and unbearably difficult." But arrangements that are messy and unbearably difficult are usually also ineffective. In the short run there is no alternative to effective arms control but the threat to match every effort undertaken by the other side.

It was just such a threat, arising out of belated American dissatisfaction with SALT-1, that has now opened the prospect for a reduction in the number of nuclear warheads. But it would be wrong to hail this as a great breakthrough. For, again, it cannot be stressed too strongly that the "national technical means of verification," as they are called in SALT— i.e., satellite surveillance—are not altogether effective even with regard to old-style ICBM's let alone in determining whether or not qualitative improvements are being made in already existing weapons systems. They cannot detect dormant warheads on the surface of the earth, especially if these are located in an environment in which there is a great deal of electromagnetic radiation. They cannot look into caves or mines or under camouflaged structures in which missiles can be hidden. There is in fact an endless number of possible ways of concealing offensive missiles so long as they are not deployed in a conventional manner—that is, in large concrete silos with uncamouflaged steel lids. Thus a truly meaningful agreement would be feasible only by reverting to the old, seemingly impossible idea of on-site inspection.

Yet even if a marked reduction in strategic arms were achieved, it would still be necessary for the West to match the general Soviet military buildup. Even in a state of equality of nuclear weapons, the Soviet Union would retain overall superiority because of its stronger non-nuclear forces. Indeed, it was the mistaken Western notion of a "cheap" (i.e., strategic nuclear) defense which contributed to the arms race in the first place. What would be most desirable is a *general,* mutually balanced reduction of forces, but here again a really effective verification system would be needed.

Other aspects of détente offer only a somewhat more encouraging picture. Soviet-American trade, for instance, has considerably increased over the last five years, but the scope of these exchanges is quite limited. Although the volume of trade went up again in 1975, this was mainly owing to grain sales; U.S. purchases of Soviet goods actually decreased in 1976. Brezhnev has complained about American restrictive measures, saying that were it not for these, American businessmen could do $10-billion worth of business in the Soviet Union over the next five years. It has even been said that trade on this scale would provide work for three million Americans. These figures are a little suspect, however, as even the most superficial analysis will show. The Russians will in the future have to finance their trade by exporting a greater volume of machinery and equipment—something that will hardly create new jobs in the United States. In addition, overall Soviet foreign-trade targets for 1975-80 are quite low, and imply a growth rate less than half of that for 1971-75. The enormous deals allegedly made by the restrictionless Germans and Japanese, and missed out on by the Americans, are for the most part mythical. Germany is historically Russia's most important Western trade partner, but even so, Russia figures only in twelfth or thirteenth place among Germany's customers—just as it did five, ten, and twenty years ago. In 1976 Germany's trade with Russia actually fell from 3.2 percent to 2.7 percent, and there may be further decline this year. Nor have there been any spectacular deals with Japan.

In 1975 and again in 1976 the USSR sustained a big hard-currency trade deficit with the West (about $6 billion each year). Soviet purchases in the West have been made possibly only by large extensions of credit on the part of Western governments and banks, and the total indebtedness of the Soviet bloc now amounts to nearly $40 billion. The international bankers are not worried—they cannot afford to be, for the climate of confidence has to be maintained at almost any price, with unpaid debts rolled over, renegotiated, or stretched out—but they have become far more cautious with regard to further loans. The credit rating of some

East European countries has also taken a plunge: Poland, Rumania, and Bulgaria can no longer receive cheap loans (Polish debts to the West are now close to $10 billion).

The prospects of American trade with the Soviet Union are summarized in a detailed 800-page study by the Joint Economic Committee of the Congress (October 1976): "Although the USSR remains an excellent credit risk in the eyes of Western bankers, heavy Soviet borrowing in 1975 may have constrained Moscow's ability to borrow as heavily in the Eurocurrency market this year. At a minimum it appears that the USSR will have to pay higher interest rates and management fees. . . ." The honeymoon, in short, is over, and it was not a wild orgy to begin with. According to *Tass,* the Soviet news agency, the enemies of détente wish to use foreign trade debts to restrain trade with the Soviet bloc. Such complaints must be a source of confusion to Soviet newspaper readers who are told daily that the Eastern-bloc economies go from strength to strength while Western economies are on the edge of the abyss.

Then there is the question of technology transfer. It is now generally accepted that Western firms have been selling technology too cheaply; even Samuel Pisar, the leading advocate of East-West trade, has written that he feels saddened by the tendency of some American businessmen to go after any profitable deal without regard to the national interest. It may well be that, as some Western economist maintain, the overall impact of American technology on the Soviet economy has not been as extensive as it has been thought to be, partly because it is limited to a few industries, and also because the Soviet system is not elastic enough to derive the maximum benefit from new technologies. But this cannot be laid at the door of Soviet-Western relations.

Which brings us to the politics of détente. The great expectations prevailing in 1971-72 have on the whole given way to a more realistic assessment. But there are still certain misconceptions with regard to what Soviet leaders have in mind when they talk about peaceful coexistence *and* the "need to continue the ideological struggle." If this merely referred to speeches and articles about the incurable ills of Western societies and the superiority of the Soviet system, Western leaders would be entitled to ignore such ritual professions of faith as matters of little consequence. What has been insufficiently understood after all these years is the simple fact that "ideological struggle" has nothing to do with philosophy but a great deal to do with a political offensive which may on occasion, as in Angola, be reinforced by military intervention. This struggle will go on in many parts of the globe, the Helsinki conference notwithstanding. Within the immediate sphere of Soviet influence, Rumania has more or less caved in under pressure, and the Yugoslavs are once again uneasy about their future. Over the last year tensions have increased between the two Germanies—traditionally an accurate barometer of the state of détente.

It would be wrong, however, to accuse the Soviet Union of not having lived up to its promises; the Russian leaders have never promised to "freeze" the global balance of power, nor have they ever said that they would not make the most of Western weaknesses and indecision. The problem is not whether the Soviet leaders have been lying (as President Carter wanted to know in his early briefings); the problem is that Western leaders have not made a sufficient effort to understand the psychology and political thinking of the leaders in the Kremlin, let alone to act accordingly.

This applies to the use that has been made of the issue of human rights as well as to every other aspect of détente. Thus, the Carter administration came into office making strong statements of support for dissidents in Czechoslovakia and the Soviet Union (including Andrei Sakharov), but it has stopped well short of threatening to impose any serious consequences on the Russians for violations of the human-rights provisions of the Helsinki agreement. The fact is, however, that in the Soviet Union and East Germany, in Poland and in Czechoslovakia, those advocating human rights are treated more harshly now than at any time in the past decade. Statements of concern on the part of Western governments may alleviate hardship in individual cases, but unless they are made an inextricable part of a larger policy they are most unlikely to affect the general drift of events.

The Soviet deployment of new weapons systems and the appearance of a strong new Soviet fleet are ominous signs, but they are not the cause of the recent Western retreat. For the latter one must look to such factors as the economic depression of the early 1970s, the divisive trends in the Western alliance, and the radicalization of some Third World countries. But it is the internal American crisis—the loss of self-confidence and the political paralysis entailed by this loss—which has been the most important factor. If there are now some signs of a recovery of spirit, a great deal of ground has still to be covered as a precondition for coping with international problems that have been neglected for too long.

More than anything else, this applies to the economic situation. The social and political consequences of the recession of 1974-75 are still felt, and there is the danger of a new downturn in 1978-79. The recovery of the world economy has been hesitant and uneven; the British and Italian economies are still in the doldrums and for France, according to all forecasts, 1977 will be a bad year. Inflation has gone down, but not sufficiently, and unemployment in the West in only twenty percent lower than at the height of the recession. Protectionist pressures are still strong (since most nations depend on export earnings more than ever before) and these pressures threaten world trade. Above all, there is the great monetary disorder, caused largely by the growth of the market in petro-dollars and the general indebtedness. There is far too much liquidity, with international bankers offering loans to all who want them and to many who do not. The accumulated debt of the poorer nations now amounts to some $170-200 billion. Perhaps half of this sum has been lent by private banks, with Brazil, Mexico, and South Korea among the main debtors. To this must be added the growing deficits of Britain, Italy, and some of the minor European countries. The pressure for "rescheduling" is growing in many parts of the globe. If, as is likely, growth in 1977 is slower than in 1976, some major nations may ask for a debt moratorium and this could lead to the collapse of leading banks and to a new reces-sion.

Coming summit meetings will be devoted to economic problems, with various rescue operations high on the agenda. The possible political con-sequences are, of course, the most worrisome aspect. While conditions vary from country to country, a policy of austerity will be unavoidable and this, according to past experience, will involve decisions that are not at all easy to make in democratic societies. There is the danger of grow-ing political polarization; whether the swing will be to the Right or to the Left depends on local conditions, and where democratic institutions are not deeply rooted or no longer function effectively, they may be replaced by authoritarian structures.

Still, the stabilization of the international currency system, however difficult, may not be beyond human ingenuity, and there is at least a chance that the ailing economies of Western Europe will eventually recover. Infinitely more difficult will be the task of improving relations between the industrialized countries of the Third World. For it is pre-cisely in the underdeveloped countries that the position of the West has deteriorated most over the last decade.

It has been said that a change in these relations can be expected only if the West accepts the new economic world order proposed by countries of Asia, Africa, and Latin America, or at the very least if new and more beneficial agreements on the terms of trade can be concluded. Such agreements should indeed be explored, but there is no room for illusions with regard to the political consequences. The experience of the Soviet Union should be pondered in this context. If the position of the Soviet bloc has grown stronger in the Third World, it is not because the Com-munists have provided more aid than the West—they have provided much less—or because they have offered better trading terms or modern technology. On the contrary, they have flatly refused to accept respon-sibility for the economic plight of the poor countries. What is perhaps even more important, they have all along limited their trade with the producers of raw materials. The Soviet Union is perhaps not greatly admired in the Third World, but it is respected and sometimes feared, much in contrast to the West, and the reason is that the growth of its military strength has not passed unnoticed. Third World leaders will not engage in campaigns to vilification against the Communist bloc because they fear that they cannot do so with impunity. There is no such fear with regard to the West.

Western relations with the underdeveloped countries are exceedingly complex because political, economic, and humanitarian considerations not only do not coincide but frequently clash. Politically, relations with the Third World could improve if the causes of tension were faced up to: this, however, might well mean a reduction in imports from these countries, which would remove the ground for complaints about exploitation and "neo-imperialism." Although costly in economic terms, such a move would be politically far more effective than any changes likely to be made in the terms of trade. There is in any case no objective standard of a "fair price" for raw materials; an increase of one hundred percent in the price of oil can be as easily justified as an increase of ten percent.

This is not to say that the terms of trade should not be renegotiated; they will have to be. But the process promises to be a long drawn-out one that may well create new tensions in place of the old. Some of the exporting nations believe not in interdependence but in a strategy of minimum cooperation and maximum confrontation; since almost all of them are dictatorships whose very legitimacy is based on an aggressive stance, the more radical members in a cartel are likely to prevail more often than not over the more moderate ones. On humanitarian grounds a good case can be made for a massive, ongoing, Red Cross-type effort for the very poorest countries. But this again would do little to satisfy the demands of the raw-material-producing nations, and the motives behind such a strategy would almost certainly be misrepresented, with America being seen to accept the historical responsibility for the plight of the very poor.

In the struggle for influence in the Third World the West faces handicaps that cannot presently be overcome. There is envy because Western societies with all their difficulties are infinitely richer than those of the Third World, and there is also a greater instinctive affinity between Third World autocrats and Eastern bloc dictators. The picture, nevertheless, is not all bleak. The anti-Western group in the UN, UNCTAD, and elsewhere consists on an alliance between the relatively rich producers of oil and some other strategic materials and the poor countries of Asia and Africa. This *ad hoc* alliance is largely based on the expectation that OPEC will obtain for the least developed nations massive financial support from the West and Japan, and also to a certain extent on racial or ideological solidarity. But as time passes and the oil producers grow richer, and as it emerges that their contribution to the welfare of the least developed nations is negligible, this alliance will falter and break—provided, of course, the West does not allow OPEC to claim credit for Western aid to the poor nations.

In a paradoxical way, the present weakness of the West in the Third World may even be a potential source of strength. As Soviet military muscles are flexed through intervention-by-proxy, Angola-style, some Third World countries may begin to feel threatened. There are Russian "parties" in almost all Third World countries but there is no "American party." Consequently (as even the Indian example has recently shown), the incumbents, especially if their country is located near the Soviet border, are bound to fear the Communists more than the multinational corporations—the latter can easily be nationalized or expelled, but the former are dangerous rivals for power. The Third World has never been a monolithic bloc, and as Soviet influence grows and the differences between the haves and the have-nots increase, there may be startling political realignments favoring the West but quite irrespective of Western initiatives.

There has been no mention of the specific problems of Central and South America, which are the problems neither of the Third World nor of the industrialized countries. It is certain, however, that they will preoccupy the United States in the years to come more than ever before. And finally there is Europe with its multiple economic and political crises, and its stalled movement toward greater unity. Of the governments of the European community only the one in Luxemburg can confidently assume that it will last the year. The French government is in grave trouble and the German coalition may fall apart; the fact that the opposition in each country is also in disarray cannot be of much comfort. Sweden, Norway, and Austria are relatively stable, to be sure, and in Portugal the worst has so far not happened; there is even a chance that Spain—despite the recent turmoil—will transform itself into a democracy of sorts without too much violence. But given the overall precariousness of the European situation, these rays of hope are not sufficient by themselves to inspire confidence.

Most European countries may indeed overcome their present political and economic difficulties; the problem is that one or two of them may not, and this would have incalculable consequences for the future of democratic institutions and of the Atlantic alliance. Ever since World War II, Western Europe has been dealing with the Soviet block from a position of weakness; if this had not been the case, there would have been no need for an American nuclear umbrella and the stationing of U.S. troops in Europe. The eclipse of even one major European country would at the very least deepen the imbalance on the continent, and the consequences could well be more far-reaching still.

In this connection one should view with skepticism Cyrus Vance's pronouncement that the participation of Communists in West European governments would upset Soviet relations with Eastern Europe more than it would upset the Western alliance. This idea seems to be based on the indisputable historical fact that the wider Communism spreads, the less unity there is in the Communist camp. To take the reasoning one step further, if Communism were to prevail in the United States, the result might well be unfortunate for the Soviet Union, for a Communist America would almost inevitably clash with Russia in the same way that China and other Communist countries have done, and would in many ways be a stronger and more dangerous rival than the present United States, hampered as it is by liberal inhibitions concerning the use of political and military power. But such a perspective is hardly reassuring if the aim is world peace, nor does it hold much comfort for the future of freedom and other such values. Eurocommunism does indeed pose problems for the Soviet Union, but the problems it poses for the West are likely to be much the more intractable.

This is not to say that the Soviet Union, or the Communist bloc as a whole, will not have real troubles of its own in the coming years. Inside the Soviet Union, succession may not proceed as smoothly as expected, and in a longer-term perspective the question of the nationalities, with the higher birth rate of the non-Russians, has potentially explosive aspects. A lasting reconciliation between the Soviet Union and China seems only a remote possibility. The Soviet position in Eastern Europe is far from "crumbling," as some oversanguine observers have announced, but the Russians certainly will have to pay close attention to sources of friction in that part of their empire. This is partly due to the desire of these countries to attain a greater measure of independence, and partly to economic pressures. For Eastern Europe too has gone through a revolution of material expectations, and at the same time has been severely hit by the recession. Still, modern-style dictatorships find it relatively easy to cope with crisis in the short run. The Soviet bloc may be handicapped or even partly paralyzed by internal convulsions in the years to come, but it would be unwise to bank on this.

New administrations always promise both to be different and to improve on the performance of their predecessors. If President Carter's own experience has not been in the field of foreign policy, the new Secretary of State, Cyrus Vance, has a reputation as an excellent international negotiator; the new Secretary of Defense, Harold Brown, has specialized in arms systems on the one hand and in arms control on the other; and Zbigniew Brzezinski, the adviser on national security, has been hailed by the press as a brilliant conceptualizer.

The new administration-will also have the benefit of advice from that segment of the foreign-policy establishment which was in opposition under the Republicans. Recent years have seen an outpouring of books, articles, and summaries of conferences held by this segment of the establishment, all offering alternative choices and strategies for American foreign policy. As some of the main authors of these alternative choices will now be in the seats of power, and as others may exercise indirect influence, it will be instructive to see which of their blueprints will be followed by the new administration.

Fewer, no doubt, than some hope and others fear, for it is one of the laws of foreign policy-making that the number of available options and the room for freedom of choice are usually even more limited than in domestic affairs. The conduct of foreign policy largely depends on the attitudes and behavior of the other players, not to mention the contingencies that may arise at any moment. In the seclusion of a university or the offices of a foundation, abstract new world orders and systems can be produced almost at will; the view from the seventh floor of the State Department (or the first floor of the Pentagon) is more restricted. Thus President Carter's new foreign-policy-makers may avoid some of the errors that were committed in the past, but they cannot pick and choose the problems with which they are going to deal.

Since Brzezinski has for many years been a leading student of world affairs, his writings over the last decade or two will be scrutinized as closely as those of Henry Kissinger once were (even though it is still not certain that his ideas will prevail in White House councils). An investigation of this kind will reveal a searching, imaginative mind but also a certain pattern of overconfidence. This refers, for instance, to his belief voiced in the 1960s, that in view of recent technological developments the position of the United States was bound to become stronger in the world, that socioeconomic reforms in the Soviet Union would lead to political reform there, and that the 1970s would witness the spread to the Soviet Union of the sorts of convulsions that Spain, Yugoslavia, Mexico, and Poland began to undergo in the late 1960s. The same pattern of imaginative overconfidence can be seen in Brzezinski's predictions concerning the far-reaching political and social effects of the new "technetronic" age, a term coined by him.

To recall such misjudgments is partly unfair, if only because Brzezinski was dealing with the shape of things to come, and it is infinitely more difficult to be right about the future than about the past. Furthermore, it is to Brzezinski's credit that at a time when transnational systems of interdependence were being offered at a dime a dozen, he drew attention to the danger of international anarchy. Brzezinski saw correctly that as far as the Soviet Union was concerned, a greater capacity for involvement in the world's trouble spots would stimulate a greater temptation to *become* involved. He also saw that the fact that the conflict between the two superpowers has become more complex in recent years does not necessarily make it any the less dangerous. Above all, if somewhat belatedly, he saw that (technetronics aside) America now finds itself facing a hostile world, at a time when its power remains central as never before to global stability and progress.[3] Even in his more adventurous moments, Brzezinski has never forgotten that power is still a factor of some importance in world affairs; the clash between this perception of his and dreams of an "emerging global consciousness" worked out by some of his colleagues is no doubt what has led to his reputation in some circles as a hawk.

But what are the policies likely to be proposed by the new national-security adviser? In his most recent essay Brzezinski has suggested that the U.S. should not support white supremacy in South Africa, should not be indifferent to the desire for greater social justice and national dignity in Central America, and should not take a cynical view of those countries of Eastern Europe that seek to enlarge their national independence. These are unexceptionable ideas, though honesty (rather than cynicism) should oblige one to admit that America will be able to offer nothing more substantial than sympathy to countries like Poland and Rumania.

In the same essay Brzezinski urges that the U.S. become cooperatively engaged with the "rising global egalitarian passions." Since most countries are ruled by dictators, a confrontation between freedom and despotism is to be avoided in favor of an attempt to accommodate the pressures for reform of existing international arrangements, in the hope that this will lessen radical passions. This view of the world scene, however, is only partly valid. "Egalitarianism" is just one of the motive forces underlying anti-Americanism, and frequently not the most important one. The inequities of the world, especially the unequal distribution of resources, cannot be seriously affected so long as nation-states, anxiously preserving their sovereignty, continue to exist. Expressions of sympathy by American leaders and trebling (or quadrupling) the amount of help to poor nations will perhaps do no harm (though even that is by no means certain), but their political effect cannot be expected to be great, either in the short run or in the long long.

Speculation about the shape American foreign policy is likely to take under the new administration is admittedly risky. An inevitable learning process must occur as statesmen and advisers adjust to the world as it is (rather than as they would wish it to be), and qualities hitherto latent may surface in unexpected ways. So far, however, from the President down, a certain alarming confusion has seemed to prevail, along with the rote continuation of old policies in new rhetoric. Early pronouncements show no sign that the administration has registered the extent to which the American position in the world has deteriorated, or the problems that this entails. Instead, there has been much sermonizing about the need for openness in the policy-making process and about the role of morality in the conduct of foreign relations. But how to combine the wish for détente, for example, with an insistence on human rights—unless one is ready to make some clear connection between progress on the one front and progress on the other, something President Carter has eschewed? Already a double standard is appearing: one for the Soviet Union and its allies, another, harsher one for the Chiles and Rhodesias of this world. In the field of nuclear disarmament, to take another example, everyone in the new administration has gone enthusiastically on record in favor of "progress," but what is the value of agreements hastily concluded mainly for the sake of "movement" if such agreements will weaken the United States and its allies without making the world a safer place than at present?

Rhetorical emphases aside, it would seem that the sum total of the new departures in foreign policy by the Carter administration can be expected to be modest. Which brings us back to where we began—to the great question of the qualities needed to face a surfeit of critical problems in a largely hostile world. Moderation, friendly gestures, negotiations in a reasonable and constructive spirit are always useful; in some instances a case can even be made for gimmicks. Still, however useful these qualities are when the going is good, at a time of danger they do not suffice. Nor can the answer be found in revolutionary new ideas or hitherto undiscovered conceptual breakthroughs. Every self-respecting political scientist has a concept for a new world order; some, for variety's sake, have offered several. What is required at a time of danger is not one new concept or several new concepts but leadership—strong leadership.

Leadership does not mean hegemony or "indiscriminate interventionism"; there is something farcical in the current invocation of these perils in view of the weakness of the American position. Leadership means clarity of vision and the vigor needed in a struggle for survival. America still is the senior partner in the Western alliance. If it does not supply the proper kind of leadership, the chances of the other partners cannot be rated high, nor, in the long run, can the prospects for world peace and for the continued existence of democratic institutions in the United States itself.

*March 1977*

## NOTES

1. The phrase occurs in Paul Doty, Albert Carnesale, and Michael Nacht, "The Race to Control Nuclear Arms," *Foreign Affairs,* October 1976.
2. Soviet spokesmen have vehemently denied all reports of a military build-up. Thus, most recently, Mikhail Lvov in *Novoye Vremya* 3, 1977: "The share of military spending in the Soviet budget is decreasing year by year. So is the amount in absolute terms." The problem with statements of this kind is that Mikhail Lvov has not the faintest idea what the Soviet military budget is, because even trustworthy party workers are not burdened with sensitive information of this kind. To reinforce his claim, Lvov quotes Brezhnev's speech at the last plenary meeting of the Communist party Central Committee. Unfortunately, Brezhnev's was more cautious in his remarks than his commentator. He simply said: "The amount spent by the Soviet Union on defense is exactly as much as is needed to insure the security of the Soviet Union and the joint defense by the fraternal countries of the gains of socialism. . . ."
3. "America in a Hostile World," *Foreign Policy,* Summer 1976.

# The Issue of Human Rights

On June 15, 1977, in Belgrade, representatives from the thirty-five signatory countries of the Helsinki pact will assemble to review the progress achieved since the final act of that agreement was signed in 1975. Helsinki established the principle that the treatment accorded the citizens of any signatory country is a matter with which any other signatory country may rightfully concern itself. At Belgrade, the Soviet Union, whose record in the area of human rights is notorious, will no doubt voice strong resentment against excesses of "concern" on the part of other signatories, principally the United States, and will protest against unwarranted American interference in Soviet internal affairs. The Russians will want to concentrate at Belgrade on the promotion of trade relations and transfers of technology—anything, in fact, but human rights. What the United States, which has made human rights a major issue, and the other Western nations will do is uncertain. If Belgrade represents a test for the Soviet Union, it represents an even greater challenge to the United States, the first of many still to come.

Human rights as an idea, as an issue in religious, political, and moral philosophy, has an ancient and illustrious pedigree; the differences between the empirical and the normative foundations of human rights, between moral rights and legal rights, between group rights and individual rights—each of these topics has been the occasion of substantial intellectual disquisition. The English Bill of Rights, and more emphatically the American Declaration of Independence and the French Declaration of the Rights of Man, were all based on the idea of inalienable, indefeasible, and absolute rights. Later, Jeremy Bentham and others were to argue, to the contrary, that there were no such rights, that the idea of natural rights was rhetorical nonsense—"nonsense upon stilts." In our time some philosophers have gone even further, claiming that the whole idea of human rights is a recent invention, alien to most non-Western cultures, and that it has been foisted by the neo-colonialist West on a more or less unwilling world.

This last position if far-fetched. Even if there were no explicit covenants to that effect in ancient Chinese or Indian culture, the idea of freedom was hardly alien to those civilizations. And as for today, were it not for the concepts of individual and group rights, the countries of the non-Western world would still be colonies. Moreover, while the distinction between (positive) law and morality has its uses in philosophy, it is safe to say that neither Bentham nor his latter-day disciples would have preferred to live under arbitrary or tyrannical government, to be arrested and tried without due process, to be tortured, maimed, or killed, to be deprived of property or sold into slavery—even if such practices were in conformity with the law of the land.

Advocates of natural rights may admittedly have had a somewhat simplistic concept of human nature, and have failed to make due allowance for the fact that political and social conditions vary from age to age and from country to country, but even so it is difficult to make a convincing case for torture and slavery. Even those purists who once argued that international law is not concerned with personal liberty have had to confront the international conventions against slavery. It is, in fact, the theory of absolute nonintervention to protect human rights that is nonsense upon stilts. Cases of such intervention have been common ever since Gelon, Prince of Syracuse, having defeated Carthage in the year 480 B.C., made it a condition of peace that the Carthaginians abandon their time-honored custom of sacrificing their children to Saturn.

In recent decades there has been a palpable shift in interpretations of international law, a shift in favor of the idea of universal human rights; few still maintain that international law concerns states alone.[1] Though the Covenant of the League of Nations did not address itself to the issue of human rights (other than the protection of certain minorities) but rather to the pacific settlement of disputes, a new approach manifested itself in the Atlantic Charter of 1941, the Declaration of the United Nations the year after, and in countless speeches of wartime leaders. This new approach found expression in the United Nations Charter and more specifically in the Universal Declaration of Human Rights, approved without a dissenting voice in December 1948. The President of the General Assembly said at the time that this was the first occasion on which the organized world community had recognized the existence of human rights and fundamental freedoms transcending the laws of sovereign states, and "millions of men, women, and children all over the world, many miles from Paris and New York, will turn for help, guidance, and inspiration to this document."

Almost three decades have passed since these words were spoken, but while millions of men and women have indeed turned for inspiration to the Universal Declaration of Human Rights, they have received precious little guidance and no help from the organization that propaged it. In fact, the declaration was flawed from the very beginning: it did not include provisions for the rights of ethnic, linguistic, and religious minorities. More important, the stipulation made in the early drafts for the right of individuals to petition the UN was deleted later on at the insistence, among others, of the United States, which believed that such a right of petition would be abused by cranks. This was a giant step backward to the old idea that international law is concerned only with relations among states, and it has enabled the UN to refuse even to acknowledge receipt of complaints by persecuted individuals such as Soviet dissidents.

Another major problem with the declaration is the question of how its provisions are to be squared with Article 2, Paragraph 7 of the UN Charter, according to which the UN is enjoined from intervening in matters which are essentially within the domestic jurisdiction of individual states. Member states switch their views on this issue as it suits them from one day to the next. When, for instance, early on in the history of the UN, India complained about racial discrimination in South Africa, the Russians argued that the issue was entirely within the competence of the UN to decide. But when Poland, or Hungary, or the Soviet Union itself has been challenged for violation of human rights, it has naturally claimed that the Commission on Human Rights (established in 1946) has no power to take action.

Since the late 1950s the debates on human rights have been increasingly dominated by a stress on economic and social as opposed to civil and political rights. This reflects the changed composition of the United Nations itself. As the Communist and Third World countries have gradually become a majority, they have insisted that economic and social rights must be attained before any other rights can even be discussed. Some have contended that civil rights might even have to be sacrificed (temporarily, of course) in order to build the economic and social foundation on which they are allegedly based. The countries promoting such views have invariably been those with the worst record on human rights.

Political and civil rights defend the citizen against arbitrary action on the part of the state; economic and social rights, to the contrary, are based on positive state action. One illustration should suffice to point up the difference: Article 7 of the International Covenant on Civil and Political Rights states that "no one shall be subjected to torture or to cruel, inhuman, or degrading treatment or punishment." This is an absolute right which can and should be universally enforced today. Article 7 of the International Covenant on Economic, Social, and Cultural Rights, on the other hand, imposes on every country the duty to grant its citizens periodic holidays with pay and remuneration for public holidays. This right cannot be universally enforced at the present time since, among other reasons, many countries do not have the resources. Moral considerations aside, it is quite clear that a law that cannot be enforced is not a law but an aspiration. But in any event, the idea that remuneration for public holidays, however laudable *per se,* should take precedence over the ban of torture, makes nonsense of the whole concept of human rights.

It is true that in a wider perspective economic and social aspirations and civil and political rights are not mutually exclusive but interdependent and supportive of each other. But they are not in the same category, and the attempt to equate universal moral rights that need to be observed here and now with the introduction of social services is simply part of the endeavor to belittle the importance of human rights, to reduce them from the level of inalienable human requirements to the level of ideals that might, or might not, be achieved at some future date. Giving priority to economic and social rights does not reflect a different political outlook, but is usually merely an alibi for states that practice oppression at home, and whose record even in the economic and social field is anything but brilliant. Among the loudest proponents of the primacy of social and economic rights there is not a single one that permits the existence of free trade unions—a principle enshrined in Article 8 of the covenant.

This is not to say that there must be in every single respect one universal standard for the most developed countries and the most backward ones; the protection of human rights has to be judged in the cultural, social, and economic context of societies in different stages of development. But it is pernicious nonsense to argue that under a certain range of per-capita income (say $500), human rights have to be dispensed with because only tyrannical regimes will be in a position "to mobilize the masses in order to attain food, shelter, and health care" (to quote Charles Yost). This argument is not only morally wrong, it is historically wrong; the per-capita income at the time of the French Revolution (not to mention the time of Magna Carter) was substantially lower than it is now in most countries whose governments claim that basic human rights can be dispensed with. Most of these dictatorships, furthermore, have not the slightest wish to "mobilize" their masses; nor is it readily obvious in what way torture and slavery will make for more effective health care. Except to the extent that slaves with a full stomach are better off than slaves with an empty stomach, the idea that full economic and social rights can be enjoyed by people who do not possess civil and political rights is a deliberate falsehood. Recent events in India have shown that illiterate peasants are better judges of what is good for them than some of their well-wishers in the West.

The real problem is that in most member states of the UN, elementary civil liberties do not exist, and, more important still, there has been little if any progress in that direction. In theory such states subscribe to principles of human freedom and civil liberties as outlined in the United Nations conventions and their own constitutions, but too often in reality the practice is oppression, persecution, and the violation of basic human rights. A new unholy alliance has come into being at the United Nations, one that has a vested interest in the denial, not the promotion, of human rights, and one that shows a great deal of solidarity in pursuit of that interest.

The meetings of the Human Rights Commission, for example, have become a farce: though appearances are still maintained, though lofty ideals are invoked, and though there is much talk about solemn obligations and human solidarity, in actual fact there is not the slightest chance of any resolution being passed that runs counter to the will of the anti-human-rights majority. Western delegates continue to participate in this farce, and from time to time they even claim to discover some grounds for hope. Thus, commenting on the last session, Allard K. Lowenstein, the U.S. delegate, said that it was "far more balanced" than previously and that "new ground was broken"—this, about a session which was not even willing to sponsor an international investigation into the situation in Uganda.

On top of everything else, the Human Rights Commission is a totally irrelevant institution. It publications are not read, its resolutions are scarcely noticed, and it makes headlines only in the case of some specific outrageous statement or resolution. But it is unfortunately true that the continued presence of delegates from countries *cherishing* human rights conveys legitimacy to an institution which deserves to be regarded as a laughingstock and a public menace. Unless they use every opportunity to speak out in the strongest possible way against the dishonesty of the commission— to counterattack constantly, castigating mercilessly the prevailing mendacity, and holding up to ridicule the whole humbug— Western representatives become accessories to the general perversion. Yet to hope for such words and actions on the part of Western diplomats seems somewhat unrealistic. They are expected to react coolly and considerately, in measured and temperate language; when they stray from those canons, as Daniel P. Moynihan and Leonard Garment did, they are upbraided for eccentricity and breach of dignity.

The old League of Nations showed weakness and cowardice, but even in its worst moments it never reached the depths of degradation achieved by the United Nations. Western representatives on the Human Rights Commission and other such bodies say in mitigation that they have succeeded in preventing even worse outrages. This does not change the fact that by playing the evil game and adhering to the perverted rules, they confer respectability on institutions whose main function is to prevent the implementation of human rights, and to justify their suppression.

The failure of the United Nations to live up to early expectations and to become an effective instrument for the promotion of human rights has induced individual governments and non-governmental bodies to take fresh initiatives in the area. In 1948 the Organization of American States passed a declaration on the rights and duties of man which has, however, largely remained a dead letter. The Council of Europe agreed on a covenant for the protection of human rights and fundamental freedoms, and established a European Commission for Human Rights as well as a European Court of Human Rights in Strasbourg which has heard many cases since it first met in 1960. But these activities concern only Europe, meaning those societies least in need of human-rights protection. Various private bodies, such as the International League for Human Rights, Freedom House, and Amnesty International, have published reports about the condition of unfreedom in various parts of the world, drawing attention to particularly flagrant violations and on occasion mobilizing public support to bring pressure on the governments concerned. But the scope of these activities and their impact are by necessity limited.

It is only in recent months and years, when public opinion in the United States and elsewhere has begun to press for new initiatives, that human rights have become a major issue in international politics. That the Soviet-bloc nations and repressive regimes generally have reacted angrily to the new initiative is not surprising, but there has been opposition also from other quarters that are disturbed by what they regard as the unwarranted intrusion of this issue into the normal political process.

To be sure, the concern shown in some quarters over the allegedly harmful effects of the emphasis on human rights was to some extent predictable. Although it has been quite fashionable in recent years to invoke human righs, enthusiasm for the cause has been rather selective in character. Some of those expressing unhappiness about conditions in the Soviet Union and Czechoslovakia or even Cuba have obviously regarded the situation in Uruguay, Chile, Iran, and South Korea as far more serious; they protest, from time to time, the arrest of a Soviet dissenter, but one feels their main passions lie elsewhere. Then there are the fair-weather protagonists of human rights, those who hold freedom's banner high so long as storms are not blowing. It is not that such people do not care about human rights, but they certainly do not like the risks involved and are bitterly opposed to any linking of this particular struggle with other political issues. There is less to be said in favor of a position of this kind—a position which reduces human rights to a matter of public relations—than for the candor of the neo-isolationists who, while they regret the violation of human rights in foreign parts, believe it is wrong to interfere in behalf of abstract ideas.

The arguments put forward against an aggressive stand on human rights have varied. There have been warnings that such initiatives will create new international tensions and perhaps a new "ice age" (as one commentator put it). It is said that the Carter administration in particular has gone too far and too fast, that quiet diplomacy can achieve more substantial results, and that speaking up will only cause greater repression in the countries singled out for attention. It is also claimed that since the United States does not have clean hands, it is not in any position to criticize others. The specter has been invoked of a new militant anti-Communism, precisely the sort of crusade that led the U.S. into disaster in the past. (Moral indignation, Arthur M. Schlesinger, Jr., has said in this connection, quoting his fellow historian, Herbert Butterfield, is corrupting; should we take it that Schlesinger himself was corrupted by his indignation over Richard Nixon?) Above all, it is maintained that undue emphasis on human rights will (and perhaps already has, as witness the breakdown of the Moscow talks last month) adversely affect arms control efforts, which are an overriding concern if the human race is to survive.

Most of these arguments are simply spurious. There is no danger that too strong an emphasis on human rights will "provoke international ideological warfare on a global scale"; the Soviet Union has never *stopped* conducting ideological warfare and has made it abundantly clear that it considers such warfare akin to a categorical imperative, détente or no détente. And if Brezhnev has not hesitated to receive Marchais, Berlinguer, and Gus Hall in Moscow, why should Western presidents refuse to see leading Soviet dissenters?

As to the dangers of causing greater repression by speaking out, Marshall Shulman, who now advises the Secretary of State on Soviet affairs, has written in *Foreign Affairs* that any easing of repression within Soviet society is more likely to result from internal evolutionary forces than from external demands for change. He does not deny individuals and groups in the West the right to express their repugnance for violations of human rights, but for governments to do so is, he contends, clearly counterproductive. Soviet dissenters, notably Andrei Sakharov, disagree with Professor Shulman. As Sakharov has said: "Resolute and ever-growing pressure by public and official bodies of the West—up to the highest—the defense of principles and of specific people can only bring positive results. Every case of human-rights violation must become a political problem for the leaders of the culprit countries."

Professor Shulman's notion of an "easing of repression" as the result of a relaxation of tension is, moreover, not borne out by the historical record. Surveying the history of détente and the democratic movement in the USSR, Frederick C. Barghoorn reaches the conclusion that the hey-day of the democratic movement was in the 1960s, and "with the blossoming of what was in the West hailed as détente Moscow was more than ever determined to crush dissent" *(Detente and the Democratic Movement in the USSR)*. Professor Shulman might counter that his own argument holds true over the long run, but this optimism is shared by few experts inside or outside the Soviet Union. Sakharov wrote in 1968, and again in 1975, that détente unaccompanied by increased trust and democratization was a danger, not a blessing, that rapprochement without democratization inside the USSR was worse than no rapprochement at all. The world, according to Sakharov, faced two alternatives: "either the gradual convergence of the two superpowers, accompanied by democratization inside the Soviet Union, or increased confrontation with a growing danger of thermonuclear war." He subsequently envisaged a third alternative—"the capitulation of the democratic principle in the face of blackmail, deceit, and violence." These are harsh words, bound to irritate Western diplomats trying not to make controversial or polemical statements. Perhaps Sakharov is not well informed about Soviet affairs; or has he too been corrupted by an excess of moral indignation?

A more weighty case against the emphasis on human rights in foreign policy has been made by the believers in *Realpolitik* who argue that, given the global balance of power, the United States is simply no longer strong enough to promote human freedom among its chief adversaries and certainly cannot afford to antagonize its allies on this score. Sooner or later, this school holds, the human-rights campaign is bound to become muted or highly selective in its targets, or both. The exponents of *Realpolitik* do not doubt the commitment of President Carter to the cause of human rights, but they know that this concern is by no means shared in equal measure by all his collaborators and advisers, and they reason that the administration's desire to reach an accommodation with the Russians will in the end prevail over other considerations (provided the Russians refrain from open provocations). In the face of Soviet charges of interference, American denunciations of Soviet infringements of human rights will become more "tactful" (as proposed by Brezhnev himself), and will focus on individual dissenters rather than on the enforced silence of the great majority. Thus there will be no sudden backdown by the Democratic administration but a gradual "slump in idealism" which will eventually affect the American posture not only toward the Soviet Union but toward other countries as well. Although human rights will still be invoked from time to time as an abstract and unfortunately distant ideal, it will no longer be a consideration directly impinging on foreign policy. This to all practical purposes will be the end of a great departure announced with so much fanfare and accompanied by so much enthusiasm.

While these fears may be quite real, it must be said that the skepticism of the proponents of *Realpolitik* is based at least in part of a misconception. The struggle for human rights in present conditions is not a lofty and impractical endeavor, divorced from the harsh realities of world affairs, but itself a kind of *Realpolitik,* one with a direct bearing on international security. This was clearly recognized by Secretary of State George Marshall in a famous speech at the opening of the UN General Assembly in Paris in 1948:

> Systematic and deliberate denials of basic human rights lie at the root of most of our troubles and threaten the work of the United Nations. It is not only fundamentally wrong that millions of men and women live in daily terror, subject to seizure, imprisonment, and forced labor without just cause and without fair trial, but these wrongs have repercussions in the community of nations. Governments which systematically disregard the rights of their own people are not likely to respect the rights of other nations and other people and are likely to seek their objectives by coercion and force in the international field.

These fears were amply justified at the time, and in the three decades that have passed since they were first expressed, the dilemma has become even more pressing. It is all very well to propose that countries with different political, social, and cultural systems should peacefully coexist, but the moment the attempt is made to translate these sentiments into the language of reality, insurmountable difficulties arise. Genuine détente has to be based on at least some degree of mutual trust.

It is in this context that the problem of arms control has to be seen. It is generally accepted that meaningful future agreements on both strategic and conventional arms have to be based on effective means of inspection. But such means do not exist, and they do not exist precisely because of the absence of democratic checks and balances in the Soviet Union and the unwillingness of the Soviet leaders to open up their country to foreign inspection and free, unlimited travel in general. Thus, the prospects for genuine progress in arms control are virtually nil unless and until the Soviet system becomes more open and democratic; the movement toward the protection of human rights is an essential part of such a process. The same applies, *mutatis mutandis,* to trade with the Soviet bloc, which at present is largely based on credits and loans. The indebtedness of the Soviet bloc now amounts to almost $50 billion; unless Soviet and East European society becomes freer and more open, the financial risk involved in such massive credits—according to some projections, the sum total might be $100 billion by the end of the decade

—will become too great, and U.S.-Soviet trade may grind to a halt.

It is quite untrue to argue, as some Western critics have done, that the human-rights campaign aims at changing the Soviet social system; the question of whether Soviet factories and farms should remain national-ized is not for outsiders to decide. The purpose of the campaign is far more modest: it simply asks that the Soviet regime live up to its own con-stitution. Until it does, there will never develop that climate of trust and confidence, so often invoked by Soviet leaders, which is a precondi-tion for effective arms control, for mutually beneficial trade, or indeed for any lasting understanding.

To be credible, the committment to human rights must be consistent. Does this mean that the same standard ought to be applied to both Den-mark and Afghanistan? Obviously not. The cultural and social context, the grade of development of each country, are factors that have to be taken into acount; and what especially has to be taken into account is the general *trend* in a country: has there been a movement toward greater human rights or away from them? The various maps and surveys pub-lished by the State Department and private bodies do not provide a guide to political action because they do not take these considerations into ac-count; nor do they make a clear differentiation between totalitarian regimes in which all aspects of society are controlled by the state, and authoritarian governments which nevertheless allow a measure of freedom. This elementary distinction is known to every student of politics, yet time and again it is blurred and obfuscated. In Professor Shulman's article, which bears the title "On Learning to Live with Authoritarian Regimes," all kinds of non-democratic governments are lumped together, despite the fact that the author is well aware that there exist "significant differences" among them.

These differences, however, are not just significant, they are crucial. In Spain, the death of the dictator constituted a decisive turning point; precisely because the regime was never quite totalitarian, a far-reaching democratization could rapidly take place. In a totalitarian regime such a development is clearly impossible, and this fact has deep implications for Western policies toward such countries. There are, admittedly, marked differences in the degree of repression inside the Communist camp as well—between countries like Hungary and Yugoslavia on the one hand, and those like North Korea on the other. But it is still true that the whole structure of all these regimes is based on the systematic denial of certain human rights, such as impartial tribunals, freedom of movement and open expression, and peaceful assembly and association (all of which, as it happens, are guaranteed in the constitutions of these countries themselves).

As for the Third World, each country has to be judged individually in the context of the considerations I have mentioned. Much depends on whether a regime respects at least *some* human rights, whether or not it is a relatively enlightened dictatorship working for political, economic, and cultural progress, whether or not it has aims other than the perpetuation of its own repressive rule. There is infinitely more freedom in Tanzania or Kenya than in Uganda, more in Iran and Egypt than in Iraq—even though all these are authoritarian regimes.

What standards, finally, are to be applied to countries that are members of the Western alliance or maintain friendly relations with the U.S.? Here again, the political context has to be taken into account. To provide an example: it is quite possible that certain infringements in civil liberties have occurred at one stage or another in the British struggle against terrorism in Northern Ireland. Such cases are reprehensible wherever they occur, but a terrorist campaign on a substantial scale constitutes a warlike act, and the standards that prevail in war are not those of peacetime. Human rights are rooted in natural law, but natural law does not prohibit free people from defending themselves against enemies hostile to the values of a democratic society. In such situations, as in wartime, certain temporary restrictions on human rights may be necessary.[2] Terrorists are a menace not because they will ever seize power, but because they provoke massive counter-terrorism which frequently leads (as in Uruguay and Argentina) to the establishment of military dictatorship, and these, having seized power, seldom, if ever, feel inclined to restore democracy.

Once terrorism has been defeated, it is indefensible to perpetuate a state of siege, and a strong stand has to be taken against regimes that show no willingness to restore basic freedoms and human rights. This goes *a fortiori* for regimes which do not even have the excuse of defending themselves against the onslaught of anti-democratic forces. In the long run, the U.S. cannot be allied with governments flagrantly and massively violating human rights. But it is also true that the prospects of influencing such governments in the Western hemisphere or in the Far East by means of quiet diplomacy are far better than with Communist countries—if only because the former are more dependent on the U.S. and the other major countries in the Western alliance. Dealing with these countries, the United States will certainly face difficulties; a price will have to be paid for forcefulness, such as losing a military base; if, on the other hand, concessions are made, they will invite accusations of a double standard. But the fact that there will be obstacles does not mean that the policy is impracticable or that the nation should desist from pursuing it.

The U.S. and the other Western countries find themselves hopelessly outnumbered in the United Nations in the struggle for the promotion of human rights, but they have many millions of allies all over the world and above all in the countries in which human rights are trampled under foot. The idea of freedom has exercised a powerful attraction throughout history, and this attraction is probably stronger at present than at any time in the past. Hence the violent reaction of the Soviet Union to the Carter administration's initiatives and the nervousness shown by other repressive governments. These regimes are well aware that Western societies have a weapon that can be used to great effect in the ideological struggle to whose continuation the Soviet Union is committed. Attempts will be made to prevent the West from using this weapon—cajolery and threats. Obviously, the United States will have to take the lead for the West as a whole, for the Western European governments (with some notable exceptions) lack the self-confidence, the determination, the solidarity, and also the political weight to act on their own. But will such leadership be forthcoming from Washington?

The new administration has committed itself to the struggle for human rights on a global basis, but so far not much thought has been given to implications and to the proper strategy. Hence the confusing and contradictory statements that have been made: three steps forward and two steps back. Thus, President Carter declares in his inaugural address that "because we are free we can never be indifferent to the fate of freedom elsewhere"; and then Cyrus Vance announces that the U.S. will speak out only from time to time, and that its comments will be neither strident nor polemical. Unfortunately, to press for human rights is by definition a provocative act even if the language used is neither shrill nor strident; to deny this, to create the impression that the aim can be achieved by platonic expressions of regret and sorrow, is to admit defeat even before the struggle has begun in earnest.

Even more detrimental is the attempt to be "evenhanded" at any cost, to establish a false symmetry. It is understandable when a private organization like Amnesty International, which does its work under exceedingly difficult conditions, "balances" denunciations of gross violation of human rights in an Eastern-bloc or Third World country with criticism of a Western government even when the cases are totally different in severity and magnitude. But a big power like the United States does not have to engage in such questionable practices in order to establish its legitimacy as a champion of human rights.

Spokesmen of the new administration have said they will place far greater emphasis on human rights than did their predecessors. But Henry Kissinger too, in his speech to the UN General Assembly in 1976, declared that human rights were of "central importance, one of the most compelling issues of our times," and the speeches made by Daniel P.

Moynihan and Leonard Garment at the United Nations, as well as the private initiatives of Ambassador Laurence Silberman in Yugoslavia, were at least as forceful as any declarations made in recent months. The real test is not speeches or even appointments, but deeds. President Carter has said that he "cannot go in with armed forces and try to change the internal mechanism of the Soviet government." No such proposal has been advanced. There are, however, a great many things that can be done besides cutting military aid to some Latin American countries. Domestically this would involve the ratification of the Convention on Genocide as well as the other conventions as yet unsigned (for the Elimination of Racial Discrimination, the Covenant on Economic, Social, and Cultural Rights, etc.). In foreign policy it would involve constant pressure for the protection of human rights through all possible channels, public statements on the highest level as well as the publicizing of gross infringements through the Voice of America and the U.S. radio stations in Europe.

Above all it means linkage—linkage, by whatever name. As El Cid said, *Lengua sin manos, cuemo osas fablar?* ("Tongue without arms, how do you dare to talk?") Resistance has been mounted to the use of U.S. resources for the promotion of human rights, and there will be more such resistance in the future. But it is perfectly obvious that unless the human-rights records of the most powerful countries are taken into account in U.S. foreign policy, fine sentiments will not have the slightest impact; they will be rightly considered by friend and foe alike as a public-relations exercise aimed at American domestic consumption. There are countless ways for linking the help sought from the United States by countries great and small to their record on human rights. Opportunities have never been lacking, only the will to make use of them.

The human-rights issue presents an immense challenge to the administration; having made it a cornerstone of his policy to restore the moral authority of American foreign policy, President Carter may stand or fall with his performance in this field. If it is mishandled, carried out without judgment and discrimination, or based on a false symmetry, a global campaign for human rights can lead to the further isolation of the United States and a further lowering of its prestige. Firmly and prudently pursued, it could give an enormous impetus to the cause of freedom all over the world and enhance American stature and influence. Excuses for inaction may be made by small countries whose capacity to influence the course of world politics is by necessity limited. But a great nation hesitant or afraid to speak up and to act on its beliefs, and values at a crucial juncture of world history is forfeiting its international standing and embarking on a course of moral and political decline.

*March 1977*

## NOTES

1. L. Oppenheim, writing his famous textbook on international law before World War I, still regarded the "right of mankind" as something more or less fictitious. The Lauterpacht edition of Oppenheim's book, published in the 1950s, took a far more positive view, noting the inauguration of a new and decisive departure with regard to human rights and freedoms transcending the laws of states.

2. President Carter, at the Clinton, Massachusetts, town meeting in March, said that he would continue to speak out against violations of human rights whether they occurred in Northern Ireland or elsewhere. He did not appear to have in mind the atrocities committed by the two warring sides in the civil war, but the few infringements committed by the British forces trying to prevent a total breakdown of public order and mass slaughter. Yet it is precisely because of the almost unprecedented restraint of the British forces that terrorism still continues in Northern Ireland; terrorists do not persist against governments that react with equal ruthlessness. If President Carter's remark was just a slip of the tongue, it shows that the administration is still at the beginning of its learning process. If it was the expression of deliberate policy, the administration would do better never to invoke the cause of human rights again.

# Third World Fantasies

## I

A recent visitor to a Scandinavian university, after a heated debate with a group of students who had complained bitterly about the lack of freedom in their own country and in the West in general, asked which country in the world they most admired. The answer was Albania. None of the students was familiar with conditions in Albania, none had been there or had the faintest wish to go, but Albania was nevertheless the name of their utopia.

This syndrome is of course not new. Throughout history men have hankered after the perfect society, and have often assumed wistfully that in some distant place it already existed or was at least coming into being. In our time Soviet Russia was once the mecca of such pilgrims, the place where not only a new social order but a new species of mankind was said to have been brought forth, free of selfishness and depravity, free of crime and even neurosis, perfect in every respect, lacking only the gift of immortality. Enthusiasm for the Soviet Union has waned in recent years, but not the need for political gods to worship. Attention has shifted to China and, to a lesser extent, North Korea and Cuba.

On the whole, reverence for China has never quite achieved the dimensions of the Soviet cult before World War II—partly because so few outsiders know Chinese and are in a position to compare the old China with the new; partly because whatever happens in China has seemed of limited relevance to the West; and partly because Chinese foreign policy, smacking too much of *Realpolitik,* has dampened the eagerness of many potential admirers. North Korea, with its cult of the individual centering on Kim-Il Sung, has not been an altogether satisfactory substitute either. Cuba at first seemed very attractive, but its glamor too has paled even in those circles which used to greet with ecstasy Castro's every speech. A repression that could be justified at the time of revolution has grown harsher and more stringent in Cuba, with estimates of the number of political prisoners ranging between 25,000 and 60,000, larger in either case than in all other Latin American countries combined; culturally the country has become a desert, with all manifestations of intellectual freedom rigorously suppressed; and as for Castro himself, if he is not just another Latin American *caudillo,* perhaps more gifted and more radical than most, he has certainly turned out to be far removed from his original image as the new revolutionary messiah.

After their disappointments elsewhere, seekers for inspiration are left with the Albanias of this world and some of the newly emerging countries. It is said that, once freed from foreign rule, these countries will find their own way toward a new dignity, a social and political order unencumbered by the inequities of a dying Western civilization. Though they are primitive, their very backwardness may well be their insurance against the evils which have led Western civilization along the road to perdition. Perhaps after all a light *will* come out of the East, a new form of community, a new quality of life, a new model providing fresh hope for mankind.

These notions, first voiced in the 1950s, have taken some hard knocks in the intervening decades, but are by no means dead—as is shown dramatically in a new book by L.S. Stavrianos, Adjunct Professor of Third World Studies at the University of California, San Diego. The professor's message is optimistic: mankind is facing a new Dark Age, but it is one which holds great promise of creative new values and new institutions of greater freedom, of real participation in public and private affairs. His is a vision of humankind at last realizing its humanity, at last sloughing off the false values of Western society with its intolerable waste and its ideology of endless consumption. And where does our author see the "grass sprouting through the concrete," the forces of regeneration? Although the Israeli kibbutzim get a kind word, and Sweden is praised as a country in which the "new person" envisaged by Lewis Mumford is more than a rhetorical phrase, the main answer is the Third World: China, Vietnam, Tanzania, Yugoslavia, Guinea-Bissau, Ethiopia, Mozambique, Somalia, Egypt (under Nasser), Cuba, and Peru.

Let us look at this list, Ethiopia and Somalia are ruled by gangs of military despots who indiscriminately kill their political opponents as well as each other; they are also bankrupt, and without outside help would be altogether lost. Ethopia, furthermore, may disintegrate from its unresolved minority problems. As for Mozambique, which Stavrianos says may have an impact on Africa comparable to that of Vietnam on Southeast Asia—he quotes President Machel giving top priority not to administrative or economic measures but to "transforming the individual thinking"—the unfortunate history of FRELIMO, the Mozambique "liberation" movement, shows that it spent as much effort in internecine killing as in fighting the Portuguese, and the transformation of individual thinking in that country means no more than a giant purge. The prisons of Mozambique are overflowing with inmates, whose numbers far exceed those under Portuguese rule. The economy of the country is a shambles, according to its own leaders, who have turned to the United Nations with an urgent appeal for massive help—hardly a shining example of self-reliance.

Stavrianos seems equally ill-informed about Egypt under Nasser and about Cambodia. He claims, for instance, that a counterrevolutionary Western strategy "lavished" aid on King Hussein of Jordan but not on Nasser's Egypt. In fact, Egypt received infinitely more money and goods from the West (not to mention Soviet billions) than Jordan; without U.S.-donated grain, Egypt would have starved. About Cambodia, a reviewer in the New York *Times* claims that Stavrianos "makes mincemeat" of standard Western perceptions of events there. A closer reading shows that his only source is a single favorable report on postwar Cambodia, one which is contradicted by a hundred unfavorable ones—a new and original recipe for making mincemeat.

This leaves Tanzania and Guinea-Bissau. In the former, President Nyerere's rule has been enlightened, for Africa; he was elected with a majority of only 93 percent and the number of political enemies executed from time to time is smaller than elsewhere. Fifteen years ago much promise was attached to the communal *ujamaa* villages, but they have not been a success; Tanzania's growth rate from 1960 to 1973 was 2.8 percent, less than its population increase, and since then the country, hit by drought and rising oil prices, has depended on aid from abroad. Guinea-Bissau, finally, is a very small country of some 600,000 inhabitants, whose leader in the struggle against Portuguese colonialism was Amilcar Cabral, a Communist and an impressive figure by any standard. But Cabral was killed, and while his successors seem to be continuing his pragmatic policies, it is far too early to conclude that they will be able to cope with the country's problems—let alone provide inspiration to others; they too have become more and more dependent on help from abroad. Stavrianos has a great many bitter things to say about the counterrevolutionary strategy of the West in the Third World, but what he does not say is that a decisive part of the aid now given to the self-styled "Marxist regimes" of Ethiopia and Somalia, and to Tanzania and Mozambique, originates in the United States and Western Europe. Without it, they would all probably collapse.

The Yugoslav experiment in workers' self-management has attracted much interest in the West, and Stavrianos expresses great admiration for it. But the results are in doubt, to put it cautiously. According to recent

Yugoslav studies, most decision-making is done by the top management. Moreover, Milovan Djilas, who was one of the chief proponents of workers' control, has said in a recent interview that it has not resolved any important problems but simply expanded the new ruling class to embrace some worker-leaders. This is borne out by Yugoslavia's general political development: where it once seemed that the country might evolve toward a greater degree of freedom, there is now actually greater repression in every field. This in turn raises the question of whether the failure of workers' self-management was not inevitable, for industrial democracy and totalitarian rule cannot coexist.

Thus, after many detours, we are left with China. To Stavrianos, "boss, bureaucrat, and expert have been demystified" in China. There, since those at the top must spend part of their time working at the bottom, the leaders learn from the masses, and "no policy decision remains fixed once it is made. There is constant testing of its reception and effectiveness among the people, reformulation, retesting, reappraisal, revoking, and so on." Although Stavrianos is not certain that Maoism can survive Mao, nevertheless Mao's China represents for him the human model *par excellence,* hardworking, dedicated, self-sacrificing, flexible, inventive, disciplined, honest, puritanical, well-motivated, cooperative, respectful of the virtues and dignity of labor. Above all, whereas in other Third World countries Western counterrevolutionary influence has simply perpetuated the rule of elites, in China (and in Indochina) power has passed into the hands of the masses, "the first anti-meritocratic revolution in human history."

What is one to say about this? Whatever the achievements of China since 1948, the belief that it is not ruled by an elite, that the "masses" have any influence on the shaping of the country's policy, that participatory democracy actually exists there, leads beyond the confines of rational discussion. China is certainly not an enormous economic success. Agricultural production during the last twenty years has averaged a two percent increase annually (despite growing investments), and has thus barely kept pace with population growth. (In 1976 it may have been actually less than two percent.) Worse, yet, from a doctrinal point of view, the production of the communes seems to be considerably lower than that of private plots. Greater investments will have to be made in the future in the development of industry, but then again, industrial workers are demanding higher wages. If Mao was incapable of persuading them that idealism and public service are more important than material rewards, his successors surely will be unable to do so.

It is perfectly true that the Chinese leaders are hardworking and have always put great emphasis on the unity of theory and practice (very much in contrast to the self-styled African or Latin American Marxists who

combine revolutionary phraseology with a predilection for material com-
forts and a profound contempt for manual labor). But all the same, they
constitute an elite which has never practiced participatory democracy as
far as important policy decisions are concerned. Neither Mao nor his
wife, neither Chou nor any other leader of the party, the army, or the
political police ever went to work in a commune or factory, and rotation
in the leadership has only come about as the result of purges in the struggle for power.

It is one thing to argue that China may eventually overcome its present
difficulties. But to regard a society of unprecedented regimentation, control, and indoctrination as the new Arcadia, a solution to the spiritual
and material needs of mankind, is a perversion of breathtaking enormity, more a symptom of than an answer to Western "degeneracy."

Quite apart from the fallacies about the actual situation in the Third
World and China, there are two fundamental issues with which writers of
the Stavrianos stripe usually fail to come to terms. One is the problem of
mass participation, which they make a fetish of in their writings. It is
perfectly true that all modern political regimes have to mobilize the
"masses" in one way or another, but the imperative holds equally for
fascism and Communism, and even for the more streamlined military
dictatorships. Historical experience has shown that such mobilization
means little more than manipulation, and has nothing to do with the
wished-for emergence of *homo humanus*. The replacement of old-
fashioned autocratic regimes by more effective, more ruthless, and more
repressive ones is not the road to progress. Iraq, which Stavrianos mentions, is a fairly typical example. "The displaced peasants [in Baghdad]
took to the streets during the revolution of July 1958, exterminated the
Hashemite royal family, and established a republic," Stavrianos writes.
In fact the Hashemite royal family was killed not by the masses but by a
group of military conspirators; a few years later their leader suffered a
similar fate. Iraq has been a dictatorship ever since, more effective and
more brutal; whether a regime of this kind is defined as a monarchy or a
"republic" is of little more than semantic interest.

The second issue is the emphasis placed on self-help and self-reliance,
on communal life and small-scale politics. This is a modern form of an
ancient idea—the idea of Natural Man—and in the last century alone it
has produced whole libraries of mechanophobe fantasies, from Butler's
*Erewhon* (where the machines are collected and deposited in museums),
to Chesterton's *Napoleon of Notting Hill* and E.M. Forster's *The
Machine Stops*. It has in fact more frequently inspired the extreme Right
than the Left. Alienated man in the big cities, the corrupting effects of
cultural modernism, the need to return to "origins," the idea of basing
the economy on self-help, on "joy in service"—all these notions occur in

the speeches and writings of Hitler and Alfred Rosenberg, of Richard-Walther Darré and other ideologists of German National Socialism. Early Nazi sects developed elaborate blueprints for communal settlements (a "new brotherhood of man") complete with nudism, homage to the sun, and bicycles instead of cars. This is not to say that because these ideas occurred to the Nazis they have to be rejected out of hand. Like the mobilization of the masses, they are in themselves neither good nor bad; everything depends on what use is made of them. Still, it is useful to bear in mind Marx's contempt, in the *Communist Manifesto,* for "promoters of duodecimo editions of the New Jerusalem," especially when such promoters are describing not some future hoped-for condition but already existing societies.

## II

Fantasies about the Third World vary greatly in character; whereas some concentrate on the alleged arcadian purity of primitive society, others, to the contrary, emphasize the growing economic and political power of the Third World and the threat this poses to the industrialized West. According to this latter school of thought, the great majority of mankind is in rebellion against political and economic exploitation, and unless the West changes its attitude toward these new and tremendously strong forces it will be doomed. The arguments that have been invoked range from considerations of economic self-interest (Third World countries hold most of the world's needed raw materials), to those of morality (retribution for past injustices), to those of military expedience (desperate nations will use nuclear blackmail unless there is a just distribution of goods). Hence the call for a new economic world order, for cartelization, for indexation (figuring-in the prices of commodities exported by underdeveloped countries against the goods they have to import), and for the cancellation of Third World debts, as well as the demand for free transfer of technology and gifts or grants.

The enormity of the economic problems facing the poor nations cannot be disputed by any sane person, and there is much to be said for their attempt to get higher prices for their products and easier access to Western markets. The unfortunate truth is, however, that the bulk of commodity trading in the world (except for oil) takes place not between poor countries and rich countries but among the industrial nations themselves. If, for argument's sake, all raw materials were to rise in price by ten or twenty percent, some industrial countries, such as Japan and West Germany, would be put at a disadvantage, but others (the United States, Canada) would benefit; among eighty-seven developing countries twelve would gain substantially, sixteen would lose, and fifty-nine would reap only marginal benefits. Moreover, many raw materials can be replaced. If the price of cotton rose beyond a certain level, artificial fibers could be used. Coffee and cocoa, if too highly priced, would no longer remain part of our staple diet. The consumption of tin could be reduced by two-thirds with the use of new technologies; copper (to provide another example) could be recycled. Cartelization might, it is true, have a salutary effect inasmuch as it would compel the industrial countries to save raw materials that are finite and that have been wasted in the past. But even in the unlikely event that unilaterial cartelization were successful, only a few of the poorer countries would benefit; those most in need would not be among them. Again, a good case can be made for the cancellation of Third World debts, but here too, with the exception of India and Pakistan, the very poorest nations would not benefit very much because they received few loans in the first place; South Korea is about as much in debt as the whole of tropical Africa, and the debts of the Communist bloc are many times higher still.

One of the arguments most frequently used in favor of a massive North-South aid effort is the politically "explosive" character of Third World poverty—the assumption being that rapid economic development will somehow defuse the explosion. But experience shows that inequality of incomes markedly *increases* with economic development, at least in the short run, and that growth would result in more turbulence rather than less. The "rebellion of the poor" now taking place is a political campaign by the top stratum of the middle-income countries, who in both relative and absolute terms are better off than the majority of the population in the industrial world which is supposed to pay for their demands.

The military argument is perhaps the most curious of all, for on the one hand it is too farfetched, and on the other hand it does not go far enough. If we assume that a desperate Ruritania would use nuclear blackmail against the United States, why should blackmail stop at a one-time transfer of resources? The demand could well be made that the citizens of the Unites States should in the future share their income on a *permanent* basis with the Ruritarians.

In short, there is no sound reason to believe that the "explosive" economic situation of the poorer countries will in any way diminish significantly on account of efforts made by the industrialized countries. The economic problems of most Third World countries are by no means insoluble, but the decisive effort will have to come from themselves. If on every occasion they invoke national sovereignty but deny this principle to others; if they continue to believe that population growth is not a critical problem; if their development efforts continue to be concentrated more and more on industry and less on agriculture, the results will be predictable, regardless of whether the industrialized nations commit 0.7 percent of their GNP to the poorer nations (as the United Nations has demanded), or seven percent, or more.

Economic issues aside, the alleged growing political importance of the Third World is also something of an optical illusion. At the recent meeting of the European Communist parties, President Tito of Yugoslavia declared that the movement of nonalignment has developed into a "powerful international factor, which independently defines its policies and positions." It is easy to understand why Yugoslavia should propagate such view; facing Soviet pressure, it is vitally interested in some kind of collective security system, however spurious. And certainly, as far as numbers go, the group of the "nonaligned" has grown by leaps and bounds since the days of Bandung (1955) and Belgrade (1961), when twenty-five countries attended their conferences. At the third conference of heads of state in Lusaka in 1970 there were fifty-one in attendance, in Algiers in 1973 there were seventy-five full members and fourteen liberation movements, and in Colombo last August the number of full members had risen to eighty-four. (On the other hand, the number of attending heads of state or government fell from about seventy at the preceding summit to forty-one at Colombo.)

Yet even a cursory look at the composition of the membership shows precious little in common. For one thing, the list of conflicts among these countries is considerably longer than the list of member states. Syria, which is a member, fights the PLO, which is also a member; and within a year or two Algeria and Morocco, Libya and Egypt, India and Bangladesh, Ethiopia and Somalia (to give but a few examples) could be in a state of war. This by itself casts a large measure of doubt on the efficacy of such proposals as the one advocated by the Yugoslavs for collective security. Nor is there any logic to the criteria for membership. Vietnam and North Korea are prominent members of the nonaligned camp, but China has not been admitted and Rumania was not even given observer status at Colombo for fear of offending the Russians. Cuba is a leading member, but so is Argentina; and so on.

Ideologically, the nonaligned movement once had anti-colonialism as a common denominator, but since vitually all the countries once under colonial domination have meanwhile attained independence, this is no longer a live issue. Member states all subscribe to the principle that economic relations should be based on equality and justice—this is the "New Economic Order" as advocated by the "Group of 77"—but the "77" also include on the one hand OPEC countries with the highest per-capita income in the world, and on the other hand the very poorest of nations. A new, all-embracing objective needs to be found to provide even a semblance of unity; this, however, seems impossible, as political, social, and economic interests diverge all along the line.

Apart from differences in political orientation and social systems, the nonaligned camp consists to all intents and purposes of four groups: the OPEC countries; the middle-income nations whose exports are of economic importance or which are at a relatively advanced stage of economic development; the very poor (the majority); and lastly those which do not fit into any of these categories. Attempts are constantly made to ignore the conflicting interests, but the widening discrepancy between declarations and realities is a source of growing tension. To give but one illustration: not so long ago it was predicted that the OPEC governments would provide support to the poorer countries, far in excess (on a per-capita basis) of that given by industrial nations. The interim balance, after three years, shows that while the OPEC countries have made promises of many billions of dollars, the amount actually paid has been a mere fraction of that. Most of it, moreover, has gone to Arab and Muslim nations and a small amount, for political reasons, to India. The poor African and Asian countries have not even been reimbursed for the foreign-exchange losses created by the oil-price increases. Nor have the poorer Arab and Muslim countries much to be thankful for. Pakistan has received little, and Egypt, with its pressing needs for economic development, has not fared much better. President Sadat's attempts to solicit help from Saudi Arabia and the Persian Gulf states have resulted in promises to underwrite Egyptian arms purchases but only negligible sums for economic-development projects. These facts of life have already had a sobering effect, and may be only the beginning of a general process of disillusionment.

What binds the nonaligned together is a lot of high-sounding rhetoric and the ambition of a few leaders manipulating the rest. President Echeverria of Mexico, who wanted to be UN General Secretary, became a great advocate of Third World solidarity; likewise Mrs. Gandhi, who uses the "bloc" to enhance India's bargaining position. As for the rhetoric, it is taken seriously in the West, which is a big mistake. Thus, at the Colombo conference France was threatened with an oil embargo on account of its trade with South Africa. A typical example of the demagoguery so frequent at these meetings was the speech of the Algerian minister of trade at the Nairobi conference in which he declared that Western aid has been totally unhelpful—which did not prevent him from asking for more of it.

There is yet another common denominator, the absence of political freedom. Most of the leaders convening in Algiers, Colombo and Havana are usurpers or were voted in by 99.9 percent of the electorate in phony elections. In no more than a handful of these countries do elementary political rights exist: a few Caribbean islands (such as Barbados, Trinidad, Tobago, and Jamaica) and places like Malta, Mauritius, the Maldives, the Seychelles, Cyprus, Malaysia, and perhaps one or two others. The total population of these free (or semi-free) countries is less than twenty million, about two percent of the total population of the nonaligned bloc. All the others are under one-party rule or dictatorships of one form or another, some of them savage, others more enlightened.

Wherever democratic institutions once existed in the Third World, they have broken down. The trend in the nonaligned camp is toward the suppression of human rights, most recently the last vestiges of freedom of the press. The process, which started a long time ago, is reflected, *inter alia,* in the shrinking number of newspapers. In the early 1960s there were still some 240 newspapers in Africa, today there are a mere hundred; there has been a similar fall-off in India, Pakistan, and Bangladesh. The planned coordination of the media throughout the nonaligned countries should liquidate the last remnants of independence. If, as is quite possible, systematic censorship is introduced and foreign journalists are excluded, there will no longer be any reports on the murderous policies of Idi Amin and President Bokassa (of the Central African Republic), nor will there be news about the systematic use of torture in Cameroon, Mali, Senegal, Lesotho, Guinea, Zaire, India, Gabon, Mauretania, and many other countries, nor about the extermination of minorities in Cameron, Ethiopia, Malawi, Iraq, Sudan, Chad, and Rwanda.

Murder and torture are crimes whether they are committed by whites or by non-whites, and racism cannot be justified even if it appears among black people or yellow. As the years pass, the argument that all the shortcomings of the Third World are the result of past colonial oppression and present Western exploitation has turned into an alibi for the failure of the new elites. But this alibi will not wash. No matter what the Western nations can and should do to provide economic aid, they cannot bring about the cultural and moral revolution which is the essential prerequisite for real change. The West can export food and modern technology, but it cannot supply new and better elites; these will have to emerge from within the developing nations themselves. The excesses of some Third World regimes are defended with the argument that these are educational dictatorships in a transitional period on the path to democracy. In fact, many of them are not educational but regressive dictatorships, whose "radical" or "socialist" declarations are a smokescreen for the leadership's desire to stay in power and enjoy the spoils thereof. In such countries political morality is low or nonexistent, and the government's ritual appeals for hard work, honesty, and austerity go unheeded because they emanate from leaders whose style of living exemplifies the opposite qualities. This is of course not true of all Third World elites—in this regard especially one cannot refuse one's respect for the Chinese—but it is true of too many of them.

Some years ago, analyzing the political prospects of the Third World in these pages ("Imperialism in this Century," May 1970), the late George Lichtheim ridiculed the fashionable dichotomy that places Western imperialism against the starving masses of the Third World. In this perspective nationalism is identified with socialism which, in turn, is a synonym for anti-imperialism and anti-colonialism. Lichtheim stressed that in principle Third World nationalism could turn "Right" as well as "Left," and that in either case there would be a revolution from above, with the intelligentsia establishing a dictatorship and turning into a bureaucracy responsible only to itself. Lichtheim thought that the Maoist model was more likely to be imitated than the fascist model, which had gone out of fashion.

Lichtheim's analysis of the dilemmas facing the Third World is still valid, although the perspective has changed since he wrote. The fragmentation of the Third World has progressed much more quickly than could have been expected even seven years ago. Some Third World countries have grown rich owing to sudden windfalls, others have fallen even further behind, and the Chinese are not in a position to claim leadership. Above all, the question has arisen of whether the Maoist model is indeed applicable to other parts of the world, for it presupposes the existence of a determined, efficient, and truly selfless vanguard. In most countries such a vanguard simply does not exist, or where it exists is not strong enough, or where strong enough it lacks the qualities for becoming an agent of modernization. Is it possible that, broadly speaking, China constitutes a historical exception to the rule? (And in the light of recent events there, can one be sure that even China is an exception?) If so, the future prospects for Third World countries which lack both resources and a "vanguard" are stagnation, regression, and a more or less permanent condition of turbulence.

In the final analysis the problem is political, not economic. Some Third World countries are so backward and desperately poor that they will have to depend for a long time on outside assistance. But for many the economic prospects are less gloomy; given the right approach, the problem of food production is a soluble one, and with the upturn in world trade and rising prices for nonferous metals and agricultural commodities, economic growth should continue. Much can be done by Western nations in this respect; Western aid, which has fallen in real terms by three percent over the last decade, could be increased, and new agreements could be concluded to offset the deterioration in terms of trade.

But before this happens, the air will have to be cleared and a fundamental reorientation in Western policies will have to take place. The United States and other Western nations, far from alleviating the international situation, have helped to aggravate it through their willingness to negotiate with a more or less artificial conglomeration of countries instead of dealing with individual nations on a bilateral basis in accordance with their needs. The motives underlying this gross error of political judgment may have been laudable—there was the wish to help the most seriously affected countries and at the same time to "de-politicize" aid, and there was the desire, again quite justified, to negotiate the terms of trade with the producers of raw materials. But this last cannot be achieved in an overall deal; it has to be done with each group of producers. Furthermore, multilateral aid, far from improving the relationship between donor and recipient, has done just the opposite. Negotiations between blocs of countries inevitably tend to ignore the interests of the truly needy. Stridently anti-Western governments, which spend far more of their considerable oil revenues on armed intervention and international terrorism than on helping their less fortunate neighbors, appear as the representatives of the "forgotten 40 percent." Anxious to prevent a confrontation with the Third World, the West has maneuvered itself into a position in which confrontation has become inescapable and the United States has been made to accept the historical responsibility for the effects of colonialism.

Sailing under the banner of international equity and a global compact, the Western governments are in fact on a collision course. Nothing constructive will be accomplished until that course is changed. Above all, no advance can be made so long as the West does not muster the courage to stop talking to demagogues with no genuine interest in economic and social improvement, for whom the nonaligned conferences, UNCTAD, the Paris "North-South Dialogue," and the Group of 77 and other such bodies are merely a platform for their own destructive political ends.

*February 1977*

# Fascism—The Second Coming

What is fascism, and have we seen the last of it?

On the precise character of fascism there is no agreement to this day. One might define it as a mass movement, headed by a leader whose command is absolute, which later turns into a state party, strictly hierarchical and elitist, ruling through terror and propanda and the monopoly of political power, on the basis of an anti-liberal, anti-democratic, rabidly nationalistic and militaristic spirit and an ideology compounded of conservative-reactionary and radical, quasi-socialist elements. Yet no two fascisms have been quite alike; some have combined religious-mystical elements, while others, by contrast, have been sharply anti-clerical. At times racism has been a central factor, in other cases it has been marginal or non-existent. Some fascist movements are barely distinguishable from old-fashioned right-wing parties, others are radical in doctrine and practice. If one takes Nazi Germany as the norm, then Italy under Mussolini was just a half-way house and Spain and Portugal were not fascist at all. If, on the other hand, Italy serves as the yardstick, Nazi Germany was an aberration, its excesses and radicalism typically German rather than fascist.

As for the historical role of fascism, the debate over this continues with undiminished vigor. According to one school of thought, fascism developed in Europe as a result of the crisis of the liberal system in the 1920s and 1930s; it was a specifically European phenomenon; and it came to an end with the defeat of Nazi Germany in 1945. This idea, that the fascist era came to an end in 1945, is, however, not accepted by orthodox Marxists, who regard fascism as the agent of monopoly capitalism: as long as capitalism exists there is a latent danger of a fascist revival. And Marxists are not alone in maintaining that we have not seen the last of fascism. Others, interpreting it as an agent not of capitalism but of modernization, and observing that modernization, especially outside Europe, is accompanied by a great deal of violence and even systematic terror, have reached the conclusion that the potential for fascism is greater in the underdeveloped societies than anywhere else in the world.

The notion of fascism as the product of a crisis of European civilization was first advanced in the 1920s and came in several variants. Liberals regarded fascism as a revolt against "Europe," meaning the tradition of the Enlightenment and the idealism of the French Revolution. Believing Christians saw it as one of the manifestations of the loss of religious faith and, like the liberals, but for different reasons, as a relapse into neo-barbarism. Rauschning, himself a former Nazi, pointed to the essentially nihilistic substance of fascism; the particular doctrine was of little consequence, he said, the exercise of total power all-important. Elitist critics saw fascism as part of the twentieth-century revolt of the masses, while others explained it as a modern version of Caesarism or Bonapartism. Some historians stressed the paramount importance of the personality of the leader: in this view, had it not been for Mussolini or Hitler, the parties they led would never have come to power.

It has been the fashion lately to dismiss these early attempts at interpreting European fascism as of purely historical interest, a little primitive, if not altogether outdated. But they all contain a grain of truth, and they compare not unfavorably with postwar interpretations, except perhaps for the fact that more recent theorists have been aware that fascism is too complex a phenomenon to be explained, as earlier theorists tried to do, by reference to a single cause.

In many ways the most consistent early theory of fascism is the one originally propounded by the Thirteenth Plenum of the Communist International in 1933, that fascism is the "openly terrorist dictatorship of the most reactionary, chauvinist, and imperialist elements of finance capital." In the world of Communist ideology, where fascism is not an independent force but a mere agent, in accordance with the basic Marxist-Leninist tenet of the primacy of economics over politics, this thesis has more or less remained in force ever since, despite sporadic attempts from within to modify it. Thus, "enlightened" Marxists like Thalheimer and Otto Bauer in the earlier period, and a few others in our own time, have maintained that fascism was a unique phenomenon in the history of bourgeois society, for in the fascist state the executive was (or became) autonomous, operating in essential respects quite independently, or even against the interests, of the capitalist "ruling class." Yet such a position, with its implication that economic factors are not necessarily the decisive ones, is clearly anathema to the orthodox Leninist conception stated above, and much effort has therefore been invested in Marxist circles to demonstrate the primacy of economics in the Third Reich as well as in Fascist Italy. This is, however, not a simple task, for it must be shown in each case that the capitalists turned to fascism when they were no longer able to cope with an acutely revolutionary situation. The trouble is that in actual fact there was no revolutionary situation in Italy in 1923 or in Germany in 1933. Moreover, although it is true that the industrialist Thyssen gave money to the Nazis and that Mussolini, through the marriage of his daughter Edda, had an interest in the Italian sugar and shipping industries, this did not prevent Hitler from detaining Thyssen in a concentration camp, nor did it hinder Mussolini from having his son-in-law shot.

In short, it is impossible to demonstrate the necessary confluence of interests within Germany industry—let alone among industrialists, bankers, and big landowners—which would have led them to join together in support of the Nazis. No matter how widely or deeply one digs, the sums paid to Hitler prior to 1933 were not only modest in absolute terms, they were small in comparison with what was given to other parties. German industrialists did not "make" Hitler, they joined him only after his party had become a leading political force, and it is possible that Hitler would have come to power even if the Nazis had not received a single *pfennig* from the bankers and industrialists.

If it cannot be shown that Hitler depended on finance capital to come to power, neither can it be successfully maintained that once in power the Nazis subordinated their policies to the interests of "monopoly capitalism." Not only were Nazi anti-Semitism and the Final Solution not dictated by economic considerations and class interests; generally speaking, Hitler's entire foreign policy was not in the best interests of monopoly capitalism; on the contrary, it ultimately led to ruin and destruction.

Hitlerian fascism, then, far from recognizing its own class interests, even acted against them. This means—and it will come as an unwelcome admission only to the orthodox Leninist—that fascism cannot be satisfactorily explained if one confines oneself to the analysis of class interests. The attempt to explain fascism in this way has the additional disadvantage of leading its advocates perilously close to an apology for fascism. For if it is all the fault of the socioeconomic "system," why blame Hitler and Mussolini, who were after all only continuing the policies of their predecessors, perhaps with a little more vigor and determination? The difference between Hitler, Himmler, and Streicher on the one hand, and Churchill, Roosevelt, and De Gaulle on the other then becomes merely one of degree, not one of substance. Besides, as a movement directed against the economic status quo, European fascism might even be defended as representing a useful stage in the ongoing conflict between the have-nots and the plutocracies. Toward some such position of veiled advocacy the strict Marxist analysis of the role of fascism would seem inevitably to lead.

To be sure, no one can fairly deny that there is a clear link between fascism and economic crisis or that the social base of fascism and its economic policy ought to be studied closely. But equally no one can be taken seriously who has not accepted the fundamental fact that fascism is "about" political power, not about profit.

During the 1950s the debate over the nature of totalitarianism generated a whole set of apparently new theories about fascism. Actually, the most striking of these, that there are strong similarities between fascism and Communism, was *not* new, having been first advanced by Italian critics like Francesco Nitti and Luigi Sturzo who, writing in 1926, called Bolshevism left-wing fascism and fascism right-wing Bolshevism. But it was at the height of the cold war that the tendency to concentrate on the elements common to fascism and Communist became most pronounced. In *The Origins of Totalitarianism,* the late Hannah Arendt claimed that Nazi Germany and the Soviet Union were "essentially identical," and Carl Friedrich and Zbigniew Brzezinski drew up a detailed outline of the characteristics of all totalitarian regimes, ranging from an all-embracing ideology to an oligarchic mass party, complete control over the media, and a command economy.

To Communists this thesis was, of course, anathema, but criticism of it came from other quarters as well. After all, the historical conditions that gave birth to fascist and Communist regimes had been altogether different. Communist regimes, moreover, aimed at the transformation of society and at a new social order, whereas fascism was essentially conservative, or, at any rate, showed much less interest in socioeconomic problems. Some proponents of the totalitarian argument had concentrated on features which, as it subsequently emerged, were not of central importance. Thus, after Stalin's death, it became clear that the charismatic leader was not a *sine qua non* for the perpetuation of a Communist regime, nor were irrational terror and indiscriminate purges (which had been stressed by Hannah Arendt and others) a necessary characteristic of Communism. In due course the pendulum of theory began to swing to the other extreme, and the idea of fascism as totalitarianism was altogether jettisoned, to be followed by a spate of new theories by sociologists, social psychologists, economic historians, philosophically trained historians, and others, many of them highly suggestive, none wholly satisfactory. Seymour Martin Lipset and, after him, Renzo de Felice, a leading historian of Italian fascism, pointed to the extremism of the middle classes which at a time of crisis turned away from liberalism to a third force, defending their interests against pressure from above and below alike. This may help to explain the social base of fascism in some countries (if not in others), but it contributes little to the understanding of the policy of fascist parties after the seizure of power. More useful was Lipset's emphasis on the populist elements inherent in many fascist movements, and the distinction between left- and right-wing fascist parties.

Another writer, Hugh Trevor-Roper, defined fascism as the political response of the European bourgeoisie to the economic recession of the 1920s and 1930s, or, in any case, to the fear caused by the recession, a response which was above all anti-Communist. This thesis too is wanting, for if Communism was perceived as an overriding menace in the 1920s and 1930s (a doubtful assumption in the first place), it was certainly a much greater danger after 1945, when no fascist response was forthcoming.

Then there was Ernst Nolte, whose contribution to the study of European fascism has been second to none, and who provided a widely quoted definition of fascism: "Anti-Marxism which seeks to destroy the enemy by the evolvement of a radically opposed and yet related ideology and by the use of almost identical and yet typically modified methods, always however within the unyielding framework of national self-assertion and autonomy." Fascism seen in this light is a revolt against secularization and democratization—in brief, against modernism. Yet the movement which Nolte took as the starting point for his argument, the Action Français, while certainly reactionary, was not in essential respects a precursor of fascism; and his argument in any case is not of much help when applied to those quite numerous fascist movements in which the anti-Marxist element is subordinate. Nor should one overrate the utopian anti-modernism of the fascist movements. However much Hitler praised the peasant way of life of ages past, he was perfectly aware of the need to develop heavy industry, if only to produce tanks and airplanes for the coming war.

Equally, one should not exaggerate the role of fascism in the process of industrialization and modernization. As long ago as 1932 Franz Borkenau propounded the thesis that it might be the historical task of Italian fascism to industrialize the country, since the Italian bourgeoisie had been incapable of doing so and since the militant working class had been "objectively reactionary" in holding up economic progress. It was a stimulating theory, but Borkenau's acompanying predictions for Germany were quite wrong and even in Italy events did not bear out his thesis, for Mussolini's contribution to the industrialization of Italy was modest, to say the least, and it was only after the fall of the fascist regime that Italy began to catch up with its northern neighbors.

After World War II the modernization argument took a different guise. Fascism (it was argued) had helped to modernize Germany and

Italy by doing away with anachronistic social structures and by promoting economic development. This is an obvious enough point, yet
oceans of ink were spilled to prove it. Any modern mass movement is a
mobilizing force—this is what constitutes the main difference between
modern and old-fashioned dictatorship. Nor can a modern dictatorship
afford to neglect economic development, which results in turn in social
changes. The problem is that the *downfall* of the Third Reich, which
coincided with the physical destruction of much of Germany, also
resulted in further socioeconomic changes, and perhaps much greater
ones. Partisans of the modernization theory might still claim that
fascism, in contrast to Attila the Hun and the Khmer Rouge, is "objectively" an agent of progress, but at this point the argument becomes a bit
far-fetched.

Has fascism, then, disappeared? There would seem to be grounds for
thinking so. Many of the regimes that have been called "fascist" by their
opponents in recent times—Chile, or Spain under Franco, Portugal
under Salazar, Greece under the colonels, or Indonesia under the
generals—have in fact been anything but fascist. Rather, these have been
old-fashioned authoritarian regimes, repressive in character yet con-
spicuously lacking the characteristics of a modern dictatorship. They
have not been populist, not even Bonapartist; there has been no state
party, not even a half-hearted attempt to mobilize the masses; and only
in exceptional cases has the state intervened in the economy.

Yet that does not quite dispose of the issue, for if it was once believed
that fascism was a specifically European phenomenon, impressing its
mark on a whole era of European history, after World War II a whole
series of regimes have emerged elsewhere in the world bearing at least
some of the distinguishing signs of European fascism. Today almost all
the countries of the Third and Fourth worlds are ruled by dictators,
about half of them military men and the rest either Communists,
autocratic monarchs, or some other kind of dictator. (The exceptions are
at present, Colombia, Costa Rica, a few little islands, some "guided
democracies," and countries such as Turkey, Lebanon, and Cyprus—
altogether perhaps a dozen.)

Conditions in Asia, Africa, Latin America, and the Middle East vary
greatly, and so does the character of the new dictatorships. Some have
been highly repressive, others only mildly so; some have made economic
progress while others have stagnated, some military juntas have been
more radical than others. Generally speaking, the effectiveness of a
regime in silencing opposition has increased much more quickly than its
aptitude in other fields.

Yet even though the new dictatorships are all different from one
another, they have certain features in common. Making allowances for

their lower cultural and social levels of development, in rhetoric they tend to resemble Communism, and in practice to display parallels with Italian fascism. They also often contain populist ingredients—such as the emphasis on *Volksgemeinschaft* and/or nationalism—which were part and parcel of European fascism. The cult of violence, which figured so prominently in Europe, has likewise reappeared here and there in the new regimes (it would be difficult to think of a more eloquent advocate of the "morally cleansing properties of progressive violence" than Frantz Fanon). So, too, the anti-imperialist, anti-Western ideology of the new dictatorships echoes the old fascist concept of a proletarian nation deprived by the plutocracies of its rightful place in the world—a concept on which the Nazis based much of their attack against the Versailles peace treaty. And finally, the racism of the Nazis and the admixture of nationalism with quasi-religious elements of other fascist movements have found new expression in Third World ideologies ranging from Mobutism to Qaddafism. The minute analysis of Third World ideologies is in general an unrewarding enterprise: the actions of the dictators are a surer guide to future developments than their announced ideas. Yet these regimes do contain fascist elements, if as yet in a primitive political framework (broadly speaking, the less developed a country the less pronounced will be the fascist character of its dictatorship).

Despite all this, there has been a reluctance to call these regimes fascist, and new generic terms have been proposed for them: developmental dictatorships, revolutionary dictatorships, or left-wing nationalist dictatorships aiming at economic development and modernization.

The search for definitions and explanations is made more difficult by the tyranny of a political language which evolved out of realities that have ceased to exist. If Marxism is no longer of much help in understanding the dynamics of Soviet or Chinese politics, what is one to make of references to "Left" and "Right" in Zaïre or Cambodia, or to "Marxist guerrillas" in Chad or Bangladesh? There is no room for conservative parties in the Third World, for there is little to conserve in an age of the break-up of traditional society. Equally out of place are liberalism and democratic socialism, the products of a long historical development culminating in the psychological attitudes of tolerance and consensus, attitudes which exist barely, if at all, in the Third World. Everyone in these countries is a nationalist and a socialist of sorts, two terms which have become interchangeable. But socialism means no more than anti-capitalism, especially where capitalism is represented by foreigners or national minorities. The leaders are intellectuals or, more frequently, semi-intellectuals ("lower mandarins") who have seized power through guerrilla movements or, more often, by transforming themselves into a military elite. Their political language borrows heavily from Marxism-Leninism, and as a result, the importance of the Communist element in Third World politics has been overrated. Nasser and Sukarno subscribed to fascist doctrines in their younger years, and there is little doubt what would have been the political credo of a Castro or Guevara and many Latin American guerrillas had they been born two decades earlier.

It was the fashion among Western observers in the 1950s and 1960s to view the emergence of the new dictatorships as a progressive and on the whole desirable phenomenon. An entire literature praised the new one-party states and military dictatorships for their vigorous dynamism and competence. It was claimed in all seriousness that these regimes would establish the necessary basis for the growth of effective representative institutions. The one-party system, as one observer put it at the time, could often be a significant step toward the liberal state. Others commended dictatorship as the only effective counterforce to Communism. Even Soviet commentators, who generally displayed greater realism, were carried away for a number of years by a new theory of "military socialism."

These illusions have more or less been dissipated. It is one thing to explain the emergence of the dictatorships in the Third World as an inevitability, in view of the backwardness of the countries concerned. It would have been a near miracle for multi-party parliamentary systems to have come into lasting existence in these parts of the globe. (In this light, Mrs. Gandhi's introduction of "guided democracy" in 1975 is not so surprising; what is surprising is that unguided democracy lasted for so long in India.) But it is another thing altogether to assume, as many did, that dictatorship would be a transitional phase, leading eventually toward freedom and greater popular participation in government. Today it is not even clear that dictatorship is conducive to economic progress, as so many observers once assumed. Brazil under Vargas and Argentina under Peron did not make substantial economic progress; Sukarno and Nkrumah led their respective countries to the brink of economic ruin; and, while there were important social reforms in Nasser's Egypt and in Ataturk's Turkey, overall development was unimpressive and it is too early to say with any certainty that their reforms will last.

In truth the record so far has shown that economic success or failure depends above all on the presence of oil or some other important minerals, or on a hard-working population bent on improving its living standard quite independently of, and frequently in spite of, the policy of the dictators. And even in countries showing substantial economic progress, there has been no advance toward freer institutions. One can think of quite a few Third World countries—not only those that produce oil—with a much higher degree of urbanization and literacy, and an infinitely higher per-capita income, than Europe or the United States had in the age of the bourgeois revolution, but which still lack fundamental structures of liberty and civil rights.

If the optimistic predictions of armies' becoming an "inculcative force for nationhood" are no longer aired with much conviction, now army seizures of power are justified as an *ultima ratio,* the army being the only institution with sufficient "legitimacy" to preserve the fabric of society. Research into the legitimacy or illegitimacy of regimes, however, will not take us very far toward an understanding of Third World politics. There has been a great deal of confusion about this subject; legitimacy usually means no more than that a regime is reasonably effective. The fascist regimes of Europe, it will be recalled, were very effective indeed, and would thus score high in any legitimacy scale. Also, both Hitler and Mussolini would no doubt have won large victories in free elections around 1935—another index of legitimacy. And citizens of Nazi Germany and Fascist Italy were allowed to travel abroad up to the outbreak of World War II—yet another evidence of legitimacy.

The fact that there have been few military coups of late in some Middle Eastern countries like Syria and Iraq, whereas a great many occurred in the 1950s and 1960s, is sometimes adduced as evidence for the growing popularity of these regimes. Actually, all it shows is that the secret police in these countries have become more effective, and the military command structure more complicated, so that not every commander of an armored division is in a position to stage a coup. Syria, and in particular Iraq, are good examples of the transition from old-fashioned military rule to a "higher" state of dictatorship in which the army shares some of its power with the state party and the security services. The Syrian regime now accuses the Iraqis, and vice versa, of having established a "fascist dictatorship." Both are correct and both exaggerate; they have rightly analyzed the tendency, but full-fledged fascism has not yet come to power in Baghdad or Damascus.

What, then of the future? As long as the rulers of the Third World are unable to develop more or less effective political institutions, such as state parties, or to generate popular participation and enthusiasm, their regimes will resemble old-fashioned dictatorship more closely than modern totalitarianism. But the logic of events is driving them toward more modern and more efficient forms of dictatorship, and all modern dictatorships are bound to have fascist features to some extent.[1] Dictatorship in the modern world cannot survive without an ideology of sorts; it has to mobilize the masses through some form of propaganda, and it has to deter its enemies by repression and terror. On the political level, modernization in the Third World means a transition from traditional authoritarian systems to more effective tyrannies. Not all countries will be able to make the grade; some will stagnate or relapse into anarchy. The more progressive ones will advance toward political systems providing greater "legitimacy."

Meanwhile, the lack of economic progress generates frustration, and this is directed above all against the West. The very existence of working democracies somewhere in the world is a provocation and a danger for dictatorships, just as it was in the 1930s. Perhaps even more so today, because whereas the old fascist regimes had doctrinally rejected democracy, the new dictatorships subscribe to it in theory (and disregard it in practice). Political opposition to Western democracy is in fact the common denominator of most Third World countries.

Thus, while the Western world sticks to its free institutions, it will face great and growing difficulties in its relations with the Third World dictatorships. The United Nations may be irrelevant in terms of political power, but it still is an excellent barometer for indicating the general trend in world politics. The fact that the West has found itself in growing isolation in the United Nations comes as no surprise. The old and much despised League of Nations, whatever its shortcomings eventually rid itself of the dictators (Germany in 1933, Italy two years later, and in the end also the Soviet Union). The United Nations, on the other hand, has been taken over by countries which, whatever their internal differences, agree that dictatorship is beautiful.

The trend is ominous, and equally disconcerting is the reluctance on the part of the West to face up to the new realities, the belief that by the ritual invocation of "common" values such as peace, freedom, and human rights, fundamental differences can be papered over. Describing an earlier age of tyranny Thucydides wrote that "words changed their ordinary meaning and took on that which was now given them." There still is the inclination, deliberate or unconscious, to deemphasize the meaning of one's own values, as if ideological confusion provided a solid basis for rapprochement between democracy and dictatorship.

Tyranny has been present throughout history, but there are periods in which it has receded and others in which it has assumed epidemic proportions. It is the great danger of modern despotisms, as of modern weapons, that they are much more destructive than in any past age. Enlightened despotism in the form of "tutelary democracy," in these circumstances, is a hope, not a forgone conclusion. Seen in historical perspective, European fascism may have been not so much the end of an era as the precursor of a new dark age.

*February 1976*

## NOTE

1. In the 1920s the concept, "exotic fascism," was used in the debates of the Communist International; it may well be resurrected one of these days.

# Peace in the Middle East

# Peace With Egypt?

Any discussion of the current prospects for peace between Israel and the Arab countries has to begin by rehearsing the history of the Middle East between the Six-Day War of June 1967 and the Yom Kippur War of October 1973. Efforts to reach a peace settlement in those seven years were protracted, highly complicated, and ultimately futile. All the many plans that were proposed—the Rogers plan, the Jarring plan, and the nameless others—seem now of merely academic interest (although it is entirely possible that one or another of them will be disinterred for future use). The story of these negotiations is a melancholy one, not least for the question it raises of possible opportunities missed by the various parties to the conflict, especially Israel. Not that Israel ignored any genuine peace overture from the Arabs; there was none. But it is another matter whether an interim accommodation might not have been reached with Egypt alone, based on a demilitarization of the Sinai, and whether such an arrangement would not have lessened the likelihood of a new round of fighting.

After the Arab attack of October 1973 it was noted in Israel that the strategic depth offered by the Sinai was in fact a lifesaver; had the attack been launched from the pre-June 1967 lines it would have threatened Israel's very existence. This is very true. But the argument assumes that the 1967 borders were the only feasible alternative to the Bar Lev Line, when in fact a demilitarized Sinai might have functioned as a more effective warning zone than did the Suez Canal. Nor can it be taken for granted that the attack itself was inevitable, since Egypt faced a great many problems at home and abroad, and had some sort of interim agreement been reached on the Sinai, the Egyptians might not have felt such an overriding urgency to recover all the lost territories.

Similarly, a settlement might have been made with Jordan; although not with Syria. Yet Syria in isolation could not have caused a great deal of damage. The same goes for Al-Fatah and its rival groups, who would anyway have kept up their sporadic attacks from across the border and the hijacking of airplanes. In the course of time, however, the Palestinians might have come to see that they could no longer rely on the Arab governments in their struggle and they too might have come to accept the existence of the state of Israel.

This particular line of thinking was dismissed in the late 1960s as a dangerous delusion by those who claimed to know Arab political psychology. Yet it later appeared that the terrorist organizations were actually afraid of a more flexible Israeli policy, lest it put them out of business. "Thank God for Dayan," wrote Yasir Arafat in retrospect:

> After the 1967 defeat, Arab opinion, broken and dispirited, was ready to conclude peace at any price. If Israel, after its lightning victory, had proclaimed that it had no expansionist aims and withdrawn its troops from the conquered territories, while continuing to occupy certain strategic points necessary to its security, the affair would have been easily settled. . . .[1]

Arafat exaggerates: the affair would not have been easily settled. Still, there was a chance that de-escalation might have worked, and the truth is that those opportunities which did exist were not explored.

The reasons for this were manifold. Deep down the Israelis have always inclined toward a "worst-case" analysis of their situation, arising perhaps from a determination (which is hardly difficult to understand in the light of recent history) not to take any risks with Jewish lives. Arab leaders had threatened Israel with extinction for many years prior to 1967, and these threats could not easily be dismissed as idle. When in the wake of the 1967 war the Arabs officially opted at the Khartoum conference for a policy of immobility ("No peace, no recognition, no negotiation") it was only natural for Israel to react accordingly. Any other course would have been interpreted as evidence of weakness, and it was well known that Arabs respected strength alone. From a military point of view the 1967 armistice lines seemed ideal. Before the war, Jordanian territory extended to within 30 km. of Tel Aviv, Egyptian territory to within 80; now the Egyptians were many hundreds of kilometers away, and the Jordanians were beyond the Jordan River. Israeli planes could reach Cairo in a few minutes' time. A good case would be, and was, made for not withdrawing from these lines—quite apart from the biblical prophecies and other divine injunctions invoked by the few Israeli annexationists.

No one in Israel expected all the territories taken in the Six-Day War to be retained, at least at first. Immediately after the war Moshe Dayan came out against an Israeli presence at the Suez Canal, Abba Eban warned against an "intoxication with victory," David Ben-Gurion on more than one occasion reiterated that a strong army, although vital, was no substitute for a political solution which in his view should include a return of the West Bank under agreed terms and a satisfactory settlement of the Sinai issue. Differences of opinion within the ranks of the Israeli government itself manifested themselves in such proposals as the Allon plan, recognizing the Palestinian Arabs' right to self-determination. But as time went on Dayan, Golda Meir, Israel Galili, and other Israeli leaders became increasingly pessimistic about the prospects of a peace settlement. As long as the Arabs were unwilling to talk, Israel had to stand fast. A growing reluctance was felt even to discuss the possible terms of a settlement. The general attitude became that the Arab-Israeli confrontation, like every other conflict in history, had to run its full course. At some date in the future, when the Arabs were psychologically ready to accept the existence of Israel, it would be possible to find mutually acceptable solutions to all the outstanding questions—but for the time being Israel had to stand firm.

This policy had much to recommend it, but it also had several major flaws. It ignored the fact that the Arab-Israeli conflict was not purely regional in character, and that with regard to the two superpowers involved, an asymmetry existed between American support for Israel and Soviet support for the Arabs: America had to consider its other interests in the Middle East whereas the Soviet Union could give all-out assistance to its clients. It underrated the effective force of the Arab armies built up by the Russians since 1967. It overrated détente. And, above all, it did not take into consideration the growing importance of the oil weapon as a means of isolating Israel on the international scene: as far as Western Europe and Japan were concerned, Israel was expendable but Arab oil was not. The international constellation, in brief, was changing, and not in Israel's favor. A major power might have stood by and watched these changes with some degree of equanimity; a small country did so at its peril.

With the end of the 1973 war came a new willingness in Israel to rethink the Arab-Israeli dispute, and to consider new ways of settling it. A spate of articles and speeches, symptomatic of the confusion caused by war, suggested all kinds of panaceas: a National Security Council, a mutual-defense pact with the U.S., a "charismatic minister of information." Only after an interval of several weeks were serious attempts undertaken to analyze the lessons of the October war in broader perspective and greater depth. This soul-searching coincided with the electoral campaign in which the parties had to clarify their policies for the future. The right-wing Herut claimed in its election propaganda that the people of Israel had won a magnificent victory on the battlefield and should not have to pay for the defeat of the Western world on the oilfields of

Arabia; but Herut also denied that it was a "war party" and asserted that it was much better equipped than the Labor coalition to lead Israel toward peace. The Liberals, Herut's partners in the Likud coalition, advocated a more moderate line, suggesting Israeli concessions in return for peace; the debate among Liberals was whether these concessions should be spelled out or not.

As for the Labor alignment, it had to accommodate conflicting trends in its declared policy. The preamble of the fourteen point program accepted last November stated that "Our platform must reflect the lessons of the Yom Kippur War." But what were these lessons, apart from the need (on which everyone agreed) to maintain the strength of the defense forces? The platform insisted on defensible borders based on a territorial compromise. There would be no return to the June 1967 boundaries; a peace agreement with Jordan would be based on the existence of two independent states—Israel, with Jerusalem as its capital, and an Arab state to the east; efforts would be made to continue settling Israelis in the occupied areas "in keeping with cabinet decisions giving priority to national security considerations." The last point was a concession to the "hawks" in the Labor alignment, but as a whole the Labor platform constituted a decisive victory for the doves and a retreat from the maximalist demands voiced before the war.

By sheer coincidence, the Labor platform was published on the same day the demands of the Arabs were made known at the Algiers meeting of Arab heads of state. These stated that the struggle against the Zionist "invasion" was a long-term historic responsibility which would call for many more trials and sacrifices. A cease-fire was not peace, which would come only when a number of conditions had been met, two among them paramount and unequivocal: first, the evacuation by Israel of all occupied Arab territories and above all Jerusalem; second, the reestablishment of full national rights for the Palestinian people. Yet inasmuch as no objections were voiced to negotiations with Israel, something which the Khartoum conference in 1967 had expressly rejected, it appeared to many observers that the "moderate" line of President Sadat had won out in Algiers. The final communiqué stated that the meeting had been a great success, but since Iraq and Libya boycotted the conference, and Syria subsequently decided not to participate in the Geneva conference at all, Arab unity could by no means be said to be complete. As the weeks passed the Algiers resolution was shrilly rejected by Arab extremists. A broadcast emanating from Baghdad on December 21, 1973 (the day the Geneva talks opened) announced: "The masses will not be bound by the regimes of treason and defeatism at the Geneva conference." Radio Tripoli asked: "Has our Arab nation become so servile in the eyes of those leaders [i.e., Sadat] that they belittle its dignity and injure its pride without fearing its wrath?''

Israel's "khaki elections" took place on the last day of the old year.[2] If public-opinion polls published last September are to be trusted, the results would have been similar even if the war had not taken place. The Labor alignment, deeply split and under fire from within not only because of the military handling of the war but for the lack of flexibility shown by Mrs. Meir's inner circle in recent years, lost ground. Were it not for the obvious necessity to preserve the unity of the alignment in view of the international situation, it is quite possible that both Mrs. Meir and General Dayan might have had to resign under pressure from large sections of their party. But Likud had no cause to be overjoyed by the results of the elections either; if the party of Menahem Begin could not overtake its rivals in such nearly ideal conditions, it never would—unless, of course, the Labor alignment should disintegrate entirely.

The campaign was confused because the Israeli voter was not given a clear choice. As one Israeli commentator wrote, "Those who want to purchase Dayan must buy Allon. Those who want the Liberals must buy Begin." In the absence of a clear choice, the outcome of the elections was bound to be inconclusive: no clear mandate emerged for any one course of action. Menahem Begin may have been relieved not to receive more votes than he did; victory would have almost certainly compelled him to make concessions in Geneva contrary to what he promised during the campaign. Yet the absence of consensus—more accurately, the sharp polarization of public opinion—will make the task of the Israeli negotiators beyond the first stage of the talks very difficult. The effect of the vote, the London *Economist* wrote, was to block any government from making the vital decisions that the Geneva talks demand. Since such a state of affairs cannot continue for very long, the deadlock will probably be broken either by new fighting or by a new election, or perhaps both.

## II

Throughout history there has been one kind of war notoriously difficult to conclude: the war of faith, the holy war, the crusade. In these conflicts it is not the leader or the government of the other side that is the enemy, but every individual in the enemy camp.

To what extent do the Arabs regard their conflict with Israel as a religious war, or a war of national liberation, to use the modern parlance? The recent Algiers summit conference proclaimed that the war aim of the Arab states was the restoration of the national rights of the

Palestinian Arabs, that the Palestine Liberation Organization was the only legal representative of the Palestinians, and that its interpretation of the "national rights" was binding. The PLO interpretation was in turn laid down in the Palestinian National Covenant of July 1968, which says that the establishment of Israel is "null and void." The Algiers resolution, in other words, as much as stated that the purpose of any peace conference would be to discuss the liquidation of Israel.

In the eyes of sòme, this means that it is pointless for Israel to attend the Geneva conference. Fortunately, however, even in the war aims of religious or quasi-religious movements a discrepancy often exists between the desirable and the possible. In theory Catholics and Protestants should not coexist to this day, nor should Muslims and Christians, or Communists and non-Communists. All such movements have come at one stage or another to the realization that with an enemy who cannot be defeated, temporary compromises have to be made. The old enmity, the *odium theologicum,* is itself subject to gradual erosion as such compromises become permanent; the formulas of hatred may linger on but they no longer carry the same conviction.

At the Geneva peace conference Israel will establish in due course whether, at this stage in the conflict, a readiness to compromise has been reached by the Arab states. With regard to Egypt in particular a peace conference may have been long overdue. So far as the psychological readiness of other Arabs to accept the existence of Israel is concerned, the conference may turn out to be premature. Geneva may be just the beginning of a long process, perhaps the first in a series of conferences that will be interrupted by crises, pressure, threats, breakdown, new fighting, new negotiations.

The Geneva peace conference opened on December 21 in an atmosphere of cautious optimism. President Nixon had said soon after the alert in October that the prospects for peace had never before been so good. Dr. Kissinger, in his opening speech at the conference, spoke of a "historic chance for peace"; there were promising noises from Jerusalem, Moscow, and even Cairo. All this optimism was based, no doubt, on the undisputed fact that immediately after a war the prospects almost always seem brightest and formerly unacceptable conditions suddenly seem acceptable after all.

It was not by chance that the conference concentrated in its first phase on Israel and Egypt; and certainly the issue of troop disengagement, an issue speedily settled in the agreement signed on January 17, was not the only motivating factor. The Israel-Egypt "problem" does not at first glance seem insurmountable. If Egyptian sovereignty over Sinai were recognized and Egypt were to accept an effective system of demilitarization, there would then remain only the matter of a token Israeli demilitarized zone and the question of the Gaza Strip and Sharm el-Sheikh. Neither side is particularly eager to accept responsibility for Gaza (though neither will admit it) and the importance of Sharm el-Sheikh to Israel has been somewhat exaggerated (the recent Egyptian blockade at Bab el-Mandeb almost nullified the strategic usefulness of an Israeli presence at Sharm el-Sheikh). Assuming that Israel were to withdraw gradually from Sinai and the Egyptians were to accept the principle of demilitarization, a settlement between the two countries could be envisaged—following hard bargaining, of course.

Israel, however, would hardly agree to withdraw in return for a mere armistice, and it is here that the real difficulties may set in. Egypt has assured its Arab allies that it will under no circumstances make peace with Israel unless Israel withdraws from all occupied Arab territories and unless the national rights of the Palestinians are restored. The official interpretation of this formula, as I have noted, means the liquidation of the state of Israel. There are, however, several other interpretations possible and there are, in addition, legitimate grounds for doubting the strength of Egypt's commitment to the cause of its allies.

For twenty-five years Egypt has borne the brunt of the struggle against Israel, yet pan-Arab feeling is less deeply rooted in Cairo than elsewhere in the Arab world. Even the late Gamal Abdel Nasser, the champion of pan-Arabism, recognized toward the end of his life that he had taken upon himself an impossible and thankless task. In the struggle against Israel Egypt has received a great deal of verbal aid and unsolicited advice, but when the hour of truth comes, as it did in October 1973, little more than token support is ever forthcoming from its Arab friends. Syria and Iraq harbor strong feelings of resentment toward Egypt; leadership in the Arab world, they maintain, should rightfully be theirs. Colonel Qaddafi of Libya has on many occasions decried Egypt's ''decadence'' and ''corruption,'' and there is not much love lost between Egypt and Algeria either. The Egyptians for their part regard Syria and Iraq as semi-barbaric lands and they have contempt for the Palestinians.

All in all, there is a strong inclination inside Egypt today to put Egyptian interests first, pan-Arab interests second. The Six-Day War came as a great shock to Egypt, and there was universal agreement that the shame of 1967 has to be expiated on the field of battle and Sinai regained. But with these aims achieved, Egypt may no longer feel an overriding obligation to champion the further struggle against Israel. To be sure, one can find hundreds of articles and dozens of books published in Egypt all proclaiming the inadmissibility of a Jewish state in the Middle East. But these declarations should not necessarily be taken at face value. If Israel could be made to disappear overnight, no Egyptian leader would object, but the prospect of many more years of hard fighting and severe damage to the country has little appeal. The Egyptian army was eager to fight for Ismailia; it is not so eager to fight (much less to die) for Nablus and Tulkarm. When addressing their more radical Arab brethren, Egyptians will stress that the final goal is the total liberation of the whole of Palestine, but this, they are apt to add quickly, will happen only in a generation or two or perhaps three. In the meantime much water will have flowed down the Nile and the Jordan.

It should have been Israeli policy after 1967—and especially after Nasser's death in 1970—to concentrate on a separate deal with Egypt, and this should be its foremost objective now. I do not wish to discount the difficulty of accomplishing this objective. Egypt is desperately poor, and financially dependent on Saudi Arabia and the Persian Gulf states. These countries, for a variety of reasons, have a vested interest in the prolongation of the struggle against Israel, which for them is tantamount to an insurance policy against the radical forces in the Arab world that threaten their own existence. Sadat's position is stronger now than before the war, but this is not saying much. Nor would an Egyptian-Israeli deal mark the end of the Arab-Israeli conflict, and in the event of a new flare-up the danger would always exist that Egypt might be drawn into the campaign. Finally, an opening to Egypt on Israel's part would involve a basic psychological reorientation: since 1948 Egypt has been *the* enemy for Israel. Nevertheless, despite all these considerations, the fact remains that the interests of the two countries are not necessarily incompatible, and normal, if not friendly, relations between them should not be ruled out as a future possibility. There will be many realignments in the Arab world in the years to come and, unlikely as this may appear now, it is by no means unthinkable that one day Israel will break out of its present isolation and align with one or more of the Arab countries against one or more of the others.

For if a settlement with Egypt entails grave risks, the two other alternatives are even more dangerous. One is not to give up anything, the other to tackle the problem at its core and strive for a settlement which would satisfy the Palestinian Arabs. As for the first, if one assumes (as some do) that any Israeli withdrawal is bound to be just the first step in the gradual dismemberment of the country as a whole by its Arab neighbors, it would of course be preferable in every respect to make a stand now, rather than later when the boundaries will be harder to defend. Israel is already isolated, according to this view, and there is no further point in trying to appease world opinion by capitulation. The U.S. in the last resort can be counted on to remain steadfast, for its prestige is deeply involved and Israel is by now a cornerstone of its foreign policy. This line of thought, if put into action, would almost certainly bring about a new war in the Middle East, perhaps within a few months, for Sadat is under considerable domestic pressure to show results or to renew the fighting. But the prospect does not deter the advocates of such a policy. A new war, they argue, might be a protracted and hard struggle, but in the end Israel would win and this time the victory would be decisive.

A more sophisticated version of the hard-line argument maintains that since the deck has been stacked in advance, it would be fatal for Israel to act "reasonably" and "responsibly" in the present situation, as it is being urged to do on all sides. A superpower like the Soviet Union can swallow whole countries and go uncriticized, while Israel is denied the right to defensible borders and is expected to conform to the wishes of the great powers. Since the game is fixed, why not behave "irrationally" —like the Arab oil producers, say, or the Arab terrorists? There would be much general indignation, the Russians would issue threats, a few more countries would break off relations, pressure would be exerted by Washington, but nothing much worse would be likely to happen. The coming years will in any case see far-reaching changes in world politics— perhaps the total collapse of Europe, or, less likely, the reassertion of Europe's power. War might break out between the Soviet Union and China. International relations are increasingly being dictated by the law of the jungle, and unless Israel adapts itself to these conditions, the argument concludes, its chances of survival will be slim. Israel should be tough, unpredictable, and to a certain degree irresponsible.

This reasoning cannot be dismissed out of hand (for the simple fact that anything is possible in politics) but the chances of such a policy in the real world cannot be rated high. It underestimates the extent of Israel's military and economic dependence on the United States, and exaggerates American readiness to help Israel in the future. But even more decisively, it is not a policy that the government of a democratic country can easily pursue.

Then there is the alternative of an accommodation with the Palestinians—in every way the ideal solution. If Palestinians and Israelis could reach agreement on the basis of the establishment of a Palestinian state on the West Bank, Israeli willingness to take back some refugees, and the resettlement elsewhere of those for whom a home could not be found, an end would be put to the conflict once and for all. For the fate of the Palestinian Arabs is the heart of the matter; without a solution of this issue, the wider conflict will not be solved.

Unfortunately, however, the Palestinian issue is also the least tractable by far of all the issues of contention between Israel and the Arab world. A Palestinian Arab state would not be economically viable, and would be heavily dependent on the other Arab countries and the Soviet Union. Moreover, the policy of such a state would most likely be dictated not the forces of peace but by the radical elements, which would consider the West Bank merely a base for the continuation of the armed struggle against Israel. Nor does the domestication of the terrorists seem a likely prospect for the near future. The main Palestinian organizations, Fatah and the PLO, deny the Israelis' right to national self-determination, and their aim is the destruction of the "Zionist state." When they speak of the "democratic secular Palestinian state" that will replace Israel, they mean an Arab state in which Jews would have the right to be buried in their own cemeteries.

Thus, whatever the Geneva conference may achieve, it will almost certainly not bring an overall peace to the area. But if the chances for overall peace are remote, there does exist now (as after 1967) an opportunity for defusing the conflict, for rendering unlikely the renewal of fighting on a large scale. This can be done principally by Israel's meeting the basic demands of the Egyptians—gradual withdrawal of Israeli forces from large parts of the Sinai and the recognition in principle of Egyptian sovereignty there, in exchange for demilitarization. Unless this demand is met, a new outbreak of hostilities seems likely, with the almost certain outcome a peace settlement dictated by the superpowers and even more detrimental to Israel's interests.

## III

The prospect of an imposed settlement by the superpowers to the detriment of Israel raises the specter of the infamous Munich conference of 1938. And, in fact, Czechoslovakia in the late 1930s has been invoked rather frequently in the last few months as offering an instructive analogy to the situation in which Israel now finds itself. A small democratic country in the center of Europe, Czechoslovakia was dismembered in two stages following a decision dictated by the powers. "Munich" and "appeasement" have become part of our political vocabulary, shorthand words connoting a sellout à la 1938. There are those who see such a sellout—of Israel—shaping up in today's Middle East.

Drawing historical parallels is always dangerous and sometimes downright misleading, but there is not denying that a comparison with Czechoslovakia is of some help in understanding the present situation. Though democratic in character, Czechoslovakia contained a substantial minority—3,500,000 Germans—which, from the very beginning, did not want to be part of the Czechoslovak state formed after World War I, gravitating rather toward Germany; the stronger Germany became, the stronger the pull toward Berlin. Hitler demanded the "return" of the Sudeten regions, where the German minority was concentrated; the

Czechs maintained that these regions were economically and militarily vital to Czechoslovakia.

All through 1938, while the Nazis were stepping up the pressure on Prague, a great deal of sharp criticism was being voiced in the West about the state of affairs inside Czechoslovakia. The British and French press published scathing condemnations of the Czechs for their treatment of the German minority. The Czech state, it was claimed, was an artificial creation, founded a mere twenty years before in what was now seen to have been a regrettable error. The idea that France should "commit suicide," or that a "single Frenchman should die for this misbegotten state" was grotesque. Not surprisingly, the Jews too were brought in; Léon Daudet, son of a famous father, wrote in 1938 in *L'Action Française:* "Peasant or worker, the average Frenchman is expected to commit suicide at the merest nod of a Jew who detests him, in some obscure and faraway village of which he hasn't the vaguest idea." Later that same year, Neville Chamberlain echoed these sentiments in similar terms: the Paris treaty-makers had committed an error, he declared, and the treaty should have been revised long ago; it was unthinkable to Chamberlain that Britons should go to war for a faraway land about which they knew nothing.

The anti-Czech comment of 1938, which bears an uncanny resemblance to remarks in the Western press, particularly the British and French, during the recent Middle East crisis and after, was by no means limited to the Right or to proponents of *Realpolitik*. The Left too castigated Czechoslovakia for not being a genuinely neutral country like Switzerland; France and Britain after all could not play the role of international policeman forever. Czech policy was called a danger to world peace; although the term "détente" had not yet been invented, the phrase used at the time was just as expressive: *"Conciliation entre les états totalitaires et les états democratiques."* The only alternative to such conciliation was the unleashing of war. What the world needed was disarmament, and in the long run Czechoslovakia too was assured it would find security in a disarmed world.[3]

The status of Czechoslovakia was supposed to be settled by the agreements reached in Munich. The Sudeten regions were returned to Germany in exchange for an international guarantee of the new boundaries of Czechoslovakia against unprovoked aggression. Yet when, six months later, German troops invaded what remained of Czechoslovakia after Munich, no one came to the rescue.

Munich provides some highly instructive lessons about the psychology of appeasement and the value of international guarantees, and as such it is useful as a warning in the present negotiations. But there is a danger in pushing the analogy too far. Not every peace treaty in world history has been violated, after all, nor every international guarantee ignored. The lessons of Munich, that is to say, are of limited value as a guide for the future and cannot in my view be used as an alibi by those who oppose any concessions whatsoever on Israel's part.

The international constellation and the balance of power in the Middle East do not resemble Europe in 1938. Czechoslovakia faced a relentless enemy who could not possibly be deflected from his course. Israel, on the other hand, confronts a coalition of states that have neither the cohesion nor the power of Nazi Germany. That this coalition should have come into being at all was unusual—to a certain extent it may have come into being as a result of Israeli diplomatic inflexibility—and it will last only by a miracle. Hitler was reasonably certain that Czechoslovakia, facing the overwhelming power of the Reich, would not fight. And as for the Czechs, surrender meant the loss of independence, in itself a national disaster but not the end of the Czech people. For many centuries the Czechs had survived under foreign rule, and the conviction was strong that sooner or late Hitler's policy would lead to a war in which the Germans would be defeated, and then an independent Czechoslovakia would rise again—as indeed it did seven years later. No such hope exists for Israel, and this in itself precludes an Israeli surrender. But Israel is not only more resolute than Czechoslovakia, it is also infinitely stronger. Even Hitler would not have attacked Czechoslovakia if, for argument's sake, it had meant risking the destruction of Berlin, Munich, and other German centers.

For Israel, the years to come, fraught as they will be with danger, will require not only constant military preparedness, a high degree of flexibility, and economic sacrifice, but also, very likely, political concessions. Nevertheless, and despite the efficaciousness of the oil weapon in Arab hands, the outlook is not all that unpromising. As long as the "Zionist menace" overshadowed all other factors in the Arab political consciousness, a certain degree of unity prevailed in the Arab world. But as the "enemy" assumes a lower profile, all the suppressed dissensions among Arab nations and Arab ideologies are bound to reassert themselves. The fact that some Arab countries will earn fabulous riches during the years to come while others will not is going to exacerbate existing divisions; sooner or later, there will be a free-for-all for the spoils. The oil-producing countries are already becoming increasingly unpopular all over the world because of their extortionist policies, and they are going to have to defend themselves and their riches against more immediate dangers than Israel. Assuming that the global balance of power does not radically change in the next decade, that America does not become substantially weaker, and that some sort of détente continues to hold between the two superpowers, the risk will be reduced of an all-out Arab attack.

But in the final analysis, Israel's fate will depend on its own policies and on its own inner character. It certainly cannot afford the luxury of an internal factional war such as once before in history caused the destruction of a Jewish commonwealth. Israel in the days to come will need unity, strong nerves, and a readiness to compromise combined with a firm resolve to repel any new threat to its existence.

*March 1974*

## NOTES

1. Quoted in John K. Cooley, *Green March, Black September* (New York, 1973), p. 99.
2. On the Israeli elections, see also David Vital's article in *Commentary,* March 1974.
3. Michael Harrington in a recent article has offered the current version of this argument. See his "Israel, the War, and American Politics," *Midstream,* December 1973.

# Is Peace Possible
# in the Middle East?

## I

One of the mysteries of world politics is the amount of attention being paid these days to the Arab-Israeli conflict. According to some estimates, almost half the time of the last session of the UN General Assembly was devoted to issues connected in one way or another with this conflict. A quantitative study of the uses of Henry Kissinger's energies would probably show a similar pattern, and so would an analysis of editorial comment on international affairs. Indeed, any unsuspecting newspaper reader would get the impression that the future of the Golan Heights and the West Bank are more important than all the other problems in the world put together. Yet it would be only too easy to point to at least half-a-dozen zones of equal or greater weight in other parts of the world, not to mention sub-acute critical trends in the political and economic sphere whose long-term effects may have the gravest results.

Of course those who put so much emphasis on the Middle East argue that it is not the future of Golan that is at stake but the general stability of the area and the securing of the oil supply. They will admit that but for these overriding considerations, the Arab-Israeli conflict would be of no greater interest than the conflict between Bolivia and Peru, or at most between North and South Korea. But unless there is some "movement" toward a "lasting peace" in the Middle East, they say, there will be another war; and a new war would trigger an oil embargo, start a world-wide depression, put at least ten million Americans out of work, destroy NATO, allow Soviet power to engulf the Straits of Gibraltar, and bring Communist ministers into coalition governments in much of Europe. If, on the other hand, Israel withdrew from the occupied territories, permanent peace would follow—Middle Eastern governments would be stable, the oil would flow, its price would go down, bankers and exporters would make profits, generals and admirals would obtain bases, and American policy-makers would be able to devote themselves to building a new and more workable world order.

Now, the resolution of the Arab-Israeli conflict would in every way be desirable. But examining recent suggestions for the settlement of this conflict, or of the hopes held out for the consequences that would follow from such a settlement, one has to cut one's way through a thicket of wishful thinking almost unique in an otherwise fairly cynical age.

To begin with, there is no cogent reason to believe that a settlement would add to the stability of the Middle East (let alone the stability of the entire world). The recent history of the Middle East is a story of conflicts: Algerian interests clash with those of Morocco and Tunisia; Libya is at loggerheads with Egypt and Sudan; there has been almost constant tension between Iraq and all her neighbors; South Yemen has a conflict of long standing with North Yemen, and is even now conducting surrogate war against Oman; Lebanon is in a state of civil war; and the survival of Jordan to this day is a miracle. The list could be extended without much difficulty. Moreover, the traditional rivalries among governments have been aggravated by the sudden influx of oil revenues.

Despite the Arab-Israeli confrontation, some of these conflicts have entered an acute phase, but thanks to the need to make common cause against the "Zionist danger," there has by and large been a truce in the Arab world. For so long as the campaign against Israel continues, Arab solidarity is the supreme necessity, and any attempt to raise other issues or press other demands is attacked as an act of treason. Once this unifying factor is removed, once the "Zionist danger" decreases, the struggles between rich countries and poor, between haves and have-nots, between pro-Soviet and pro-American regimes are bound to escalate; and so are the grave domestic tensions between "moderates" and "radicals" within each country. The Arab world would then be rent by bitter civil strife and, very probably, war; and it is the oil countries like Saudi Arabia and Kuwait which would be in the gravest danger. For while it is sometimes argued that in the absence of progress toward peace in the Middle East, moderate policies and leaders will be superseded by more radical ones, this is far more like to happen as the *consequence* of progress toward peace between Israel and the Arab countries and the resulting increase of tension elsewhere in the Arab world.

Almost everyone believes that Israel's return to the 1967 borders and the establishment of a Palestinian state are necessary to a settlement in the Middle East. Of course the basic issue in the Arab-Israeli conflict is not the border problem or a Palestinian state—the conflict existed before there were occupied territories and before there was a demand for a Palestinian state. The real issue, as Elie Kedourie puts it, is the right of the Jews, "hitherto a subject community under Islam, to exercise political sovereignty in an area regarded as part of the Muslim domain." Why, Professor Kedourie asks, should the Arabs, who have been unwilling for twenty-eight years to grant this right to the Jews, suddenly be willing to do so just when Arab power and influence have so greatly increased?

But let us assume that the Arabs *are* willing to do so. Let us even assume that the PLO no longer regards the destruction of the State of Israel as its ultimate aim, that it is ready to accept the Jewish state, and peacefully to coexist with it in a Palestinian state of its own. What would be the nature of such a Palestinian state?

A look at the map shows that it would consist of two separate parts. One part would be the West Bank, bounded on the east by the River Jordan and including Samaria and Judaea; the western border would run west of Tulkarm and Kalkilya, east of Lod and Ramla, from there to Jerusalem, then south to Hebron and the Dead Sea—altogether some 2,165 square miles. In addition there would be the Gaza Strip. The West Bank has a population of about 600,000, the Gaza Strip of some 300,000. The two sections are not connected, and they remind one of what the late Viscount Samuel said about an earlier partition plan: it would have the effect of creating a Saar and a Polish Corridor and half-a-dozen Danzigs and Memels in a country the size of Wales. If it is argued that Israel in its 1967 borders cannot be defended, a Palestinian state would be even less defensible.

Nor would such a state be economically viable. Annual rainfall in the northern part of the West Bank is fairly high, which has favored local agriculture, but industry is all but nonexistent except for some olive-oil and soap factories in Nablus. Hebron produces glass as well as wooden and mother-of-pearl souvenirs. Bethlehem and Ramalla cater to tourists. The Gaza Strip, whose population density is one of the world's highest, has no industry either; there are citrus groves and some summer fruits such as watermelons. Given this economic situation (which has already forced many workers from the West Bank and the Gaza Strip to work in Israeli industry and on building sites), the new state would not even be able to absorb more than a token number of Palestinian refugees.

Some Arab spokesmen have recently argued that the issue of non-viability is not really a very important one, since a great many countries in the modern world are not viable either. But this, though true, is hardly a reassuring argument. Arab spokesmen also claim that the Palestinians are a hard-working people (which is correct), that they have a great deal of know-how, and that they would get support from the oil-rich countries. According to various research papers prepared by the PLO studies center in Beirut, a Palestinian state could be economically viable—provided the Saudis gave billions for an unlimited period. Past experience has shown, however, that Arab solidarity does not extend to sharing oil revenues, except perhaps for the purchase of arms. Egypt in particular, which has received no major investments from Saudi Arabia and Kuwait, has learned this lesson the hard way.

In addition to being unviable, a Palestinian state in the West Bank and Gaza would have all the makings of a permanent irredentism. If any single thought has gone into the proposals for establishing such a state (and this, unfortunately, cannot be taken for granted), it is apparently the idea that a partial fulfillment of Palestinian demands would lead to a deradicalization of the PLO. Thus it is said that once the Palestinians had to assume responsibility for a state, however small, they would have to drop their maximalist program for the conquest of Israel; nor could they afford to engage in terror any more. Yet even if one believes that there is a moderate element inside the PLO genuinely willing to coexist with Israel on the basis of the 1967 frontiers—a daring leap of faith indeed—it seems almost a foregone conclusion that the logic of events would drive those moderates toward extremism.

Once the state were founded, there would almost certainly be a struggle between the different PLO wings and, of course, the "Rejection Front" (primarily Iraq) and various Communist organizations. These groups, which stand for divergent political aims, deeply distrust one another, but the stakes are not at present sufficiently high to warrant open warfare. With control of a state in the balance, however, a bitter internal battle would begin. Units of Fatah and the PLPF stationed in the new state would regard it as a mere interim arrangement, a milestone on the road to the liberation of the entire homeland. Other Arab countries, weary of carrying the burden of Palestine, might well advise the Palestinians not to pass immediately on to the next phase of the struggle but to let a decent interval elapse. However, in the fight against Israel this would be dangerous for the Palestinians, for once the momentum were lost, it would not easily be regained. It is doubtful therefore whether they would be ready to listen to outside advice. And as to internal advice, though the merchants of Nablus and Jenin would certainly be interested in a climate conducive to business as usual, they could no more be expected to prevail against the irredentists than the bankers of Beirut have been able to do against the terrorists.

In some ways, indeed, it would be easier than in the past for the Palestinians to conduct their operations against Israel. With artillery and missile bases, physical infiltration would be largely unnecessary, while Israeli counter-shelling would be less effective since there would be fewer targets on the other side. Israeli retaliatory raids, on the other hand, would be severely condemned by world public opinion and sanctions might be taken against them.

Nevertheless, there is a limit to what the PLO could reasonably hope to achieve. The Israelis are not a minority like the Assyrians or the

Kurds, nor is there any similarity between their position and that of the Maronites. Israel has a considerable military potential, and it would be unwilling to play according to rules established by the PLO. Fighting would not be limited to border skirmishes; there would be a general escalation involving other Arab armies and possibly also the Soviet Union, and the use of nonconventional weapons would not be ruled out.

In short, the moment one begins to scrutinize the practical implications of establishing a Palestinian state on the West Bank and the Gaza Strip, it becomes abundantly clear that such a state, far from contributing to a peaceful solution of the Arab-Israeli conflict, would more likely exacerbate it.

Many among those in the West who favor the establishment of a Palestinian Arab state genuinely believe that it is the only way to peace, stability, and justice in the Middle East. Others are aware of the dangers ahead but see no alternative in view of the seemingly overwhelming pressures from all quarters; they have persuaded themselves that the worst does not always happen. Then there are those who have no illusions about the outcome of this policy, who know that it will lead to a new war, or wars, but who regard this as both inevitable and desirable, on the theory that a Middle East settlement (as they see it) will be possible only after further bloodshed. Finally, there are those who, unwilling to accept these as the only alternatives, have cast about for variants on the idea of a Palestinian state.

One such variant, a way of coping with the problem of viability, is federation with either Israel or Jordan. At the present time, one cannot envisage a scheme, however ingenious, of federating Israel and a Palestinian state that has a realistic chance of working. The "Jordanian solution," which involves returning the West Bank to Jordan and which Israel now favors, might have worked in 1968, but it is unlikely at this point to break the deadlock. The Palestinians are against accepting Jordanian control in the short run, and King Hussein knows that in the long run a merger between the West Bank and the Hashemite kingdom (the majority of whose inhabitants even now are Palestinians) would make Jordan a Palestinian state.

Hussein's loss, however, would not necessarily be the Palestinians' gain. Even adding Jordan to a Palestinian state on the West Bank still would not provide sufficient scope for a large-scale resettlement of Palestinian refugees. For Jordan is a poor country. Its per-capita income is $270, lower than any other Arab country except the Sudan and Yemen; between 1965 and 1972 (the last figures available) it experienced minus economic growth. Whichever way one looks at it, a merger between the West Bank and Jordan would be no great bargain. Hussein and the Jordanians would lose, the Palestinians would not gain much, and Israel would still be threatened, only this time by one state rather than two.

Besides federation, there is of course the idea of a bi-national state. The establishment of such a state ("democratic and secular"), which was rejected for decades by the leadership of the Palestinian Arabs, is now the official aim of the PLO. The PLO formula should not be taken quite literally, for it clashes with two other Palestinian demands, namely that the character of the state must be Arab, and that the state should be integrated into the area and not remain an "outpost of the West." But a democratic and secular state could not possibly integrate itself into an area that is neither democratic nor secular. Such a state would invite envy and hostility and would be regarded as a foreign body.

With these reservations, it may be quite true that the PLO wants a binational state of sorts, but does not know how to achieve this aim in the present circumstances. One of its chief spokesmen in the West recently stated in an interview that if he waved a magic wand and Israelis and Arabs would live in a democratic, secular state, this would more or less immediately lead to a civil war: "All these years of conflict and tension are not a good background for the establishment of a peaceful and harmonious coexistence between two communities."[1] Said Hammami is of course quite right; historical experience, including some of very recent vintage, shows that bi-nationalism works only very rarely.

It will be argued that these speculations and objections are all too pessimistic, that the conflict will not necessarily escalate, that the Palestinians may well put up with the existence of Israel (and the Israelis with the existence of a Palestinian state), that there may be isolated acts of violence but no movement toward full-scale war. Yet even if an optimistic scenario for achieving a settlement is assumed, there would still remain the problem of guarantees by outside powers.

Who would these powers be? Among the various nominees who have been put forward, the United Nations and Europe can be dismissed without further comment. As for the Soviet Union, it is indeed true (as a recent Brookings Institution study group has noted) that the Russians, because of their relations with Syria and the PLO, have a considerable capacity for obstructing peace or even blocking further progress toward an overall settlement. Or to put the case even more bluntly: the Soviet Union could probably torpedo any settlement not to its liking. But is it at all certain that the Soviet Union would prefer a peace settlement to the present state of affairs? Those who argue that a new Middle Eastern war would be a disaster for the West and would greatly strengthen Soviet influence, paradoxically also maintain that it is in the interest of the Soviet Union to help make peace in the Middle East and to guarantee it. The logic underlying this argument is not readily obvious; governments seldom act for any length of time contrary to their own interests, and the Soviet government in particular is not known for excessive altruism in world politics.

This is not an abstract issue: if the Soviet Union had wanted to make a contribution to Middle Eastern peace, it could have put some pressure on the "Rejection Front" to moderate its opposition to any political solution of the conflict. This would certainly have made it easier for Arafat to produce an ambiguous formula satisfying the State Department (though not Israel) that the PLO might be willing under certain circumstances to consider according Israel something that could be interpreted by unsuspecting third parties as *de facto* recognition. But the Soviet Union has refrained so far even from making this minor effort. It is unlikely therefore that the Soviets will extend a bona-fide guarantee to a settlement which gives their Arab friends and clients less than they want. (This is not to say that the Soviet Union might not look with favor upon the establishment of a non-viable Palestinian state, assuming with some justification that it would sooner or later gain a foothold in this state.)

American guarantees are almost equally problematical. A guarantee that does not make provisions for military intervention is worse than useless, and given the isolationist mood of Congress, this is about all that can be expected. But even if a real guarantee should be provided, it would obviously apply only in the case of an extreme violation of the agreement, such as an all-out military attack. This, however, is a less likely eventuality than the kind of shelling across the border which has been practiced in recent years from Jordan and Lebanon. Israel would find such shelling intolerable, but would the United States? And even if there were a clear case of aggression, would there not be cries of "No more Vietnams" and the like? And even if all these fears were to prove groundless, it is still true that if present trends continue, America may no longer be in a position actively to intervene even if it wanted to, simply because it is steadily falling behind the Soviet Union in military preparedness.

## II

To accept the inherently unstable nature of the Middle East politics and the intractability of its problems is not to preach defeatism and opt for inaction. It is, however, to ask for an end to false hopes in the West generally and in the United States in particular. For it is important to understand that even if there should be a settlement between Israel and the Arabs, major conflicts in the Middle East would persist. And so far as basic Western interests are concerned, these might be in even greater danger after a settlement were reached than in the present situation.

Yet whatever the consequences for other countries, it is certainly in Israel's interest to work for a lessening of tensions in its relations with its Arab neighbors. There are things Israel can do, but these options cannot be discussed without reference to the immobilism of Israeli policy after 1967 in which they have their roots.

Psychologically, this immobilism is easy to understand. The 1967 victory had been complete, and it seemed only reasonable to assume that the Arabs would be willing to discuss peace terms. The old borders had been a nightmare, and since Arab leaders had threatened Israel with extinction so many times, it seemed right to insist that a return to these borders was out of the question. But the Arabs refused to meet Israel halfway, let alone to discuss a firm and lasting peace. In the circumstances, the military victors saw no reason to seize the political initiative. No Israeli leader was ready to take risks with the security of the country. It was the "safe-border" argument, not the mystique of the "Land of Israel" movement, which underlay Israeli policy between 1967 and 1973.

In retrospect, however, it is clear that this approach ignored the wider context of the world politics. It underrated latent Arab power (economic and political rather than military); and giving absolute priority to security, it made the defusing of an inherently dangerous situation impossible. Again, it is easy to point to mitigating circumstances. Few countries in history have made unilateral concessions after a brilliant military victory. Psychologically, it would have been difficult to persuade the Israeli public to pursue such a course of action, especially since there was no guarantee that unilateral Israeli concessions would be reciprocated, and that the Arabs would not go to war again after a few years.

Mitigating circumstances, however, count for little in politics, and we now can see that greater risks should have been taken. Time was not working in Israel's favor, and it would have been preferable to part with at least some of the occupied territories, unilaterally if necessary, from a position of strength rather than weakness. To be sure, territorial concessions might not have prevented a new war; in that case Israel's position would have been worse. But it need not have been much worse, especially if arrangements had been made for the demilitarization of border zones. It is true that the Arab countries might still not have accepted the existence of the Jewish state. Certainly there would have been bellicose speeches and threats on the part of the Arab governments. Acts of terror would have continued and Israeli goods might not have passed through the Suez Canal. But not all the Arab governments would have felt the same overriding urgency to go to war and recover the lost territories. And since the Israeli problem was not the only one preoccupying the

Arab world, the conflict might well have lost some of its acuteness. Israel would still have figured high among Arab grievances, but it might no longer have had top priority.

Israel, in other words, could not possibly have relied on Arab good will, but it could have relied on Arab disunity. It was this failure to accept anything less than peace, the insistence on a policy involving no risks, which paralyzed Israeli foreign policy between 1967 and 1973.

Some now agree that mistakes were made, but maintain that a democratically elected government could not have carried out a policy rejected by the majority of the population. Such fatalism is unfounded; public opinion would have accepted almost any policy advocated by a strong leadership, just as it accepted Ben-Gurion's decision to withdraw Israeli forces from Sinai in 1956.

Others believe that nothing Israel might have done would have made the slightest difference. They are certain that no opportunities were missed during the interwar years—which is true in the sense that the phone call General Dayan expected from King Hussein never came, and that the Arab leaders decided at Khartoum not to negotiate with Israel. But the decisive question is, of course, whether it was indeed impossible to create opportunities, thus reducing the likelihood of a new war, and whether it would not have been worthwhile to pay a price to attain this end. There are no certainties, but it seems very plausible that Israel's international position would have been considerably stronger today had it after 1967 pursued the policy it is now being forced to carry out, if it had made voluntarily and from a position of strength the concessions it has made (and is going to make) under pressure. At the very least, Israel's position would not have been worse.

Of course not even clarity about the past can produce a magic formula that will show the way out of the present impasse. This applies especially to the view that Israel should at all costs stand firm against outside pressure in the present circumstances and should not give up an inch, on the ground that the compromises suggested will lead not toward peace but to a new war under less favorable conditions.

There are serious problems with this approach, but to reject it out of hand for ethical reasons, as certain commentators do, is to apply moral standards to Israel that are not applied to any other country. After all, it was not the fault of the Israelis that the Arabs went to war against the Jewish state in 1948 and that, as a result, new realities came into being which can no longer be undone. The Arab argument that the injustice done to the Palestinians is somehow unique is based either on ignorance or on hypocrisy. All over the world many millions of people have had to leave their native countries in recent decades without hope of repatriation. Nor have the many millions of square miles of territory conquered

in war over the same period been subject to demands that they be returned. As to the case for a greater Jewish state, it was put most succinct-
ly by Jabotinsky in his evidence before a British Royal Commission on
the eve of World War II:

> . . . I do not deny [that] the Arabs of Palestine will necessarily become a
> minority in the country of Palestine. What I do deny is that this is a hard-
> ship. That is not a hardship on any race, any nation possessing so many na-
> tional states and so many more national states in the future. One fraction,
> one branch of that race, and not a big one, will have to live in someone
> else's state; well, that is the case with all the mightiest nations of the world.
> I could hardly mention one of the big nations, having their states, mighty
> and powerful, who had not one branch living in someone else's state. That
> is only normal and there is no "hardship" attached to that. So when we
> hear the Arab claim confronted with the Jewish claim—I fully understand
> that any minority would prefer to be a majority: It is quite understandable
> that the Arabs of Palestine would also prefer Palestine to be the Arab state
> No. 4, 5, or 6—that I quite understand—but when the Arab claim is con-
> fronted with our Jewish demand to be saved, it is like the claims of appetite
> versus the claims of starvation. . . .

Today a Palestinian state would not be the fourth, but the twenty-
fourth Arab state. The Palestinians may reason that they are as much entitled to their own state as all other Arabs, but all Arab leaders and
political movements have solemnly declared on many occasions that the
Arabs are one nation, divided by artificial frontiers; if so, the Palestinians are at home in every Arab country. Nor is there any lack of space in
the Arab world. When it was decided to partition Palestine in 1947, less
than one-sixth of one percent of the territory inhabited by the Arabs was
set aside for Israel; one-half of one percent of the Arabs was to become a
minority and to live in the Jewish state. This compromise was accepted
by the Jews and rejected by the Arabs.

Shorn of certain dubious historical-religious arguments, then, the case
for Israel to stand firm and refuse to give an inch is not a weak case at all.
The difficulties arise on the level of reality and power, not on that of
morality and reason. For the truth is that there is not one law for strong
and weak alike. When the Soviet Union and its East European satellites
expelled many millions of Germans after World War II, world public
opinion expected the Germans tacitly to accept their fate. When they
protested, they were denounced as fascists and warmongers. But Israel is
not a power like Russia, and the Palestinians have stronger protectors
than the Germans from Poland and the Sudeten region. The fate of the
Palestinians is regarded by world public opinion as a grave injustice, to
be remedied as quickly as possible. If the Palestinians were politically

weaker, and Israel were stronger, less dependent financially and militarily on outside help and good will, it could sit out the storm a few years or even a few decades. Such a policy would find few supporters outside Israel, though; the idea frequently voiced by Herut and its supporters that all Israel needs is *hasbara*—more effective political propaganda—is quite illusory. What really matters in the last resort is whether Israel could get along without outside financial support, whether it could accept the risks of political isolation, whether it could produce at home all the arms that are and will be needed for its defense.

But even if it could do all these things, the size of the Arab minority in the Jewish state would still be a major problem. It is unlikely that the Arabs living in a "greater Israel" would be assimilated; there would always be a strong pull toward the other Arab countries. The improvement of Arab living standards in Israel would do nothing to assuage Arab nationalism or contribute to the solution of what is essentially a political problem. Thus a "greater Israel" would, to put the point bluntly, either cease to be Jewish or cease to be democratic.

Except for the idea of standing firm, there is no coherent strategy being advocated within Israel, and for a long time now there has been no overall concept behind the government's foreign policy. This is a general weakness of democratic societies, what with conflicting domestic pressures and the absence of strong leadership preventing major foreign political initiatives. There have been no such initiatives in Israeli foreign policy for a long time, merely responses to the actions of others. But historical experience has shown that a free society is not doomed to impotence; a democratically elected leader, or group of leaders, need not be unsure and indecisive, they need not be dependent in their every action of public-opinion polls and popularity contests, they can act without paying undue attention to their own political careers.

What, then, might Israel do? It would be a realistic policy on Israel's part to reaffirm unequivocally in conformity with Resolution 242 that there is no intention of incorporating Arab territories into the state. Israel could also declare that these territories will be evacuated step-by-step over a period of five to ten years within the framework of a general peace settlement involving recognition of Israel and a regulated rectification of the 1967 borders in the interest of security. Each Israeli concession would depend on Palestinian and Arab willingness to carry out the terms of the settlement. If, for instance, acts of terror were to continue, Israel would no longer be bound to fulfill its part of the bargain. (Such arrangements have been made before in history; they were used, for instance, in Central Europe after World War I.) Israel would also have to insist on transferring these territories to a representative Arab body—it would be pointless to deal with leaders whose authority is not recognized by the Palestinians. This would mean free elections, under the supervision of Israel, the Arab states, and some third parties. The PLO would of course compete in these elections, but it is obvious that there could be no dealings between Israel and the PLO unless and until the PLO were ready to accept the existence of Israel.

A procedure of this kind would not by itself solve any of the difficulties that have been mentioned. But it would to a certain extent reduce the risks, and it would make it possible in the interim period to work for a more lasting solution, either in the form of a confederation or some other framework that would safeguard the security and the political and economic viability of both states.

It is a long time since Israeli leaders have made concrete proposals to the Arabs for coexistence. This is not surprising, for such proposals would probably have fallen on deaf ears. The Arab-Israeli conflict may well have been inevitable; it is not inevitable, however, that it go on forever. It has to be recognized at long last that the Zionist attempt to "solve the Jewish question" resulted in the emergence of a Palestinian Arab question, and that Israel has to play its part in helping to solve *that* question. This does not imply that Israel has to sacrifice its own existence. Many Palestinians know quite well, and the others will learn, that speeches about the "total liquidation of Israel" will get them nowhere, for the present-day armies, unlike the Crusaders, fight not with swords but with weapons of mass destruction. The PLO and the Rejection Front may want to destroy Israel, but they do not want to pay for it with the annihilation of their own people and their own future. Once they realize that the only alternative to coexistence is mutual extinction, a solution of the conflict will become possible. One hopes, though there can be no confidence, that this realization will come without recourse to yet another war.

But if one asks whether a lasting peace is possible in the Middle East at the present time, the answer must be no—whichever way one looks at it, and least of all as a result of the measures suggested so frequently these days with so little thought of the consequences. All one can hope for is the absence of war. If that can be achieved, the time gained can be used for thinking about new ways and means to find a stabler basis for coexistence between Israel and its Arab neighbors.

*March 1976*

## NOTE

1. Said Hammami, quoted in *New Outlook,* October-November 1975. (Said Hammami was killed by an Arab terrorist in London in 1977.)

# Is Peace Still Possible
# in the Middle East?
# The View from Tel Aviv

## I

Tel Aviv. To comment today, and from Israel, on the prospects of peace and war in the Middle East has become a more painful endeavor than at any time in the past. It is easy enough to point to mistakes that have been committed in recent months, infinitely more difficult to point to realistic alternatives. And the task of commenting is made all the harder by the rapidly polarizing climate of opinion both in Israel and in the West, especially the United States.

Many friends of Israel are reluctant to admit even the possibility of error on the part of the Jerusalem government. As for Israel's critics, this is a large company indeed. There are those who may sincerely want to "save Israel in spite of herself"; there are erstwhile supporters who have been waiting for the chance to dissociate themselves from a cause no longer fashionable; and there are still others who would not be greatly perturbed if Israel were to disappear. The last group includes "petro-conservatives" on the one side, radical revolutionists on the other, and—a relatively new phenomenon—some open anti-Semites sniffing for the first time in years the prospect of a fair wind. Most numerous of all the critics, perhaps, are the men and women of good will but impaired vision, aware of current opportunities, oblivious of the pitfalls and dangers.

President Carter, addressing a group of Congressmen, remarked of Menachem Begin that he "had peace within his grasp and he let it get away." But it is one thing to criticize the Begin government for various sins of omission and commission; it is quite another to believe, as Carter seems to do, that "peace" in the Middle East hinges simply on one man and his followers. In the chorus of condemnation, it is all too quickly forgotten that even if the government of Israel were headed by Noam Chomsky, with I.F. Stone as his foreign minister, the Middle East would still be plagued with problems to which no one, except fools and fanatics, has found the answer—and a host of new problems besides.

Any review of the current state of affairs between Israel and its Arab neighbors has to go back to the Six-Day War of 1967, which, in retrospect, can be seen as the true turning point in Arab-Israeli relations. Before that date there had indeed been, to use the popular Israeli saying of the time, "nothing to talk about." The Arab governments were unwilling to accept Israel within its then-borders. The moderates among them were, at most, willing to consider a return to the original UN partition plan of 1947; the less moderate, who were the majority, advocated the destruction of the Jewish state. After the Six-Day War, however, Jerusalem was for the first time in a position to make moves which might have brought about some Arab acceptance of Israel's legitimacy; for reasons that are all too understandable, Israel did not make the most of these opportunities.

True, from time to time there were concrete Israeli initiatives—such as Moshe Dayan's plan of August 1972, aimed at giving up half of the Sinai; or the Allon plan, which envisaged autonomy for the West Bank, provided the Jordan River remained Israel's security border; or the Labor Alignment resolution of December 1973 in which a Palestinian identity was recognized for the first time. Yet no real action was taken along any of these lines, and in the meantime Israel adopted a negative attitude toward the various peace initiatives of the U.S. and the United Nations. Again, it is easy to see why: among the Arab governments there was still no apparent willingness to accept Israel regardless of any concessions it might make. This was most clear in the threefold resolution of the Khartoum conference, held shortly after the end of the Six-Day War: no negotiations, no recognition, no peace. While Nasser was riding high on the wave of radical pan-Arabism, the prospects of even a limited arrangement were vitually nil. And after Nasser's death, those opposed to recognition of Israel still carried the day; the Rabat conference (October 1974) proclaimed the PLO as the only legitimate representative of the Palestinian people, and the PLO stood for the destruction of the "Zionist entity."

Thus, there seemed at the time no alternative to official Israeli policy. Yet the dangers of that immobilism were nonetheless real, and costly. It was, for instance, largely as the result of Israeli occupation of the West Bank and Gaza that the PLO, now the main stumbling block on the road to any settlement, became a major political force. Inside Israel, an unwillingness grew to give up the conquered "territories." (It ought to be recalled that before 1967 there was no irredentist party in Israel, and that not even Herut, let alone the religious parties, ever proposed the conquest of "Judea and Samaria.") The idea that these regions should not be given back was never part of official policy, but the longer the occupation lasted, the more difficult it became even to envisage that they should one day be surrendered. This also meant that the Jewish state was saddled with a very substantial minority of reluctant inhabitants, and one which, given demographic trends, could well turn into a majority in the not too distant future—with grave consequences for both the Jewish and the democratic character of the Jewish state.[1]

Whatever the mitigating circumstances, a price had to be paid for the lack of initiative on the part of successive Isreali governments, and that price was the Yom Kippur War. It is, in fact, possible that the 1973 conflict could have been averted had Israel made far-reaching concessions to Egypt along the lines of the Dayan plan of 1972. This would not have resulted in a formal treaty, but it would have removed the inducement for Egypt to go to war; and without Egypt, the other Arab states would not have attacked. It is true that Israel's concessions would have had to be unilateral, but they would have been made from a position of strength. Unfortunately, there was a fixation within Israel on a formal peace, with all its trappings—trade, tourism, and the exchange of ambassadors—and in the absence of Arab readiness to reciprocate, this fixation was allowed to dominate political thinking. As a result, the depth of the hostility toward Israel in some of the Arab states was overrated, and the fact was ignored that the Arabs faced problems other than Israel, and that their relations among themselves were anything but cordial. Israeli foreign policy, in short, made no use of existing opportunities but followed the line of least domestic resistance. The shock of the Yom Kippur War showed that its assumptions had been mistaken.

## II

To dwell on lost opportunities may seem of little topical relevance. Certainly, the situation now is quite different from what it was six years ago. But if circumstances have changed, underlying political attitudes are more or less the same, despite the coming to power of a new government in Israel in 1977.

The reasons for Menachem Begin's victory in last year's elections to the Knesset are not to be sought in a sudden conversion of the electorate to the domestic and foreign-policy program of the Herut party. The reasons are more prosaic, having to do with the scandals, or alleged scandals, affecting some leading members of Mapai, and above all with the general feeling that one party had been in power for too long. In fact, foreign-policy issues played scarcely any role at all in the election results. True, the National Religious party had veered to the Right in recent years, but the Liberals, who were Herut's partner in the Likud coalition, advocated a rather moderate foreign policy and so, emphatically, did the Democratic Movement for Change, another partner in the new coalition, consisting mainly of former members or sympathizers of Mapai. Still, however heterogenous the composition of the Likud coalition, there was no doubt from the first moment that Begin would impose on it his own foreign policy.

Begin had been a key figure in Israeli politics from the very beginning, yet little was known about him outside a small circle of friends and admirers. He led a quiet life, he was not a prolific writer, and his speeches in the Knesset usually dealt with matters of current concern and were not meant to provide inspirational guidance. (It is perhaps significant that the only collection of Begin's speeches at present available is the one in Arabic published by the PLO head office in Beirut.) His personality provoked sharply divergent reactions. His friends and admirers maintained that he was a political genius. Others took a less sanguine view. Ben-Gurion, himself no dove, always regarded Begin as the most dangerous man in Israeli politics, a "fascist," who, if he came to power, would bring about Israel's destruction through a reckless and adventurist foreign policy.

It is true that in the past Begin was given to outbursts of wild demagoguery. But he was not, and is not, a fascist, and he did not aim at establishing a dictatorship. In the 1950s he organized a famous campaign in the Knesset to defeat the reparations agreements with Germany, but in the end, despite his dire threats, he did not go underground or unleash a "civil war." On the contrary, he mellowed into a stalwart of democratic rule, taking an inordinate pride in his intimate knowledge of the intricacies of parliamentary procedure.

The main formative influence on Begin is Zev Jabotinsky, leader of the Revisionist movement within Zionism. But there are some important differences between the two men. Jabotinsky was essentially a nineteenth-century romantic liberal, in the tradition of Mazzini, and he had nothing but contempt for religious "obscurantism." Zionist society, as envisaged by Jabotinsky, was to be liberal, not clerical. Begin, by contrast, has systematically cultivated Orthodox rabbis, and not just for tactical reasons—it is said that even now those who combine Orthodoxy with a belief in the "Land of Israel" concept are the only people to whom he is willing to lend an ear. Jabotinsky, to take another point of contrast, never denied the existence of a Palestinian-Arab people; in a series of articles in the 1920s he made clear his belief that there was indeed such a people, proud of its traditions, eager for national independence. But it was Jabotinsky's view that since the Arabs already had to many states of their own, whereas the Jews had none, elementary justice demanded that the claim of the Jews be honored before that of the Palestinians. Begin, on the other hand, has denied the existence of a Palestinian Arab people with an identity of its own.

Yet for all his single-mindedness, Begin too is in the tradition of nineteenth-century integral nationalism—a tradition that puts the interests of the nation above all other considerations, but that is also democratic in inspiration. (Begin has shown more politeness, even friendliness, to allies and enemies alike than almost any leading figure in Israeli politics in recent memory.) Like Churchill and de Gaulle, Begin believes that a head of government should be free to concentrate on foreign policy and defense, and that domestic issues can safely be left to the experts. In an age of pragmatism, Begin is a man of firm, deep, and sincerely held convictions, including the conviction that the whole historical Jewish homeland belongs to the people of Israel by right.

Unfortunately, none of this—neither his intellectual and ideological background nor his three decades in parliament as the main spokesman of the opposition—really prepared Begin for his responsibilities as head of a government coalition. And what is worse, there was no one to initiate him into the realities of world politics and power. Over the years Herut had undergone successive splits and purges, and many of those who had shown any inclination toward independent thought had left the party. Intellectuals were never strongly represented in Jabotinsky's movement, and the same was true with regard to Herut. There was a sprinkling of scientists, technicians, lawyers, and journalists, men and women of accomplishment in their own fields but with no specific competence or knowledge in politics. And so when he became Prime Minister, Begin assembled around him a group of young people who are vaguely reminiscent of the aides who entered the White House, the National Security Council, and the State Department after President Carter's election. These are people who might acquit themselves creditably as managers of a chain of supermarkets, as professors, or as partners in a law firm, but who have suddenly found themselves in positions of power and influence well beyond their capabilities.

Their influence, to be sure, does not extend to the Prime Minister himself, who has not been open to persuasion except perhaps on a tactical level. When confronted with unpleasant facts and figures, Begin likes to maintain that he is by nature an optimist. A true exchange of opinions is hardly possible in these conditions. Begin's interlocutors are tempted to gloss over differences rather than go over the same ground for the second or third time, and this, in turn, creates the mistaken impression, as far as Begin is concerned, that his own arguments have prevailed. For the Prime Minister is a greater believer in the power of the spoken word. His legal training in Poland seems to have persuaded him that, in politics as in jurisprudence, arguments are of paramount importance; he also tends to attribute enormous significance to legal formulations in the conduct of foreign policy. This is not just a matter of style;

Begin's approach has had a decisive impact on the negotiations in Ismailia and Washington.

III

Despite his reputation for inflexibility, it appeared at first that Begin was actually willing to make more far-reaching concessions in his search for peace than any previous Israeli leader. Even before President Sadat's mission to Jerusalem, he made it known that he would consider a general peace settlement. On September 11, 1977, the Israeli cabinet approved the text of a proposed treaty between Israel and the Arab states on just these lines.

Nor has the whole history of Sadat's visit to Jerusalem on November 19 yet been told; once all the details are published, Begin may well emerge with more credit for the early stages of the talks than has so far been given him. There were, in fact, several preparatory meetings, ranging in location from Tangier to Teheran, and details of the statements made "independently" in Jerusalem by the two leaders were closely coordinated, including even Begin's remark that he preferred a general peace settlement to a separate treaty with Egypt. Sadat's later statement to an interviewer—"I gave him everything, he gave me nothing"—is quite untrue. The fact that Begin did not accept a total withdrawal to the June 1967 lines, and rejected the establishment of an independent Palestinian state, could not have come as a surprise to Sadat in November. All this has been made clear by Foreign Minister Dayan in his preliminary meetings with various Arab leaders, and it had been stated publicly by Begin a week before Sadat's visit.

What, then, went wrong during the weeks after the meetings in Jerusalem? When Sadat and Begin met in Ismailia on December 24, 1977, they failed to agree on a "declaration of agreement on principles" because of differences over the Palestinian problem. By January 14, Sadat announced that he had "absolutely no hope" that anything would be achieved at the forthcoming meeting of the political committee in Jerusalem, and he did in fact recall his delegation four days later, accusing Israel of proposing mere "partial solutions."

Various therories, many of them quite far-fetched, have been propounded to explain the breakdown. Some argue that the reason Sadat went to Jerusalem in the first place was that he feared an impending Israeli military attack, and that he drew back the moment he realized no such attack had been contemplated. Others claim that Sadat was acting in bad faith from the beginning, that his visit was a clever tactical move aimed at driving a wedge between Israel and the United States.

These explanations are not really convincing. There is every reason to believe that Sadat's initiative was genuine. Egypt, after all, had borne the brunt of the Arab struggle for three decades, had sacrificed more than anyone else, and was truly inclined now to bury the hatchet with Israel. Sadat's initiative was based on the assumption that Begin was a stronger political leader than his predecessors, that he could make concessions which they could not have made. This assumption was at least partly correct, for Israeli foreign policy under Golda Meir, Yitzhak Rabin, and Shimon Peres had indeed been paralyzed—not least because the Labor leaders were afraid of Begin. And there may have been other factors behind the Sadat visit. United States policy-makers, in one of their periodic fits of lunacy, had approached the Russians in September 1977 with a view toward giving them a greater share in the Middle East peacemaking process, and in October the two superpowers signed a joint statement that harked back to a similarly ill-starred initiative undertaken by Secretary Rogers in 1970. Sadat clearly wanted no part of harebrained schemes of this kind. It was better, despite the risks involved, to talk directly to the Israelis.

Sadat had two demands as a precondition for peace: Israeli evacuation of Sinai, and agreement on some formula regarding the future of the Palestinians. It is true that, after his visit to Jerusalem, Sadat's position hardened on some issues—he began, for instance, to insist on Jordanian participation in the talks. Perhaps he had started to feel the pressure of the radicals in the Arab camp, perhaps he hoped that America would force Israel to make greater concessions. But Jordanian participation was apparently not an absolute for Sadat, and there are grounds for thinking that but for the vacillation of the Israeli government on some issues, and the amateurish way in which the negotiations were handled, the original momentum of the peace initiative could have been preserved.

To Sadat's now somewhat hardened position Begin responded in Ismailia with a detailed twenty-six-point plan for the inhabitants of the West Bank, which was bound to create friction precisely because it spelled out what should have remained vague, at least for the moment. Far from clarifying the issues, these proposals provoked endless semantic discussions over the meaning of autonomy, self-rule, limited self-rule, and other such terms. Lawyers stepped in where politicians had feared to tread, and from that moment the talks entered a cul-de-sac.

But this was not the only stumbling block. While the negotiations were going on, General Sharon, Israel's Minister of Agriculture, gave a green light to those Israelis who wanted to establish new settlements in Sinai, and Begin declared that these settlements would not be given up and were to be protected for all time by the Israeli army. The Prime Minister also offered a new interpretation of UN Resolution 242, claiming that it did not necessarily apply to the West Bank. This interpretation was not only rejected by every government in the world, it also differed from the interpretation provided by all previous Israeli governments, including Begin's own (joint U.S.-Israeli declaration of October 5, 1977). In April 1978, this reinterpretation of Resolution 242 was again reinterpreted in a more moderate, or in any case, more obscure way, but by then the damage had been done.

The impression was thus created among Israel's friends and enemies alike that the Likud government was not really interested in pursuing the peace initiative. True, Begin continued to claim that "everything was negotiable except the destruction of Israel." But this formula, which encountered disbelief even inside Israel, was naturally given little credence elsewhere. In fact, although Begin did want peace, and although he was aware that he faced a unique political opportunity, he was not clear in his own mind what price he could afford to pay for it in the way of concessions.

Begin's misgivings in this regard were reinforced by attacks against him at home, which began almost immediately after the Jerusalem meeting. The main attack emanated from the "Rejection Front," comprising most of Herut, most of the Le'am ("For the Nation") faction, Gush Emunim ("Bloc of the Faithful"), and the Greater Israel group. They based their opposition to possible concessions on the West Bank not on consideration of security but on the belief—to which Begin also subscribes—that Judea and Samaria are the historical homeland of the Jewish people and should under no circumstances be given up. And they were almost equally reluctant to make concessions in the Sinai, because they did not believe that the essential Arab hostility to Israel had changed or that the Arabs had ceased to aim at Israel's destruction.

There was also criticism from certain circles in the Labor Alignment. Some, indeed, tried to outflank Begin on the Right; others, willing to make concessions on the West Bank, were not so willing to do so in Sinai, and pointed to the undeniable military importance of the airfields there; lastly, there were those (in the "agricultural-military complex," as one unkind critic put it) who had a vested interest in preserving the status quo because of the extensive use they had been making of relatively cheap Arab labor.

The settlements were perhaps not the most important bone of contention, but they caused the greatest opposition inside Israel and created the most political damage abroad. The basic facts are these: since 1967, 76 settlements have been established beyond the "Green Line," with some 6,500 inhabitants. They are located in the Golan, the Jordan Valley, in Judea and Samaria, in the Rafiah region, and in the Sinai. Most were set up openly, with the permission and support of the Labor and/or Likud governments; others were established semi-legally, as temporary work camps, or within army bases. And a few, connected with Gush Emunim, were founded against the express wish of the authorities. Successive Israeli governments have closed their eyes to these last settlements, while demanding on occasion that they be evacuated.

The purpose of the settlements has never been made altogether clear. It might be argued abstractly that Jews do have the right to settle wherever they want in historic Palestine (and perhaps also in Transjordan). But given political and military realities, as well as the small number of people in Israel willing to join any new agricultural settlement, it is still hard to understand why priority should have been given for a decade to settlement beyond the Green Line. For during this same period, only 2,000 settlers have pitched their tents *inside* the 1967 borders, despite the fact that there is sufficient land and that unless new settlements are soon established, Western Galilee will have an Arab majority. From a military point of view, the settlements are of no value; on the contrary, they are likely to hinder operations in a time of war. Economically, many of them are not viable, in view of the high cost of water and the poor quality of the soil.

The problem with most of the settlements is not that they are illegal, as claimed by Secretary of State Vance, but that, with notable exceptions, they have been a waste of people and resources which are in short supply. The Gush Emunim settlements, in particular, are little more than Potemkin Villages. Of the few families living in them, some regard their presence as a political demonstration and have no wish to settle permanently, while others continue to work in Israel but return to the settlements for nights and weekends.

That the settlements were ever allowed to become a major political issue is in a way unforgivable. But a major issue they did become. Ezer Weizman, Minister of Defense, and not known as a dove, told the Prime Minister in a stormy telephone conversation from the United States early this year that he would resign if "one more bulldozer moved in the Sinai." There were other voices of warning from within the government coalition, too, until it was finally decided to freeze construction of new settlements in the Sinai for the time being but to continue to expand existing ones, with Begin again emphasizing that no settlement would be surrendered in the framework of a peace treaty.

And so the stage was set for Begin's disastrous visit to the United States last March. In early private meetings with Senator Henry Jackson and former Secretary of State Kissinger, Begin expressed dismay that the plan which he had submitted to President Carter in December, and which had been (he thought) approved by the President, was subsequently rejected. Carter, for his part, claimed that he had thought Begin's plan merely a preliminary negotiating position, not a rock-hard stance. He complained that the Israelis had taken a slight nod of the head for a ringing endorsement. At the end of the meetings, Carter listed Begin's "no's," which, in addition to the issue of the settlements, all concerned the meaning and scope of Resolution 242. Begin, according to Carter, had refused to commit himself to withdrawing from any portion of the West Bank or the Gaza Strip at any time, irrespective of security arrangements that might be included as part of an agreement. He had rejected the American proposal for a limited-choice referendum on the West Bank and Gaza Strip following a five-year transition period. And he had refused to acknowledge the legitimate rights of the Palestinians because, he claimed, this would lead eventually to an independent Palestinian state threatening Israel's heartland.

President Carter's summary of Begin's position, while unfairly stressing the negative, was basically correct. A glum Begin returned to Israel, and the dispatch of Weizman to Cairo on March 31 did nothing to remedy the situation. Weizman had gotten along considerably better on a personal level with Sadat and the other Egyptian leaders than had Begin and Dayan, but this time his reception was brusque, even unfriendly. As for Begin, upon his return he received an overwhelming vote of confidence in the Knesset. But even among those who expressed their confidence in him, there were many who felt great unease about the record of his government.

They were uneasy about more than foreign policy. When the Likud assumed power, it had been widely believed that at long last Israel had a government with a strong sense of purpose. It was expected that an end would come to the strikes which had paralyzed the economy, that bureaucratic interference would be reduced and incompetence stamped out, that a stop would be put to the chronic overspending which had resulted in an inflation rate of forty percent. And indeed the new government did take some daring steps during its first months. The pound was floated, most exchange controls were abolished, and there were massive cuts in subsidies. Simha Ehrlich, the new finance minister, did sincerely try to reduce spending and balance the budget. But after a short time he found himself confronting the same pressures his predecessors had faced, and he was not notably more successful in dealing with them. During the winter and spring, strikes spread throughout the public sector, and while the government held out in some instances, more often it had to give in to wage demands. Hoped-for investments from abroad failed to materialize. In short, after a promising beginning, the Likud government came to look no different from what had come before.

Even more disconcerting was the political disarray within the coalition. Ezer Weizman quarreled with both the Prime Minister and General Sharon; Moshe Dayan, who had some of the qualities needed by a foreign minister but lacked others, was bitterly attacked by Moshe Arens, the new head of the Knesset Foreign Affairs and Security committee, and an expert in aricraft technology rather than in world affairs. Shmuel Katz, an old Herut stalwart who had been made special adviser on information, resigned from the government and frontally attacked Begin, Weizman, and Dayan. In this he was joined by other influential Herut supporters and new converts like Moshe Shamir, the novelist, who demanded Dayan's resignation.

By the end of the first year, the Liberals, one element in the coalition, were manifesting distinct unhappiness. The Democratic Movement for Change, another element, found itself in a state of disintegration. There were many resignations, and of the remaining party, half was in favor of staying in the government while the other half pressed to dissolve the partnership. As for Labor, it had yet to recover from its 1977 defeat or to constitute itself as any sort of alternative in political life. And meanwhile, outside the traditional political structure, a new movement came into being, "Peace Now," led by army reserve officers who questioned Begin's policy vis-à-vis Sadat and announced that peace without settlements beyond the Green Line was preferable to settlements without peace.

This was the situation in April. Begin again visited Washington in early May, when the atmosphere seemed friendlier and the differences between the Carter administration and the Israeli line seemed to have narrowed down considerably. It was made clear that according to the American blueprint, Israel would be able to retain military outposts on the West Bank during the interim period and beyond, and that a permanent settlement there would be based substantially upon the home-rule proposal put forward by Begin.

Yet if there was some advance in this direction, there were setbacks in another context. The package-deal sale of fighter planes to Israel, Egypt, and Saudi Arabia was an issue which Israel could not win, and the political defeat was only aggravated by the disproportionate significance that was attached to it. Still, the implications of that defeat for the future are ominous, and the same may be said of the open dissent now being voiced in Israel and among American Jews over Israeli policy. Israel can ill afford a "second front" at this time, and Israel's enemies will be only too eager to publicize these critical voices. But the dissent should be taken seriously, for it reflects the erosion of an earlier consensus. That consensus existed so long as Israeli foreign and defense policy was based on the legitimate security interests of the state. Once an attempt was made to shift the emphasis, to base foreign policy on, in effect, the platform of a single political party, polarization in public opinion became inevitable. That Begin is not a consensus politician has always been one of the main sources of his political strength. But at the same time it is this which jeopardizes the Israeli position at a time when unity is needed more than ever before.

## IV

For a few weeks in November and December 1977, there was a chance for an agreement between Israel and Egypt. Once the settlements became a bone of contention, once legal formulations became as important as matters of substance, the opportunity receded. Sadat reverted to his old demand that Israel withdraw from *all* territories, and Begin went back to quoting Scripture.

Today, it is still the case that a separate peace with Egypt is the most desirable of outcomes. There is, of course, no certainty that such an agreement with Egypt would hold. Sadat could suddenly disappear from the political scene, and a more radical or aggressively pan-Arab leadership might take over in Cairo. Israeli withdrawal from the Sinai would involve palpable risks. But the conduct of policy always involves risks, and in this case the risks are not that formidable. There was, and is, a great deal of support in Egypt for a settlement with Israel, and a great deal of discontent with the other Arab countries whose solidarity with Egypt has been mostly of the verbal kind. Sadat's successor could fairly be counted on to take a line similar to his, and to put Egypt's national interest before that of the Arab "cause."

A successful outcome to the negotiations with Egypt would remove the prospect of war in the Middle East, and would strengthen Israel's position both in the Middle East and in the world at large. Whether it would lead to a settlement on the West Bank is far less certain. It is Begin's misfortune to have become Prime Minister precisely at a time when the hard choices more or less successfully postponed by his predecessors were at last put on the historical agenda. And it has to be said that even if Begin were to demonstrate all the qualities of a Richelieu, a Disraeli, or a Bismarck, even if he had at his disposal the best advisers and assistants in the world, even if his course of action were not dictated by the dead hand of the past (or the voice of the Scripture), it is difficult to see how he could resolve the problem of two peoples claiming the same land.

It has been said in Washington that no one really expects Israel to withdraw from the whole of the West Bank and Gaza, and no one really expects that an independent Palestinian state will be set up. According to the various schemes that have been proposed in recent years, the West Bank and Gaza would be demilitarized; Israel would not claim sovereignty over the area but would merely retain some defensive outposts; self-rule would be granted to the Palestinian Arabs under the tutelage of

Israel, Jordan, and, if necessary, Egypt. But would Palestinian Arabs accept a scheme of this kind, which would leave them with less territory than a West Bank-Gaza mini-state, with no control over defense or foreign policy, with their citizenship determined by Jordan, a country only slightly less resented than Isreal? It seems unlikely in the extreme. The Palestinians are told that these schemes should be considered provisional; after five years there would be free elections in which they would have the right to decide freely their own future. If true, this would be a sensational new experiment—the first free elections for a very long time anywhere in the Arab world.

Anyway, this plan is opposed by the Israeli government because it would be nothing but a roundabout road toward the establishment of an independent state run by the PLO, a solution opposed by virtually all Israelis for reasons which have nothing to do with the theological beliefs of Begin and Gush Emunim. It is all very well to argue that under the American plan the Palestinians would be part of Jordan; what would prevent them from taking over and radicalizing a country in which they would constitute a majority? And Jordan, too, has so far shown no willingness to be party to a deal of this kind. Hussein already has too many Palestinians in his kingdom, and his past experience with them has been none too happy.

To break the deadlock, the idea has been broached of American guarantees for Israel and some Arab countries, with the overall aim of a regional nonaggression pact. The United States, according to this blueprint, would have an air base in Sinai and a naval base at Jaffa or Haifa, and would in turn enter into specific treaty obligations with regard to the territorial integrity of the countries involved. But there is little enthusiasm for any such plan in Israel and Egypt, even if one takes for granted congressional approval and an American ability or willingness to live up to such a commitment five or ten years hence, in an area much closer to the Soviet Union than to the United States. Given the reluctance of the present administration to match the continuing Soviet military build-up, the question arises of how much any U.S. guarantee is likely to be worth in the 1980s. There would, in addition, be the greatest reluctance in Egypt to accept any scheme that smacks of nineteenth-century "capitulations." It took the Egyptians a long time to get rid of their British bases; they would be unlikely to welcome new ones. Nor would such bases be welcomed in Israel; psychological considerations apart, it is not at all clear what security they would provide. They might be of help against a full-scale attack, but they would be of no use against missiles fired into Tel Aviv or Ben-Gurion airport, operations sufficient to cause grave dislocation but not sufficient to invoke the treaty obligations. Not that the idea of a base or a defense treaty should be dismissed as out of hand; but it is an idea which would make sense only as one component of a general settlement, if acceptable to all concerned.

What, then, is to be done about the West Bank? The hard truth is that there is no fully satisfactory solution, only a choice among various evils. Begin has said that everything is open to discussion except the destruction of Israel; this means, necessarily, that annexation of the West Bank by Israel is ruled out. And since Israel cannot occupy the West Bank indefinitely without clarifying its status, this in turn means that what must be envisaged is some form of autonomy and, indeed, independence.

According to some observers, the PLO has changed over the last year or two and become more moderate; according to others, it has been weakened through internal splits. But in its new program (March 1977) the Palestinian National Council made no attempt to modify the provisions of its charter, which are incompatible with the continued existence of Israel, and it rejected Resolution 242. Meeting again in August 1977, it failed to pass even a modified version of Resolution 242. Ever since Sadat's visit to Jerusalem, it has been the prime mover against Egyptian "treachery" and for the establishment of an "Arab Confrontation and Resistance Front."

Not too much importance, perhaps, should be attributed to the PLO's public announcements. Even an endorsement of Resolution 242 could be a mere tactical move, or perhaps signify the temporary victory of a moderate faction. The decisive test is not what the Palestinians say about recognizing Israel, but what they do. Nor is it of paramount importance what *kind* of constitutional arrangement would be made for a Palestinian Arab state. The military danger it would present can be reduced not by constitutional guarantees but only by a security pact—for instance, a treaty of friendship, cooperation, and mutual assistance between it and Israel similar to that concluded between Poland (1956) or Hungary (1957) and the Soviet Union. According to those treaties, the temporary presence of Soviet troops does not lead to interference in the domestic affairs of the countries concerned; no Soviet troop movements outside specified areas are permitted without the authorization of the local government. It goes without saying that the treaties preclude the establishment of any third-party military bases or the presence of any foreign troops.

An independent Palestinian entity would obviously entail serious dangers, and not just for Israel. It is possible that the Palestinians, if given a mini-state of this kind, would start fighting each other—as the Irish did after gaining independence in 1921. Although some Arab countries would lose interest in the Palestinian cause once there was a state, others would certainly be tempted to intervene, and the result could be a new Lebanon on a larger scale; again the Irish precedent is anything but encouraging. And how could one reasonably expect the Soviet Union to pass up the opportunity to acquire an ideal base of operations, extending help to a defenseless state in need of a strong protector? In short, the prospects that a state of this kind would constitute a permanent irredentist force are greater than the chances of peaceful coexistence. For all these reasons, it is most unlikely that any Israeli government would accept the establishment of a Palestinian state unless it had guarantees reducing the dangers to a minimum. And the only effective guarantee one can envision at present is a long-term military presence.

But it should not be forgotten that if a Palestinian state would create dangers for Israel, such a state would itself be in an exposed position. If it engaged in military adventures against Israel, it would suffer at least as much as southern Lebanon has. Colonel Qaddafi of Libya recently told a German correspondent that Israel could not possibly permit the establishment of a Palestinian entity because it would mean the beginning of the end of the Jewish state. It may not have occurred to Qaddafi that attacks against Israel would also be perilous indeed for such an entity.

Recently the PLO has drawn much closer to the Soviet Union, but this rapprochement has also isolated the PLO, for many Arab countries have become increasingly apprehensive about Soviet intentions in the Middle East; events in Africa have shown that the Soviet Union now feels strong enough to engage in military intervention by proxy. The attitude of Saudi Arabia toward Israel is anything but friendly, but Saudi Arabia does not feel threatened by Israel; it *would* feel threatened by an irredentist Palestinian state representing Soviet interests in the Middle East. The same refers to Egypt and even the United States. To survive in a hostile climate, a Palestinian Arab state would have to be on its best behavior. One should not underrate the political intelligence and the instinct for self-preservation of the Palestinians, including perhaps the PLO.

All this is not to minimize the dangers involved in granting even limited autonomy to the West Bank. Why, then, should it be tried? Because there is no other way, and it should be done from a position of strength rather than weakness; the errors of omission between 1967 and 1973 should not be repeated. Because the demographic factor, the presence of a million Arabs, cannot be forever ignored; because for a majority of Israelis, national security, and not the voice of Scripture, is the decisive consideration as far as borders are concerned; because the national security of a small country depends not only on territories but on a great many other things, including some measure of foreign support; and because Israel, unlike China, cannot withdraw into total isolation and defy the rest of the world. General Eitan, the new Chief of Staff, recently claimed that Israel cannot be defended without the West Bank, Gaza, and the Golan Heights. Most of his predecessors seem not to agree with him. And in any event, provisions for the defense of Israel will have to be made irrespective of whatever political solution may be arrived at; what is more to the point than territories, Israel cannot be defended without a steady supply of modern weapons systems—systems which are not produced in Israel.

It is one of the ironies of history that Israel may one day have to grant to the Palestinian Arabs the very autonomy which the Arab governments refused to give them between 1948 and 1967. From that stage on, it will be up to the Palestinians themselves to decide whether the experiment leads to some form of uneasy coexistence or to further bloodshed ending possibly in the destruction of their homeland.

*July 1978*

## NOTE

1. The demographic problem facing Israel is briefly as follows: within the pre-1967 borders there now live 3 million Jews and about 600,000 Arabs (17 percent). If we add those living on the West Bank and in Gaza, the total number of Arabs amounts to 1.7 million (36 percent). The growth rate of the Jewish population is 1.75 percent, that of the Israeli Arabs is 4 percent; the rate is 3.75 percent on the West Bank and Gaza. Projections show that in thirty years, or less, there will be more Arabs than Jews in the areas at present under Israeli control. It is likely that the Arab birth rate will decline, but such changes usually take place over longer periods.

# Judaica

# The World of Mr. Begin

Menachem Begin has never had a good press outside Israel but this has done him little harm at home, although even there his foreign policy has been critized, and his domestic record considered undistinguished. Some of his appointments have ranged from the ludicrous to the absurd. It has been argued that Israel's prime minister came to power too late in life, and that plagued by illness, he is no longer able to cope with a punishing job which might have proved too much even for a man in the prime of life. But he still seems to be firmly in the saddle, a phenomenon among contemporary politicians: a true believer in an age of pragmatists and opportunists; far too well-read and well-behaved to qualify simply as a fanatic, yet quite inflexible; a man of exquisite politeness, yet innately incapable of engaging in a dialogue, or of accepting advice.

It seems only a question of time before the psycho-historians step in but meanwhile Mr. Begin's electoral victory last year has already produced several biographies. Richard P. and Irving A. Greenfield, with the help of an encyclopedia and a handful of standard works on modern history, have provided a competent running commentary to the few autobiographical notes which they have gleaned from Mr. Begin's own writings. Thus the fact that Mr. Begin was born in Brest-Litovsk presents an occasion for seven pages of information about its geographical location, the agricultural importance of the black earth of Poland, the economic significance of the Baltic port of Danzig, and the Brussilov offensive in July 1917; there is even a quotation from Trotsky giving his impressions of Brest-Litovsk. All this is very illuminating, but it is also true that were it not for these and similar details the authors would have found it difficult to expand their book beyond ten pages. (They do make one contribution to modern historiography: what was hitherto known as the propaganda of the deed becomes in their book "the propaganda of the dead".)

Harry Hurwitz, a former South African newspaper editor, has known and admired Mr. Begin for more than three decades. His is in some ways a touching book; Mr. Hurwitz is to political writing what Grandma

Moses was to painting—a real primitive. In this age of the anti-hero some may find it refreshing to read about a man who has always been a political genius, a visionary, a brilliant and courageous leader, who has already established himself as one of Israel's greatest prime ministers, who is destined to be one of the leading world statesmen in the last quarter of the twentieth century, and who accomplished in five months things that were regarded as impossible; a man who was born to be great, and has already profoundly influenced world history. Mr. Begin, according to this source, is an exceptional and charismatic leader, the outstanding Jewish personality of our day: "the most maligned has become the most beloved". Mr. Begin is not a "faultless superman", but Mr. Hurwitz, no muckraker he, refuses to spell out his shortcomings which, in any case, he says, are insignificant. Such adulation would be more bearable if there were some meat to it. But there isn't.

Unlike the Greenfields, Mr. Hurwitz does not use an encyclopedia for padding, but Begin's speeches, articles and Herut manifestoes are all of them rendered in full. Following the publication of this book, Mr. Hurwitz was invited to move from Johannesburg to Jerusalem and to become Begin's chief publicity adviser.

In comparison with these two efforts Etan Haber's biography stands out as a monument of judicious scholarship, detachment, erudition and wisdom. An Israeli journalist who is familiar with Begin's role in Israeli politics over a period of thirty years, he brings much that will be new to those who have not followed the Hebrew press. But Mr. Haber contributes little to an understanding of the formation of Begin's views, his policies, the sources of his popular appeal and the reasons for his electoral victory.

Begin came to power as the result of something akin to a cultural revolution and because of demographic change. The origin of both can be traced back a good many years. Before the state of Israel was founded the dominant trend in Zionism was socialist; the stereotype was an agricultural pioneer, wearing a blue shirt and dancing the *hora*.

Stereotypes apart, it is of course true that these admirable young men and women had a historic opportunity to try out a new life-style long before this became a fashionable thing to do in the West. This was the time when no one bothered to lock the front doors of apartments in Tel Aviv and Haifa, when people regularly read books and went to concerts after a long working day, intellectuals picked oranges, and so on. There was then a great deal of cohesion and solidarity in Israel; it was what sociologists call a face-to-face society. Leadership for this small community of half a million was provided by socialists from Eastern Europe—they were, typically, long-winded and impractical, but most were steadfast in the pursuit of their ideals, incorruptible men and women of considerable moral stature and vision.

Another important political tradition is that of the Revisionist movement led by Vladimir Jabotinsky, an exceedingly gifted, if erratic, Russian-Jewish intellectual with great personal magnetism who drew his political inspiration largely from the Italian Risorgimento and preached "integral maximalist" Zionism. Jabotinsky's appeal in Palestine was directed mainly to the middle class—small shopkeepers, independent farmers, and workshop owners. In Eastern Europe Revisionism's social appeal was much wider—there it was a genuinely populist movement.

But the middle class in Mandatory Palestine—as Jaakov Shavit has shown in his excellent study *Merov Limedina* (Revisionism in Zionism)—was small; it welcomed the appearance of the Revisionists as a counterweight to Labour Zionism but it also distrusted their rabid slogans and violent practices. In the first elections to the Israeli parliament in 1949 the Revisionists (Herut) obtained some twelve percent of the vote; in the second elections their share dropped to eight percent, which was a true reflection of their political strength. This was in spite of the fact that the Irgun had just emerged triumphant from the "national liberation struggle" of the Jewish people, which, according to Mr. Hurwitz, Mr. Begin and his comrades had won practically single-handed.

The state was founded in 1948. But David Ben Gurion, who dominated the Israeli political scene for more than two decades, was firmly convinced that it still faced a race against time and that it would last only if the number of its inhabitants increased at the fastest possible rate. Thue the "in-gathering of the exiles": and the population of the country quintupled within thirty years.

It was obvious that a process of this kind would involve major strains and stresses, but Ben Gurion and his contemporaries were reasonably confident that the newcomers would be socially and culturally integrated and that the transition from a small elite community to a more "normal" society would be accomplished without too great a loss to its aims and values. It was a noble dream, but how could it possibly succeed? As hundreds of thousands of new immigrants streamed into Israel—the survivors of the holocaust in Europe, and the huddled masses of Oriental Jewry—the character of Israeli society changed. Idealism began to fade, the old leaders gradually disappeared from the political scene and were replaced by a generation of pragmatists (or *bizuists,* to use the Israeli term) on the one hand and an omnipresent and intensely detested bureaucracy on the other.

There were other disturbing features at this time: Herzl once wrote in his diary that in the coming democratic Jewish state the rabbis would be confined to their synagogues and the generals to their army camps. He could not have been more mistaken, for organized religion and the military were to play an increasingly important, and by no means always constructive, role in the political life of the country

There was a deterioration in the moral fibre of the nation and here and there a new chauvinism manifested itself, inevitable perhaps in a beleaguered country, but repugnant and politically dangerous.

Above all, there was the painful issue of integration. The assumption that the problem would be solved when a second and third generation had gone through Israeli schools and the army was not borne out by subsequent events. On the contrary, the problem was aggravated by the emergence of the second generation of some of the post-1948 immigrant communities. This topic has largely remained taboo in Israel to this day. Generalizations about "Oriental" Jews are quite misleading in this context; Jews from Iraq, from Yemen, from Egypt and other Arab and Mediterranean countries did adapt to conditions in the new country. But Moroccan Jewry, the most numerous group by far, was a special case. Beset with all the consequences of loosened family ties, spiritually uprooted, this group was further weakened by the fact that many of its community leaders had emigrated to France and other countries, not Israel.

Many Moroccan Jews have adapted successfully to Israeli life—and not only in material terms. However, there has frequently been failure to adapt, and this is reflected, inter alia, in crime statistics. There have been problems with prostitution and drugs; too much dependence on state welfare handouts; and difficulties in schools. The story is a familiar one —a similar state of affairs prevails in all countries with substantial immigrant communities. But Israel, it had been thought, would be more successful in absorbing newcomers, and the higher the hopes, the greater the subsequent disenchantment. There has been greater assertiveness on the part of the second generation Moroccans compared with similar immigrants in other countries, for they feel that Israel is, after all, their rightful home; and since there are so many of them it is natural that they should want to have a substantial voice in the country. This has had important political implications: Jews from Arab countries frequently expect the worst so far as Arabs are concerned, because their recent experiences in Arab countries have not been pleasant.

Once upon a time Arabs and Jews lived harmoniously together, but that was in the Middle Ages and the fact is no longer of political relevance. For many years Arab leaders and many of their Western well-wishers have admonished the Israelis for not shedding their Western (European) heritage and have urged them to become spiritually and culturally part of the region in which they have made their home. This is now happening, to a certain extent, but the result is not at all what had been anticipated. The high hopes attached to the growing political role of the "Arab Jews" sprang from a monumental misunderstanding.

In the 1950s Moroccan, and to a lesser extent other Oriental Jews, regarded Ben Gurion as their leader; his style was authoritarian and there was something in him of the prophet. But they could not bring themselves to transfer their allegiance to Ben Gurion's weaker and far less inspiring successors. These factors do not of course fully explain Mr. Begin's electoral victory in May 1977. Even in the 1930s, when the composition of the Oriental Jewish community was very different from what it is today, more of them sympathized with the Revisionists than with any other party—they had never had much sympathy for Labour Zionism.

A great many factors were involved in the defeat of the Ma'arakh—the quality of the leadership, the rivalries in its top echelons, the minor and major scandals that shocked Israel in 1975 and 1976, and the inevitable erosion of the strength and cohesion of a party which had been in power for four decades. Perhaps the election campaign, ably described by Alex Ansky in *Mehirat Halikud* (The Selling of the Likud), also played a part, though the evidence is far from conclusive. Likud, the coalition of parties headed by Mr. Begin, availed itself of the services of Dahaf, Israel's leading public relations firm. The glimpses behind the scenes of the hectic campaign are fascinating, with the Rabelaisian language used by Ezer Weizmann, who directed the campaign, providing some light relief. But did the campaign really have a decisive impact on the outcome? Zhurbin, who was the head of Dahaf, candidly stated that Likud would have won in any case. As in Italy and France, there was the widespread feeling that the time for change had come and since, in contrast to Italy, there was a democratic alternative, many erstwhile supporters decided to give their vote to the party of the founding fathers no longer.

Some of the protest vote went to Samuel Flatto-Sharon, a businessman from Paris, about whose identity and activities the French police and Interpol were better informed than the Israeli electorate. His election was part of the process which brought Likud to power, but it was overshadowed by Mr. Begin's victory and it is only lately that the enormity of this scandal has fully registered. This then in outline was the background against which Mr. Begin's triumph took place after eight consecutive defeats. Only in this light can it be understood, for the Jabotinsky heritage was virtually forgotten and Likud's electoral platform—which, as is usual in such cases, promised everything to everybody—did not matter in the least.

Thus in May 1977, Mr. Begin became prime minister of Israel. He had arrived in the country thirty years earlier from Russia, a private in General Anders's Polish Army, His name was known at the time to only a handful of Jabotinsky's disciples in Palestine, who had heard of him as one of the most promising young leaders of their movement in Eastern Europe.

They were looking then for a new head of the Irgun which, after the death of its commander David Raziel in 1941, barely continued to exist. Begin was elected and his release from the army arranged. In early 1944 the new head of the Irgun declared a revolt against Britain, and this was followed by attacks against the British Mandatorv immigration offices in Tel Aviv, Haifa and Jerusalem. The rest of the story is known; a detailed account was recently provided by J. Bowyer Bell in his book *Terror out of Zion*.

Like other terrorist movements Irgun certainly attracted publicity, but the sound and fury it created was far in excess of the political impact of its activities. Former members of Irgun have long complained that their part in the struggle that led to statehood has not been sufficiently appreciated in Israel. Mr. Begin's government is now trying to make amends for this alleged conspiracy of silence, and the history of these years is gradually being rewritten. Most observers now agree that Begin's main contribution was probably the prevention of a civil war—out of a feeling of national responsibility, his admirers claim; out of fear that the Irgun would be smashed, according to his critics.

For a new immigrant to have imposed his authority on a group of militants was no mean feat. How was it accomplished? Begin had neither the appearance nor the bearing of a military man; in fact he had never been involved in military operations. But he was a great speaker, persuasive, devoted to his cause, totally sure of himself, and his guidance was only too eagerly accepted by young people thirsting for action. He certainly had charisma, to use that greatly overworked term. Natan Yelin-Mor, once the head of the Stern Gang—the "Fighters for the Freedom of Israel", Irgun's more extreme rival—tells an illuminating story. In the days of the underground there was a dispute between the two groups and eventually they agreed on arbitration. To Yelin-Mor's consternation, Begin tried to appoint himself the arbiter. When asked how a member of one side in the dispute could possibly act as an arbiter, Begin answered that this did not at all disqualify him, for how could anyone doubt his objectivity?

In Begin's speeches there has always been a great discrepancy between the delivery and the substance; they do not read at all well. A comparison with the speeches of Moshe Sneh, the other brilliant orator of the period, is of some interest. Sneh also arrived in Palestine from Poland during the war. A middle-of-the-road Zionist who was made a Hagana commander, he later became a staunch supporter of the Soviet Union, but eventually lost his faith in orthodox communism. Both men were natural talents of the first order, but while Sneh first and foremost appealed to reason even during his worst, Stalinist, period, Begin did not, playing with great skill on his listerers' emotions. There were logic and consistency in Begin's speeches, too, but only if one accepted his basic tenets. For those not in tune with Begin's beliefs the charm did not work; they dismissed his histrionics as those of a second-rate actor, a not-too-successful provincial advocate or, at worst, a dangerous demagogue.

But oratory does not wholly explain the Begin phenomenon, certainly not during this early period, if only because in the underground years there were no mass audiences. In the final analysis it was his single-minded, uncompromising nationalism which was his great strength at a time of confusion and crisis.

Keynes' description of Clemenceau's attitude at the Versailles Peace Conference comes to mind: nations are real things—you love one, and for the rest feel indifference or hatred. Begin felt about Israel what Pericles felt about Athens—that there was unique value in her, and that nothing else mattered. ("There is no morality higher than the morality of the Hebrew freedom struggle": *Bemahteret,* Volume 1, page 218.) He had one illusion—Israel, and one disillusion—mankind (not excluding the Israelis, even his own colleagues).

The young Begin of 1944 may have been less of a misanthrope than the old Clemenceau. Early on, however, he expressed the fear that the Jewish nation was totally isolated, that it had no friends, that the whole world was against it. In a famous encounter in pre-war Poland, Begin is reported to have given vent to these feelings, only to be told by Jabotinsky that the logical course of action for him would be to drown himself in the Vistula.

Begin, as we know, did not follow this advice: his despair in any case was not consistent and quite frequently his black moods would give way to extravagant optimism. When he came to power he promised to solve most problems in the near future and he told his advisers that there was no reason at all to fear that a conflict with America was inevitable.

There are more examples in Polish history than in Jewish history of such single-minded nationalism. It has fortified him all along, but it has also made it impossible for him to understand the national ambitions of other people—or of those of his own people who failed to share his convictions. In a recently published collection of his manifestoes, articles and illegal broadcasts during the underground period (1944-48), Britain time and again appears as the reincarnation of Nazi Germany: British rule since 1920 had been a pogrom: "but for our resistance they would have slaughtered our children". Begin was then at war with Britain and hence it was not a good time for writing history, but one still wonders whether his reputation will be enhanced by disinterring propaganda speeches made in the heat of the battle. Begin did not hate the Arabs, but thought there would be sufficient room for both Jews and Arabs (on both sides of the Jordan, to be sure). On at least one occasion he stated that a population transfer would be immoral. If there was Arab resistance to the Jewish national home, it was simply the action of misguided people incited by the British. And as late as 1947, in his meeting with the members of UNSCOP (the United Nations Special Committee on Palestine) he flatly stated that Arab threats were empty and that they would not go to war.

Since then Begin's attitude to Arabs and British alike has changed. He has been eager to establish a special relationship with Whitehall, and the epithet "Nazi" is now applied to the PLO and to the more radical Arab terrorist organizations. But had he not been a terrorist himself? Such comparisons are indignantly rejected by Mr. Begin. He was a fighter for the national freedom of his people, he and his comrades-in-arms engaged in military operations, not in terror, least of all against the civilian population. But such protestations carry little or no weight, for the Arabs too have claimed all along that they are conducting a national liberation struggle. Mr. Begin was, of course, head of a terrorist organization; so was Sean MacBride, who subsequently received both the Lenin and the Nobel Peace prizes, and a great many other people now highly respected.

With more justification Begin could claim that his form of terrorism belonged to a different era, with something of the "terrible beauty" of the Easter Rising of 1916, and not to be identified with the indiscriminate slaughter of innocents that has become the hallmark of contemporary terrorism. True, a great many innocent people were killed in the bombing of the King David Hotel, and there was mass murder at Deir Yassin.

But Mr. Begin could claim that these were regrettable, unplanned incidents; and that they were not an integral part of Irgun strategy, for otherwise there would have been many Deir Yassins. Mr. Begin has claimed that Irgun made an all-out effort not to attack non-combatants; and whether the effort was really all-out or not is a matter of legitimate dispute. There is no denying that there are fundamental differences between the Irgun (and most other old-style terrorist groups) and the deliberately indiscriminate murder perpetrated by their present-day successors.

In 1948, with his election to the first Knesset, Begin became a parliamentarian and, in the course of time, an accomplished one. For a while, after the Six-Days War, he served as a cabinet minister without portfolio. His legal training in Warsaw had awakened his interest in parliamentary procedure, and he became something of an expert in the field. In parliament he has seldom spoken about social or economic issues; he firmly believes in the primacy of foreign policy. Yet over a period of thirty years his contribution to foreign policy has been modest; he seems to be more interested in legal formulations than in ideas. He would oppose the policy of the government and admonish it regularly to "make the most of the opportunities". What these opportunities were and how they could be exploited he has never quite made clear.

On one famous occasion he attacked the government head on, threatening to overthrow it by extra-parliamentary means. This was on the issue of German reparations in 1952. Accepting "blood money", Begin said, was the ultimate shame. There were fiery speeches, Begin announced a fight to the death, and there were violent demonstrations in front of the parliament building. For a moment it seemed quite possible that the mob assembled outside would storm the Knesset. But in the end Begin retreated; there was no return to the underground, no civil war.

Ben Gurion and most other leaders of Mapai never forgave Begin. Years later Ben Gurion wrote in letters to Moshe Sharett, the foreign minister, and to Haim Guri, the poet, that if Begin ever came to power he would bring about the ruin of the state, or, at the very least, make it an abomination. But in the years that followed Begin stuck scrupulously to the ground rules of democracy, and among his supporters who had hitherto blindly, unquestioningly followed him, there were murmurings about "Begin-Cunctator" who had seemingly lost his enterprise and his daring.

On rare occasions he would suggest some new political initiative. Thus in the 1960s it occurred to him that it was necessary to improve relations with the Soviet Union. This, he suggested, could best be achieved by closely cooperating with the Soviet Union in opposing West German nuclear rearmament. But Germany had no such intention in the first place, nor would the Soviet leaders have needed Israeli support for a campaign of this kind.

The idea, based on a serious misreading of the world situation, was typical of his limited outlook; it seemed the main lesson he had learnt in his underground days was Danton's, "l'audace, l'audace, encore l'audace". The years of opposition did not help to broaden his horizons, and brief visits to Western capitals were not sufficient to provide an education in world politics. The idea that the policy of a small country such as Israel had to be attuned to the interests of at least one great power, that it needed international support, undoubtedly occurred to him, but there was no sign that this insight meant much to him. This is not to say that he was a blind believer in military power; he had always attached enormous importance to *hasbara,* which can be roughly translated as information or explanation, or propaganda, in a constructive sense. He had deeply believed in the force of his moral and legal arguments, and being himself a master of the spoken word, he has been firmly convinced that if only Israel's case were put forcefully it would eventually be accepted by all men of good will. He has been quite blind to the fact that other people have arguments too, and that, in any case, in international politics, unlike in the legal profession, it is not necessarily the strongest argument which wins the day.

He carried on the political struggle almost singlehanded. There had been some men of ability in the Herut, but they drifted away or were purged: few could accept the fact that all important decisions (and many unimportant ones, too) were taken by one man. In later years Begin's intervention in internal party affairs diminished and eventually virtually ceased. But in the Herut, internal party democracy seemed to consist of a struggle as to who would get what: there were no serious discussions of the political issues facing the country at home or abroad. After the electoral victory, there were constant complaints on the part of old Herut stalwarts as to why the top bureaucrats of the old regime had not been replaced by those who had faithfully served the national cause for so many years. The obvious answer was that there were few capable people in their ranks. It was not that there was a surfeit of capable people in other political parties. But in Herut even more than in the other parties the presence of one man who was the ultimate authority on every issue prevented the emergence of a younger generation of leaders. The Herut did not have much intellectual support. A Mapai leader had once noted the fact that there were more voters in one single immigrant camp than among all the university professors, journalists and actors. And this, to, formed the basis of Begin's political attitude.

He had the traditional Jewish respect for learning, but he was not at all anxious to have the benefit of the intellectuals' political advice. He failed to realize that although intellectuals in a democratic society cannot help politicians very much in practice, as makers of public opinion they can certainly cause them a great deal of harm.

Mr. Begin's performance in his first year in power was quite different from what had been expected of him. The transformation of the terrorist leader into the elder statesman was complete and his ascendancy over his colleagues in the cabinet undisputed. But far from revealing dictatorial ambitions he showed signs of weakness and indecision. His mandate was by no means as sweeping as has been generally assumed. His own party did not even have a majority in the ruling coalition, and it was riven by internal strife, with its lunatic fringe calling for the immediate cessation of negotiations with the "Hitler from the Nile". The only interest of the Liberals, Begin's major coalition partner, was in "business as usual", and the generals in his cabinet behaved with a remarkably unmilitary lack of discipline, pulling the coalition in different directions.

Initially there had been much public support for Begin—perhaps he was the one to cut the Gordian knot, as de Gaulle had done in Algeria. And it is perfectly true that during one period at least in autumn last year he did show enterprise. The "Sadat peace initiative" was to an equal degree Begin's; the pre-history of Sadat's visit to Jerusalem remains as yet to be written. Perhaps his inflexibility had been exaggerated: he did, after all, accept relations with Germany, just as he had given up the old Revisionist dreams about Trans-Jordan ("Our flag will fly over Amman": *Bemahteret,* Volume 2, page 119). In the negotiations with Sadat he expressed willingness to give up all Sinai, a concession which no previous Israeli government had been willing to make. But there was still the question of Judaea and Samaria; how could he surrender the idea of Jewish settlements in these regions without betraying the Jabotinsky legacy and indeed his whole past? Thus the issue of the settlements, which were quite irrelevant compared with the larger issues at stake, became a major bone of contention, and the talks were bogged down in futile attempts to find legal definitions concerning the future of the West Bank's status.

In the eyes of the world Begin became the man who had thrown away the chance of peace, and the Israeli public too became deeply divided on the issue. There was the case of Shilo. A small group of religious fanatics had squatted in West Bank territory; the government opposed the move but did not dare to remove them. Thus, according to the official version, they became "archaeologists" overnight even though they did not know the difference between an antique earthenware vessel and a contemporary *djara*. A growing number of young people were asking: "Mourir pour Shilo?" Perhaps in his heart Mr. Begin had accepted the necessity that ultimately there would have to be concessions on the West Bank too; perhaps he preferred that these decisions should be taken by his successors.

Despite such irresolution there was still support for him. Most Israelis would prefer peace to their "historical rights", but the majority also think that peace is not at hand. Everyone agrees that without a solution to the Palestinian issue there will be no peace, but it is also certain that a solution acceptable to the PLO would mean war. Recognizing that the dangers are about equal, large sections of the Israeli public prefer that there should be as little change as possible for the time being and this, broadly speaking, is Mr. Begin's line too. Why give up the hills of Judaea and Samaria, if the Palestinians do not even recognize Israeli rights to Tel Aviv and Haifa?

Perhaps there will be a change in the world situation; perhaps, with the new aggressiveness shown by the Soviet Union in Africa and Asia, Arab countries will no longer see in Israel the main threat to their existence. It is true that the Palestinians have a right of national self-determination;

and it is also true that the presence of a large and hostile minority is not in the best interests of Israel. In a similar situation in the 1930s Czechoslovakia refused to let the Sudeten Germans exercise the right of self-determination and return to the Reich, for this would have left the country defenseless. There are alternatives to Mr. Begin's policies, but they all involve risks. Many Israelis, neither nationalist nor religious extremists, are reluctant in the light of recent Jewish history to take risks, and this reluctance is, in the last resort, the main source of Begin's popular support.

Thus Mr. Begin's government has been reduced to a policy of immobilism. The prime minister, quite obviously a disappointed man, is seldom heard. The years and illness have taken their toll; there are no long and fiery speeches any more and instead of the Latin quotations once so dear to him there are frequent invocations of the Almighty.

But God does not supply the F-15, nor can he prevent a confrontation with the United States. It was Mr. Begin's historical misfortune that he came to power when it was no longer possible to ignore some of the agonizing questions which his predecessors had avoided for years— partly no doubt out of fear of Begin and his supporters.

Many of Mr. Begin's domestic critics, in disagreement with his principles and fearful of the consequences of his policies, quite readily admitted that the situation facing him is anything but enviable. They would greatly prefer to see him reaching a settlement with at least some Arab countries. For statesmen and many observers in the West he remains a riddle or an anachronism: full-blooded nationalism is no longer in fashion (since de Gaulle's death it is seldom found outside the Third World and the communist countries). Nationalism is, of course, by no means dead in the West. But it is of a different character: a nationalism of resentment and weakness, the aims of which are strictly limited by both geopolitical and economic considerations.

The stature of a political leader can be measured synchronically or diachronically. In comparison with the Weizmanns, the Ben Gurions or the Jabotinskys, Mr. Begin does not fare too well, but when judged in the context of his contemporaries, the condescension shown towards him by many seems less justified. He is not stupid nor does he lack character, and in an age of mediocrity and defeatism these attributes can no longer be taken for granted. Seen from Israel the counsels offered by some of Mr. Begin's opponents seem at times a little suspect: what are they to learn from Dr. Nahum Goldmann, venerable Zionist leader and great raconteur, whose political judgment during a long career has been almost invariably wrong? What are they to make of the many Western politicians and commentators, full of good advice and stern admonitions— some of whom at least would be happier if the state of Israel did not exist? They would no doubt mourn its demise, but Mr. Begin and most Israelis prefer their complaints to their condolences.

All this does not make Mr. Begin's policies right and a heavy price may have to be paid, not only by those who elected him. Even if a war is unavoidable it is not wise to create a situation in which one's country will be virtually isolated, but this has been the result of Mr. Begin's policy. He became prime minister at a difficult and intensely interesting time. The social and cultural processes that carried him to power were essentially negative. But if there has been a deterioration in Israel there still is idealism and enormous vitality. Israelis are a people of extremes: so gifted and so stupid, so brave and selfless in the face of danger, so quarrelsome and irresponsible at most other times. It is certain that Israel will have to live dangerously in the years to come, and precisely for this reason the survival of the country seems assured. But outside dangers are not the only, and perhaps not even the main ones threatening Israel at the moment.

*July 1978*

# Hannah Arendt in Jerusalem— The Controversy Revisted

It is difficult to think of a book in living memory that stirred up as much controversy as Hannah Arendt's *Eichmann in Jerusalem*. Mrs. Arendt still has her angry detractors and fanatical supporters, but on the whole, I believe, it is easier now to understand what made the late Hannah Arendt write this book and why it provoked so much criticism. It is also possible to comment on the impact of this controversy on the subsequent historiography of the holocaust.

## I

Hannah Arendt, thirty-five years of age at the time, arrived in the United States in 1941, having escaped from France. Her main intellectual interests had been philosophy and modern literature. She had written a doctoral dissertation on the concept of love in the work of St. Augustine; her first articles, published in Germany, were on Rilke's Duino Elegies and on Kierkegaard. She belonged to a generation and a milieu that was basically unpolitical but which had developed a passionate interest in politics—in the widest sense—following Hitler's rise to power and the outbreak of World War II. Soon after her arrival in the United States, she began to publish articles, first in the German language weekly *Der Aufbau,* later also in other periodicals. Her early journalistic work in the United States has been almost entirely neglected (or forgotten), yet it provides essential clues to the genesis of the book that created such a furor two decades later.[1]

What emerged from these articles was that Hannah Arendt always had doubts about Zionism and that gradually she came to believe that Herzl had been a crackpot, that Zionism was a chauvinistic, fanatical and hysterical phenomenon, and that it had never been a popular movement. At the same time she insisted on the establishment of a Jewish army to fight Nazism 'for the glory and the honour of the Jewish people.' This was the theme of her very first article in the U.S. and of many that were

271

to follow. Her demand was based on something like a neo-Bundist ideology. An army is usually the function of a state—except perhaps in the case of Prussia, where according to an old saying, the state was a mere appendage of the army. But Hannah Arendt did not want a state for the Jews, and her demand for an army in these conditions was curious, to say the least. She was at this time very much preoccupied with the fate of the Jews in Europe and, above all, with Jewish resistance.

A report published in *Aufbau* about the Musterghetto Theresienstadt provided an occasion to develop a theory to explain Nazi policy towards the Jews: Jews are tolerated, and sometimes even protected, where their presence will create antisemitism among the local population; they will be deported from regions which are not antisemitic. Jews are deported from areas where their very presence could lead to resistance. ('If Mrs. Mueller in Germany sees that her neighbour, Mrs. Schmidt, behaves decently to Mrs. Cohn, she knows that she must not be afraid of Mrs. Schmidt—she may even talk openly to Mrs. Schmidt')[2] An ingenious theory no doubt, but quite wrong. On another occasion writing on the 'part of the Jewish partisans in the European uprising,' Hannah Arendt noted that the European Jews were not doomed: the Jews of Europe no longer faced a separate fate if they refused to accept it. *('Die Gesetz-maessigkeiten des juedischen Sonderschicksals verloren immer ihre Gueltigkeit wenn Juden sich weigerten, es als Schicksal zu akzeptieren.')*[3] Or to put it into more simple language: the Jews did not have to die if they did not want to die. A small minority of Jewish millionaires and scoundrels had acted as traitors, but a very substantial part of the people had chosen the road of armed struggle. She wrote about a 100,000 Jewish partisans in Poland, 10,000 in France. . . fighting the Nazis in the streets, fields and forests.

Even before the war ended Hannah Arendt gave her mind to the question of guilt, noting that the number of those responsible and guilty among the Germans were relatively small; hence the conclusion that there was no political method for dealing with German mass crimes, 'where all are guilty, nobody in the last analysis can be judged'. Even in a murder camp, Mrs. Arendt noted, everyone, whether directly active or not, was forced to take part in one way or another in the workings of the machine—'that is the horrible thing'.[4] This brief outline was the origin of the concept of the 'banality of evil'. (I recently came across the phrase in Josef Conrad's preface to *Under Western Eyes,* written well before World War I, but it may have been used before.) Hannah Arendt was fearful of the great opportunities that would exist in Europe after the war for the re-emergence of an international fascist organization. The arch evil of our time had been defeated but not completely eradicated—except in the areas under immediate Russian influence, where the 'forces of yesterday' had been destroyed once and forever.[5]

I have concentrated on the issues that have a direct bearing on the controversy of the early 1960s. A reading of Hannah Arendt's political journalism shows that she was far more often wrong than right both in her analysis and predictions. There was always an inclination on her part to exaggerate as well as to generalize (and theorize) on the basis of a slender factual basis. She had a great deal of intelligence but little common sense and apparently no political instinct—she was a philosophical not a political animal. The case of Theresienstadt is an extreme case in point. The obvious explanation provided in *Aufbau,* that of a Musterghetto was quite right, which is more than can be said about the theories about 'selective deportation'. Again, the fears of a great revival of fascism after the war are psychologically understandable, but they were not at all borne out by subsequent events. But the fact that she had so often been wrong did not shake Mrs. Arendt's confidence in her own judgment. In one of her very last essays Mrs. Arendt wrote that 'Anti-Communism' was 'at the root of all theories in Washington—in sheer ignorance of all pertinent facts'.[6] This from the woman who had been one of the most influential architects of the totalitarianism concept, who had explained in *Burden of our Time* that Nazi Germany and Soviet Russia were 'two essentially identical systems'.[7] True, Mrs. Arendt later retracted this; after the Hungarian revolt in 1956 (which profoundly influenced her) she wrote that the closed system of the Soveit Union was no longer totalitarian in the strict sense of the term. One of the reasons given was the food supplies sent to the Hungarians; another was the flowering of the arts in the Soviet Union. Mrs. Arendt had exaggerated in 1951, and again after 1956, without, however, lasting damage to either her self-confidence or her reputation.

There was a general tendency during the war and indeed for quite a few years after to overrate the importance (and the numerical strength) of Jewish resistance in Europe. The same is true, incidentally, with regard to war-time resistance in general—excepting only Yugoslavia. I have dealt with this topic in a recent study ('Guerrilla'); all that need be said in this context is that resistance was physically possible only in a few countries to begin with. The reports about tens and hundreds of thousands of *maquis,* Jewish or non-Jewish, were of course sheer fantasy. Thus, seen in retrospect, European Jews did not live up to Mrs. Arendt's expectations as fighters for the glory and honor of their people; as a result they were punished for if they had fought they (or at least many of them) would have survived. Since most of them did not fight, five or six million were killed. Mrs. Arendt found mitigating circumstances for non-Jews. Everyone in a murder camp was forced to take part in the working of the machine. She did not make such allowances for her fellow Jews.

## II

Mrs. Arendt attended the Eichmann trial as a journalist, and her account was published in five installments in the *New Yorker* in late spring of 1963. It became a *succès de scandal* from the first moment. Some critics were shocked by the periodical chosen by Mrs. Arendt—witty, entertaining, frivolous, intellectually pretentious and quite unserious. An investigation into mass murder in between Mr. Arno's cartoons; the advertisements for Cadillacs and Oldsmobiles, gin, holidays in Bermuda; a little bit of holocaust; a little bit of Tiffany and Saks Fifth Avenue—it was quite a remarkable mixture. Others complained about her style, the snide remarks, the flippancy and superciliousness—the heartlessness. Yet others pointed to the unfortunate tendency on the part of the author throughout her book to use terms that were emotionally highly charged and to apply a double yardstick. Thus, when Gideon Hausner, the chief prosecutor, asked some of the survivors of the death camps why they had not offered armed resistance, Mrs. Arendt expressed indignation about cruel and foolish questions of this kind. But her own critique of the Jewish leadership rests precisely on the same basis: those who did not fight were guilty.[8] Again, any form of contact between Jewish leaders and the Nazis, even when the aim was to make the emigration of Jews possible or to save lives, was 'collaboration' as far as Mrs. Arendt was concerned. But the term collaboration in the context of World War II has a certain connotation of which the author was no doubt quite aware. If she believed that Jews should not have talked to the Nazis under any circumstances, she should have said so. But she did not and for this reason the indiscriminate use of the term was irresponsible. A German critic was taken aback by the fact that Mrs. Arendt had singled out two Germans who had resisted—one was the right-wing writer Reck Malleczewen, the other the philosopher Karl Jaspers.[9] Reck Malleczewen had died in a concentration camp, but there is no known evidence whatsoever that Prof. Jaspers ever uttered a word of criticism between 1933 and 1945. Why then was he singled out? Because he was Mrs. Arendt's teacher to whom she remained devoted to the end of his life—he died in 1969. This little episode is revealing. While in no way central to Hannah Arendt's arguments, it was typical of her approach to history. But there is yet another aspect which, to the best of my knowledge, has not so far been noted, the curious resemblance between master and disciple. Both were philosophers, both felt from time to time obliged to comment on politics, frequently in a high pitch, bordering on an hysteria—from which their philosophical writings were quite free. Thus Jaspers, during the height of the cold war, was one of the people advocating West Germany's nuclear rearmament. In the 1960s, on the other hand, he published a treatise in which he demonstrated that West Germany was well on the way towards abolishing parliamentary democracy, and to all intents and purpose, to becoming fascist again. This book was published in the United States with a preface by Hannah Arendt in which she stated that 'politically [this is] the most important book to appear after the second world war.'[10] Had Hannah Arendt really believed this, she would certainly have published at least an article in the same vein. She did not, which shows that she had reservations. But filial piety nevertheless prevailed over intellectual integrity.

Among Hannah Arendt's critics, apart from those already noted, Gershom Sholem and Manes Sperber ought to be mentioned, as well as Norman Podhoretz' essay, the Bettelheim review in the *New Republic* and the ensuing polemic with Judge Musmanno.[11] The most detailed and ambitious, but in many respects, least effective reply to Hannah Arendt was the late Jacob Robinson's *And the Crooked Shall be Made Straight,* a book of more than four hundred pages published by Macmillan in 1965. The late Dr. Robinson probably knew all there was to know about the factual background and with his training as a lawyer he was also an expert on the legal implications of war crime trials. His technique in the book was that of the lawyer who wishes to discredit a hostile witness by showing that he is not really master of the subject. And so he relentlessly subjected every word of Mrs. Arendt to critical examination, pointing out that the correct spelling of a certain SS Obergruppenfuehrer should be Hanns—not Hans as given by Mrs. Arendt—as if mistakes of this kind necessarily disqualified her from commenting on SS policy. Dr. Robinson's book was a case of overkill; he demonstrated that Mrs. Arendt had indeed committed many mistakes, partly in view of a cavalier attitude to facts, partly perhaps out of genuine ignorance. She knew, after all, neither Hebrew nor Yiddish, neither Polish nor Russian, and most of the relevant literature was at the time in these languages. She had to rely basically on Prof. Hilberg's book (a book on the Nazis, not on the Jews) and on what she learned during the Eichmann trial. But Robinson's book, hastily written, also contained factual mistakes, it failed to tackle important issues, it was inconsistent, claiming at one and the same time that much further study was needed on collaboration—and that there had been no collaboration and treason at all among the Jews. Above all, Dr. Robinson, in the light of his background, training and interests, was quite obviously the wrong person to 'refute' Hannah Arendt. Plodding, immersed in questions of detail, he could not possibly follow her to the rarified heights of abstractions where the moral philosopher could engage in a virtuoso performance, but where poor Dr. Robinson would be quite lost.

I should perhaps mention in passing my own involuntary involvement in the affair. I had reviewed Dr. Robinson's book at the time and had noted its shortcomings.[12] This produced an irate reply from Mrs. Arendt, far longer than the original review. It dealt largely with Dr. Robinson's book rather than my review, which mainly served as a peg for her rejoinder. My review had been more moderate than most and there had been no anger in it. But Mrs. Arendt was far from satisfied; she was at the time already something of a cult figure among the New York intelligentsia. She did not mind being attacked, but she evidently disliked not being taken very seriously as a student of contemporary Jewish history. She imputed to the reviewer sinister motives: Mr. Laqueur, she implied, was dependent on Dr. Robinson, a vassal jumping to the aid of his seigneur. My relations with the late Dr. Robinson were neither close, nor, for a variety of reasons, friendly. Mrs. Arendt, who did not know me at all, could not possibly know about my relations, if any, with Dr. Robinson and yet she was quite ready to assume the worst, to insinuate and to incriminate. Her reaction greatly intrigued me, even though I knew of course that statements made in the heat of a polemic should not be taken too seriously nor remembered for too long. Mrs. Arendt was certainly at the time in a state of near panic, as her writings show, firmly convinced that the Elders of Zion had conspired to 'get her.'

### III

Hannah Arendt's main arguments are widely known and can be summarized therefore in briefest outline. Eichmann was guilty and deserved to be executed, but he was an idealist in a perverted way. He had no criminal intent; he was basically a normal human being acting under the pressure of a totalitarian regime for which he was not personally responsible. Hence the conclusion that justice was not done in Jerusalem—it was the wrong court condemning him for the wrong reasons. He should have been hanged as *hostis generis humani,* rather than *hostis Judaeorum.* Mrs. Arendt attributed to this distinction enormous importance; I failed to see the crucial significance of this issue at the time and I have not become any wiser in the years between. Far more important are the charges she made against the Jewish leadership and its responsibility for the catastrophe. Without their active collaboration ('mere compliance would not have been enough'), the destruction of so many millions of Jews would not have been possible ('there would have been either complete chaos or an impossible severe drain on German manpower.')[13] The ghetto police, Mrs. Arendt reports, was an instrument in the hands of the murderers. The actual work of killing in the extermination centers was usually in the hands of Jewish commandos, who also dug the graves and extinguished the traces of mass murder, and had built the gas chambers in the first place. Thus Jewish cooperation put an end to the clear cut division between persecutors and victims. There was a moral collapse among the victims. The leadership, almost without exception, cooperated in one way or another, for one reason or another, with the Nazis. If the Jewish people had been unorganized and leaderless, there would have been chaos and plenty of misery but the total number of victims would hardly have been between 4.5 and 6 million people. Hence the conclusion that to a Jew this role of the Jewish leaders in the destruction of their own people is undoubtedly the darkest chapter of the whole dark story.

Some of these allegations are true, some are wrong, most are half true. There is no reason to assume that if the Jewish people had been leaderless, the Nazis would have found killing more difficult or even impossible. It has frequently been pointed out that the extermination proceded quite smoothly even where there were no Jewish Councils—or where the Jewish Councils were not required to collaborate with the Nazis in the preparation for the final solution. Nor is it true that the division between murderers and victims was obliterated. But even if resistance would not have meant survival, this still leaves the painful issue of 'Jewish appeasement.' Hannah Arendt's condemnation of appeasement is basically correct as a rule of political behavior when dealing with enemies of this kind. It is inexplicable how Dr. Robinson could possibly write in 1965 that 'there is no evidence that the motivation in accepting and maintaining membership in the Judenraete was not generally honorable.'[14] There was a great deal of such evidence. But there was no conspiracy of silence, no deliberate attempt to whitewash villains and make heroes out of doubtful characters, as Mrs. Arendt seems to have believed. She saw herself, no doubt, as a champion of truth, which had been suppressed too long. There was a certain reluctance to deal systematically with the most tragic subject of all, for the very same reason that there has been reluctance in every European country (including the neutral ones) to come to terms with the many manifestations of 'collaboration' in the Nazi era. The Jewish case was different, to be sure, because Frenchmen or Dutchmen—for instance, had freedom of choice: they did not *have* to collaborate. A recent French writer notes, 'le collaborationisme n'était pas une fatalité. Un Louis Marin ou un Louis Vallon adhéraient en 1939 aux memes partis qu'un Philipple Henriot out un Marcel Déat.'[15] The Jews did not have to collaborate either, but the alternative was considerably more unpleasant.

There had been books and articles, countless autobiographies and memoirs on the Jewish Councils in Poland (by Philip Friedman and others), in Holland (by Abel Herzberg and others), in Theresienstadt (by H.G. Adler) and elsewhere. Professor Hilberg's book, which had many harsh things to say about the Jewish reaction, had already appeared, and it was Hannah Arendt's main source. The facts were known but they had not fully registered even though, as in the Kastner trial, the basic issues had been discussed. If many of the facts referred to in Hannah Arendt's book had been known for a long time, what made so many people so angry about *Eichmann in Jerusalem,* and why did the book become a *cause celèbre?* Her series of articles, and the book that subsequently emerged, were of course far more widely read than the scholarly articles or monographs dealing with the same subject. The scholars, among whom there were, and are, quite a few not less extreme in the final analysis than Hannah Arendt in their condemnation of collaboration, were more cautious in stating their conclusions, not because they were afraid, but because they were more aware of the complexity of the situation—the terrible pressures under which the Jewish Councils had been acting. Hannah Arendt's book, on the other hand, was impressionistic, subjective. There was her usual tendency toward exaggeration. She attacked without discrimination the entire Jewish leadership in Europe and made some exceedingly silly remarks which she probably later regretted (the reference to Leo Baeck as the 'Jewish Fuehrer'—without quotation marks). She attacked Zionism in view of its collaboration with the Nazis (meaning the organization of illegal immigration) and also because of certain ideological similarities, real or imaginary. Thus she antagonized all Zionists and pro-Zionists. But this again does not explain the vehement reactions triggered off by her book. The most telling criticism came from non-Zionists (such as Eva Reichmann) or anti-Zionists, or Zionists such as Ernst Simon, Buber and Scholem who had belong to Brith Shalom, which stood for Arab-Jewish collaboration and which had been actively supported by Hannah Arendt. Her attitude toward Zionism was by no means as consistent as commonly believed. While she supported Ichud, she also had sympathies for Mr. Begin's Irgun Zvai Leumi, which (in her words) attracted the most decent and idealist elements. This apparent paradox is not difficult to explain. Arendt hated 'conciliators' and 'appeasers' such as Weizmann, but she always had a weakness for those who fought and resisted. She belonged to those intellectuals about whom it has been said that *ils n'aiment que les trains que partent*—the direction of the departure being a secondary consideration.

Hannah Arendt was bitterly attacked precisely because she was held in such high esteem by many of her contemporaries—*corruptio optimi pessima.* This, in a way, was quite unfair, for she had, after all, not made her name as a contemporary historian. She had moved very far from her national Jewish enthusiasm of 1942-43, but no one expected that she would want deliberately and unnecessarily to cause offense and pain. Hannah Arendt's attitude toward her people (her personal 'Jewish problem') was complex, and there is little doubt that this had a bearing on the writing of this book. Sooner or later, someone more familiar with this subject than the present writer will deal with this aspect of the affair.

Hannah Arendt was mainly attacked not for what she said, but for how she said it. She was a highly intelligent person and at the same time exceedingly insensitive. She would not, or could not, discriminate, see the nuances—and this in a context in which nuances were all important. She certainly had the intellectual equipment to deal with the subject, but not the temperament. She was one of the most clever writers of her generation, but the holocaust is a subject in which cleverness can be a positive disadvantage. Her memory was selective: when she wrote about Eichmann, she had forgotten almost all she had written about the human condition in a totalitarian state. The holocaust is a subject that has to be confronted in a spirit of humility; whatever Mrs. Arendt's many virtues, humility was not among them. 'Judge not that ye not be judged' says the New Testament. But Hannah Arendt loved to judge, and was at her most effective in the role of *magister humanitatis,* invoking moral pathos. Thus she rushed in where wiser men and women feared to tread, writing about extreme situations which she in her life had never experienced. She was a writer always inclined by temperament to overstatement, most at ease when dealing with abstractions, at her weakest when analyzing concrete situations and real people. The constellation was unfortunate, and the result predictable.

The Eichmann controversy did not do any lasting harm to Hannah Arendt's reputation. On the contrary, at the time of her death she was widely thought to be one of the most original and influential thinkers of our time. She was an erudite and brilliant woman, she wrote well, her ideas appealed to left and right alike—an almost unique case at the time. Even her confusion seemed attractive in the New York of the 1960s. The fact that that her political comments and her historical *obiter dicta* were often wrong was quite immaterial. One can easily think of professional politicians being wrong most of the time; they seem not to be worse off as a result. In politics it is far more damaging to be right at the wrong time. Nor should it be forgotten that she had made her name as a political philosopher, not a political journalist. True, Hannah Arendt's political philosophy has also baffled admirers and critics alike. One of them, a highly sympathetic commentator, admitted that most of what she had written about totalitarianism had been wrong, but still her book was a 'considerable work of art, vivid and enthralling, intensely reflective. Even when it fails as history it succeeds as reflection.'[16] It is certainly true that when *The Origins of Totalitarianism* appeared it was more enthusiastically welcomed by literary figures than by students of history and politics. The romantic streak in Hannah Arendt has been noted by many. Perhaps *Eichmann in Jerusalem* too should be treated as a work of art rather than historical analysis? If so, it may well remain the only work of art inspired by that trial. There still is a last paradox, the relationship between the political philosopher and the political journalist. Is a political philosopher to be relied upon who can be trusted only on the level of abstraction? I have been assured that there is only a tenuous link between these two activities, just as a great art historian is not necessarily the best expert to establish the provenance or genuineness of a picture.

## IV

It has been argued by Leni Yahil among others that it was the merit of Hannah Arendt's book to provide fresh impetus to the study of the Judenrat phenomenon and, more generally speaking, the issue of 'collaboration.' This is, I believe, correct only in part, for even before *Eichmann in Jerusalem* appeared there had been a great deal of comment on the subject. Solomon Bloom had written a memorable essay on Rumkovski and the Lodz Ghetto as far back as 1949, Friedmann had written on Gens (of the Vilna Ghetto) and Merin, Nahman Blumenthal on Bialistok, and there were many more studies both for the general public and of a more specialized character. Two of the most important books on the Jewish Councils appeared in 1965 and 1972 respectively; this refers to Presser's *Ondergang* and to I. Trunk's *Judenrat*. But both had been many years in the making. Presser owed nothing to the Arendt controversy, and Trunk, I suppose, very little. During the last fifteen years there have been more specialized studies on the Jewish Councils in Holland, in Hungary (Braham), in Theresienstadt and above all in Poland.

Following the publication of the Czerniakov diaries, there has been much illuminating comment on the Judenrat phenomenon. Some writers have recently tried to draw an interim balance, comparing the findings of various studies.[17] Most of this work, I suppose, would have been done in any case and thus the impact of the 'controversy' consists mainly in having compelled her contemporaries to rethink the whole issue of Jewish collaboration and resistance during World War II. Whether anyone basically changed his views as a result, I doubt. There are some such as Dvorzhetzki and Eisenbach who see the Judenrat vitually without exception in a negative light. Nathan Blumenthal in his investigation of the Lublin Judenrat reaches the conclusion that not all were criminals and traitors, but that even those who were not, objectively served as Nazi tools. Others, such as Z.A. Braun, Weiss and Kaplinski maintain that a wholesale condemnation of the Judenrat distorts history.[18] They argue that there were enormous differences between conditions in one ghetto and another, that in a few the Judenrat closely collaborated with the resistance, that in some (perhaps twenty percent according to Trunk) the German orders were carried out with excessive zeal and no attempt was made to circumvent and sabotage them, and that in most places the general strategy was to gain time. Yehuda Bauer has noted that if—I quote from memory—the Soviet army had reached Lodz a few months earlier Rumkovski, the 'king' of the local ghetto, would have entered the annals of Jewish history a hero, not a traitor. It is also true that one has to differentiate between the period before the deportations started, when the Judenrat engaged in the administration of the ghetto and the time thereafter when the Jewish leadership actively participated in the selection of the victims that were to be sent to the extermination camps.

Thus fifteen years after the controversy we are no nearer to a consensus than before and it is quite likely that there never will be agreement partly because, as has been noted repeatedly, conditions varied so much from place to place, partly also because there are genuine differences of opinion with regard to what could have been expected from Jewish communities facing the Nazi terror machine. But if in many cases mitigating circumstances can be found, if some leaders in fact behaved heroically, the Judenrat phenomenon, as a whole, has acquired a negative connotation, and rightly so. From the moment at the very latest that the Jewish Councils were used by the Nazis to help in the 'final solution', their action became indefensible. True, it can always be argued that they acted to prevent worse persecution, but this argument has been heard too often. Why was there so little resistance? The question deeply bothered Hannah Arendt and most contemporaries. The answer is in many ways obvious given the isolation of the Jews, the demographic structure of the Jewish communities, the lack of psychological and organizational preparation, the hostility of the non-Jewish population in Eastern Europe, the lack of arms, the unsuitability of the surrounding terrain. There could not have been much resistance—certainly not successful resistance. But there could have been more resistance than there was, and why did Jews let themselves be slaughtered like sheep? Hannah Arendt was doubly shocked —partly because during the war she had imagined that there had been a great deal of resistance—only to find out later that this had not been the case. But she was also by temperament one of the intellectuals who had great admiration for men or women of action (preferably intellectuals who were doers such as Rosa Luxemburg, even if the results were disastrous). The meekness of the Jews seemed intolerable in retrospect. She looked for a scapegoat and found it in the Jewish leadership.

Sixty years before Hannah Arendt published her book the greatest living Hebrew poet, after the Kishinev pogrom, wrote his *Ba'ir Ha'hariga [In the City of Slaughter]:* 'Great is the sorrow and great is the shame—and which of the two is greater, answer thou, O son of man ... The grandsons of the Maccabeans — they ran like mice, they hid themselves like bed-bugs and died the death of dogs wherever found.' Bialik's indictment was far stronger than Hannah Arendt's but there were no irate reviews, no protests, no contradictions. His poem, unlike Hannah Arendt's book, influenced a whole generation. Was it because Arendt's book, pretending to be an objective historical account, contained much that was unfair or untrue? I do not think that this was the main reason, for her book also contained much that was true. His contemporaries felt that Bialik's attack was born out of agony. Hannah Arendt's reproaches were those of an outsider, lacking identification, they were almost inhumanly cold and they were in part, at least, rooted in an aesthetic approach. She would have hailed a great Jewish uprising, I suspect, for the same reason that Yeats welcomed the Easter Rising in 1916, for its "terrible beauty."

*November 1978*

**NOTES**

1. The only exception known to me is a Ph.D. dissertation, R. Meyerson, *Hannah Arendt, Romantic in a totalitarian Age, 1928-63.* Ann Arbor, 1972. There is a Hebrew dissertation by Yerahmiel Cohen (Jerusalem, April 1973) on H. Arendt that does not, however, deal with her early writings.
2. "Musterghetto Therensienstadt," *Aufbau,* 35, 1943; 'Die wahren Gruende fuer Theresienstadt' 36, 1943.
3. "Die juedischen Partisanen im europaeischen Aufstand," *Aufbau,* 36, 1944.
4. H. Arendt, "Organized Guilt and Universal Responsibility," *Jewish Frontier,* January 1945.
5. "The Seeds of a Fascist International," *Jewish Frontier,* June, 1945.
6. *Crises of the Republic,* New York, 1972, p. 39.
7. Arendt, *Burden of Our Time,* London, 1951, p. 429.
8. H. Trevor Roper, *New York Times,* October 13, 1963; E. Simon, *Nach dem Eichmann Prozess,* Tel Aviv 1963.
9. *Golo Mann, Die Neue Rundschau,* 4, 1963 and *Die Zeit,* January 24, 1964.
10. K. Jaspers, *The Future of Germany,* Chicago, 1967.
11. *Neue Zürcher Zeitung,* October 19, 1963; *Der Monat,* May 1964; *New Republic,* June 15 and 29, 1963; *Commentary,* September, 1963.
12. *New York Review of Books,* November 11, 1965.
13. Arendt, *Eichmann in Jerusalem,* New York, 1964, p. 115, 117.

14. Robinson, *And the Crooked Shall Be Made Straight,* Macmillan, 1965, p. 169.

15. Pascal Ory, *Les collaborateurs,* Paris 1976, p. 268.

16. Margaret Canovan, *The Political Thought of Hannah Arendt,* London 1974, 47.

17. For instance, A. Weiss, articles in *Gilead,* Jerusalem 1976; and in *Moreshet,* November 1969 and November 1972.

18. For instance, Z. A. Braun, *Hahanhaga-darkeha ve'akhariuta,* Jerusalem.